The Fastest Ship in the Fleet

The story of HMS Cavalier and her men

By Barry Knell

Published by Chatham Historic Dockyard Trust (2014)

Barry Knell.

Published by:
Chatham Historic Dockyard Trust
The Sail and Colour Loft
The Historic Dockyard
Chatham
Kent ME4 4TE
Tel: 01634 823800
Email: info@chdt.org.uk

The Chatham Historic Dockyard Trust is a Registered Charity no. 292101

First published 2014
1st Edition April 2014

ISBN 978-0-9534260-1-0

British Library Cataloguing in Publication Data
A catalogue record for this book is available from the British Library

Cover Design by Arc Creative Solutions, Chatham.
Designed and typeset by Arc Creative Solutions, Chatham.
Printed by Cliffe Enterprise, Eastbourne.

The publication of this book has been made possible through the generous contributions of the following:
Arts Council England
Bell Glass & Glazing
Chatham Branch - Royal Naval Association
The Marsh Christian Trust
Peel Ports

Acknowledgements

It was the long held ambition of Mike Fleet ex RN and the 'go getter' for the 'Cavalier' volunteers at Chatham, to see a book written about her. Mike had joined the Royal Navy in 1951 as a Boy Seaman. This was the start of his 12 years of service to King, Queen and Country. His training at HMS St Vincent was to be the first of six "Stone Frigates" (shore establishments) and he went on to serve on-board nine warships including Britain's last Battleship, an Aircraft Carrier, two Battle class Destroyers, three Anti-Submarine Frigates and an Atlantic Escort that featured in the film "The Cruel Sea".

He approached Richard Holdsworth, of the Chatham Historic Dockyard Trust (CHDT) and the committee of the HMS Cavalier Association, chaired by 'Tony' Cox, all of whom agreed that a book should be written. In true naval fashion I was 'volunteered' to write it! I didn't need much persuading as I believed that the ship and her crew's story should be recorded, so it turned out to be a bit of a labour of love.

There are far too many contributors to be able to thank them all here personally; but most of those appear in their own right within the narrative. Some need special mention for their help with research: 'Carrie' Westwood of the Isle of Wight Heritage Service, Ron 'Sally' Rymer, old shipmate and Archivist for the HMS Cavalier Ass. David Thompson OA RN, last commission and Admiral Sir Jeremy Blackham for the loan of his Midshipman's journal. Caroline Barnsley of South Shields Heritage, Central Library, Mark Beswick, Meteorological Office Archives, Andrew Chapman for his reading, Hugh Alexander PRO and Richard Holdsworth and Paul Barnard of The Historic Dockyard Chatham. I would also like to thank the many people who submitted articles and photographs which I was unable to use. Thank you also to 'Spell' Checker for his help! Last but not least my wife Val who spent many lonely evenings whilst I tortured the computer.

Most of the photographs are from members of her crew which have passed from hand to hand and are not attributed to individuals. Where copyright is known it is shown, where it couldn't be found please accept my apologies.

To all our shipmates who are no longer with us.

Foreword

Royal Navy warships – especially those built of steel – normally, have quite a short life and are high maintenance. Their existence is marked in records by their date of First Commissioning (Birth), when they first fly the White Ensign and the date of their Final Paying-off at the end of the Last Commission (Death), when the White Ensign is lowered for the last time. The ante-natal period, during which the ship is ordered, built, launched and completed may last years but is seldom thought worth a mention. Although a few warships do get sold to other Navies after paying off, the vast majority are broken up for scrap – after a period during which they are used as a source of spare parts for other ships. There is no after-life and these ships exist only in the memories of those who served in them. So, her people almost invariably outlive the ship.

HMS Cavalier is a splendid exception to practically all these rules. She was built in a shipyard that was frequently under air attack by bombers based just across the Channel. Then, whilst still on Contractors Sea Trials, with chaps in bowler hats on board, she was diverted to go to the assistance of a ship torpedoed off the French coast and did sterling work there. So quite an interesting ante-natal period. Once in commission in 1944, she gave the nation twenty eight years service, finally paying off in 1972. But this was not the end because she is still around, aged 70, back here in Chatham, where she paid off 42 years ago. She is flying the White Ensign again – as part of the National Destroyer Memorial. Practically all her equipment is intact and she will now probably outlive all of us who served on board her.

In this very well researched book, Barry Knell covers all aspects of the ship's story, before 1944 and after 1972, explaining how the ship was saved for the Nation thanks to having many friends in high places but also some very hard work by ordinary mortals, who continue to give their help voluntarily. For those parts of the story when HMS Cavalier was fully in commission, Barry lets members of the ship's company give their recollections of what it was like to serve aboard – vivid and amusing memories of the various incidents which occurred.

Perhaps the best description of HMS Cavalier to leave in your memory is the remark made by Lord Ironside when speaking up in the House of Lords in favour of saving Cavalier for the Nation as the last of the Second World War Destroyers: She is a Survivor.

Rear Admiral John Hervey CB, OBE
Commanding Officer, HMS Cavalier 1966-67
President, HMS Cavalier Association 1995-2010

Contents

INTRODUCTION

The main aim of this book is to give readers an insight into what it was like for men to live and work onboard a destroyer such as HMS Cavalier in war and peace, or more accurately, constantly training for the next war. It also records for posterity a way of life that is fast disappearing into history. So many people, naval personnel and civilians, at home and abroad, were touched by the destroyer HMS Cavalier in her twenty eight years in service, several lives were lost and many more saved.

This is not a day to day diary of events; a book could be written about each one of the seven commissions but that would take volumes. Each one lasted between eighteen months and two years, there is only room here for a few highs and lows of each.

Before coming to the different commissions and some of their stories it may be easier to explain how a sailor was trained, the relatively hard life he endured and what made him the way he was. Much of their lives were little changed from the days of Nelson, sleeping in hammocks, eating on crowded mess decks and holding Sunday divisions to show the captain that the men had shifted into clean clothes, a left over from the 18th century! Matelots or 'Jacks' as they were referred to, developed a keen sense of humour to make light of difficult situations, they had their own language and terminology, much of which cannot be repeated in polite society.

They learned fair play, to support those weaker and more vulnerable than themselves and having seen the wonders of the world and experienced the violence of nature were quite covertly religious (*These have seen the works of the Lord and his wonders in the deep, psalms 107 verse 23*). And like the PO Instructor at HMS Ganges training school who marched his boys into church one Sunday morning, one of them forgot to take his cap off, the instructor bellowed… '*That man there, take your F…ing 'at orf in the 'ouse of the Lord.*'

They worked hard, and certainly played hard when the opportunity arose, they were a special breed.

Technical detail will be kept to a minimum except where it is necessary and a glossary appears in the rear of the book. There will be errors in this book (not mine of course!), some people see the same situation differently as much of what is written here took place some time ago.

The crew's name lists have been compiled mainly from memory or from other sources as the Admiralty did not archive these lists, even so they are quite comprehensive. Names have not been changed to protect the innocent… or the guilty!

It should perhaps be explained why 'Cavalier' spent much of her post war time in the Far East. Briefly there were the Goodies, us, and the Baddies, the Reds. Britain kept a large fleet east of Suez to protect the smaller countries, our trading partners, many still governed by Britain; these were the dying days of Empire. This you will understand when you see all the countries that 'Cavalier' and other RN Ships constantly visited. They were showing that there was an alternative and free way of life; we called it 'showing the flag'.

The British Pound Sterling was, next to the American dollar the strongest currency in the world and although Jack wasn't paid a lot he was able to enjoy most of the countries he went to, a reasonable night out in Hong Kong could be had at the time for 10/- shillings (50p).

Although we had a large fleet out in the east we were still outnumbered and that is how the atomic tests at Christmas Island, which 'Cavalier' took a small part in, came about.

Many of the stories and some of the pictures used here are from the 'commissioning' books and from members of the crew.

For those not familiar with the black art of Imperial measurement a basic conversion table appears below.

Imperial	Metric
1 inch	2.54 centimetres
1 foot	0.30 metre
1 yard	0.91 metre
1 land mile	1.609 kilometres
1 pint	0.568 litre
1 gallon	4.54 litres

1 Nautical mile/2026 yards = 6080ft
1 land mile/ 1760 yards = 5280ft

THE SHIP
HMS CAVALIER

Admiralty order, Job No. J6099, 24.03.1942
Keel laid February 1943
Launched 07.04.1944
Commissioned 22.11.1944
Final paying off 07.06.1972

THE SHIP
HMS CAVALIER

In February 1942 the Admiralty authorized the building of thirty two large emergency class destroyers as they desperately needed more escorts capable of crossing the Atlantic Ocean without having to refuel. By today's standard they were not that large. These ships were to become the 'C' class. The first eight started with the letters 'CA' and were named 'Caesar', 'Caprice', 'Cavalier', 'Cassandra', 'Cambrian', 'Carysfort', 'Carron' and 'Cavendish'. The other sets of eight started with 'CH', 'CO' and 'CR', all the 'CR's' were completed after the war and were mostly sold off to other Allied or foreign navies. Two of the 'CA's, 'Cavalier' and 'Carysfort' were built at J. Samuel White & Company Ltd Yard at Cowes on the Isle of Wight, the other six were built at Northern yards.

J. Samuel Whites & Co Ltd logo

On the 24th March 1942 'Cavalier' had been ordered as job number J6099 and started to take shape with a few strokes of a pencil on the drawing board. Initially these eight were given different names but that was changed when they decided to start the entire group with names starting with 'C' to identify them as a class. 'Cavalier' was the first Royal Navy ship to bear the name 'Cavalier'. Originally a cavalier was a type of horseman, but was later used to describe a supporter of King Charles I and II during the English civil war from 1647. They were described as being 'Dashing men of honour with a loyal heart' and 'gallant and chivalrous gentlemen, especially when escorting a woman'!

White's drawing office early 1940's (Norman Barton).

Being war time her keel was laid without much ceremony in February 1943 and after her basic hull was completed she was ready for launching and to be fitted out.

Norman Barton apprentice, White's yard: I was apprenticed to the yard in August 1943 straight from school aged sixteen, I was paid £1.0s.10d (£1.05) a week. We worked five and a half days a week and if we had to answer the call of nature we were timed … we were allowed seven minutes! I worked in the mould loft; we had to make full size templates of all the parts in wood of the ships being built. Nothing was regular shaped and we had to learn how to 'lay them off the ship'. There was little communication between the different shipyards throughout the country in those days and therefore, although of the same class the ships varied slightly in size and shape. The hulls were constructed on the east side of the river Medina and after launch were moved to the west side for fitting the engines and weapons.

Some of the young apprentices who worked for Samuel Whites Yard and who built 'Cavalier' in 1943/4 (Norman Barton).

Back: Johnnie Haines, Norman Green, Tony Boutland, John 'Mac' McKeown, Arthur 'Garth' Brudenell, Bill Bailey. Front: Wally Allen, Johnnie Mercer, Brian Wescombe. John Mercer joined the RN rising to the rank of LT CDR.

Patterns for large castings, such as the hawse pipes and engine castings were made in our shop, a mock up of the ships frames were constructed to make sure they fitted correctly. The ships were built out in the open with planking laid on wooden staging around the side of the ship. There was no such thing as health and safety so you looked out for yourself. The steel for the ships came from Sheffield by rail to Portsmouth and Southampton and was sent onward to Cowes by the I.o.W. Transport Company, a subsidiary of Whites. The weapons came from Priddy's Hard by way of the RN transport and were lifted into the ships by the hammerhead crane. Despite a shortage of labour, and apart from one or two key personnel the crew for the trials was supplied by Whites yard. Being war time the trials were kept to a minimum of about ten days. Although there was no 'health and safety' then I was denied seeing the launch clearly from my vantage point high up on the hammer head crane, because I was told to get off it.

16 year old Norman as an apprentice

Later during fitting out a group of girls from the typing pool (including my future wife Audrey) demanded to see the end product of all the technical letters and forms that they had been typing out. Unusual as it was then they were invited to visit the ship and were given tea on the messdeck.

The building of 'Cavalier' was considered to have been very quick'. In April and May 1942 Whites yard had been badly damaged in three bombing raids by the German Luftwaffe. Over two hundred tons of bombs and incendiaries were dropped and over one hundred thousand square feet of buildings were totally destroyed. It would have been considerably worse had it not been for the Polish destroyer in the yard, the 'Blyskawica' (Lightning). She had been built there in 1936 and was now back in the Yard refitting, having had to leave Poland. She had retained her ammunition onboard, which was not normal practice because of the obvious danger to the local inhabitants; however during the raid she was able to use her anti aircraft guns to good effect to help defend the town. ('Blyskawica' is now a preserved ship and lies in dock at Gdynia in Poland). The Yard was almost destroyed but was rebuilt with government help and was re-equipped with new welding equipment. Being lighter work this had the added bonus that women could be employed to do it. 'Cavalier' and 'Carysfort' were among the first Royal Navy ships to have some of their component parts welded. HMS Contest, another 'C' class, was the first all welded warship constructed in this country.

Whites' machine shop, where most of Cavalier's parts would have been manufactured. (Isle of Wight Heritage service)

The huge hammerhead crane at Whites yard; it was capable of lifting in excess of two hundred tons and was used in the construction of 'Cavalier'. Its size can be gauged by the two men standing near the top. It still exists and is now listed. (Isle of Wight Heritage Service).

The ship was launched at a ceremony on the 7th April 1944 by Lady Sibell Glyn, the wife of Lord Ralph Glyn a director of Samuel Whites yard. After the ceremony she presented a silver cigarette box to the ship as a trophy (Now back with the ship).

HMS Cavalier, bow shrouded in red, white and blue, is launched on 7th April 1944 by Lady Sibell Glyn. (Isle of Wight Heritage Service)

Silver cigarette box, the trophy presented to the ship by Lady Glynn. It is inscribed;

*'God Speed Cavalier
Launched by Lady Glyn 7th April 1944'*

Opposite page: Another C&A hull takes to the water and is ready to be fitted out.

The ship was then taken alongside to be fitted out, painted and made ready for the rest of her crew to join. It was the Admiralty's practice to have key personnel 'standing by' ships whilst they were being built; they would have joined her about two or three months before completion. This was in order that they became totally familiar with all the equipment that was being installed and would get to know the ship intimately. They would live in local accommodation, either a hotel or a boarding house until the accommodation onboard was ready.

Clyfford Arrowsmith and John Mercer were young lads working at Whites yard as apprentices during the fitting out. John told us that although you cannot see him he is on the photograph below which was taken on her trials, he is standing behind the ship's whaler. He felt privileged because he was only an apprentice at the time and they were not normally allowed to go to sea on trials.

HMS Cavalier undergoing trials in the Solent in December 1944.
After the war her pennant number R73 became D73 to conform
to the NATO destroyer designation. (Beken's of Cowes)

At 1500hrs 28th December whilst at sea off the Isle of Wight on acceptance trials, and still flying the Red Ensign they intercepted a radio message from a warship escorting the Empire Javelin, a troopship, that she had been torpedoed off Cape Barfleur, France. She was sinking by the stern and had onboard 1,500 troops and crew. The skipper checked that they had sufficient fuel and ammunition onboard for all the weapon systems and then radioed the C in C and the escort that they were making their way to assist. They left the Solent at high speed with Whites civilian staff still onboard, much to their consternation as they hadn't brought their toothbrushes and weren't paid to fight wars anyway! Several other warships arrived in the area and between them saved the survivors from the original attack. The area was searched for the submarine, later believed to have been U772, and many depth charges were dropped during that night and following morning. It has never been proven that the U-Boat was sunk that night but it was later established that it did not return from its patrol. Seventeen men died and many were wounded on the Empire Javelin, but many more would have been lost had it not been for the prompt action of the rescuers. 'Cavalier' returned to the Solent the following day to continue her trials, much to the relief of the civilians onboard.

Before moving on it should be explained that from the time of her build to her final paying off she never had any power to the boats davits or the torpedo recovery davit. Although weighing three and half to four tons the boats could be lowered quite easily by two or four men using ropes round the bollards. However, to raise them, the lower deck was cleared of all men not engaged elsewhere (usually about a hundred and fifty men) and, with half on one line and the other half on the other their efforts coordinated by a Petty Officer, the boats would be raised by hand.

Throughout this book the ship's speed is referred to in knots. It may be a good time here to explain to the uninitiated what constitutes a knot as a measure of speed. A land mile equals the average of one minute of latitude, 1,760 yards; however the nautical mile was set at 2,020 yards. Hence the nautical mile is longer. So if a ship is shown as travelling at 30 knots the rough equivalent would be nearer to 36 miles an hour.

Ship's badge

These badges were more commonly known, incorrectly, as 'Crests'.

The original badge, believed designed by CDR McBarnett and produced by Whites on the 3rd August 1944, was given the motto 'Cavalier's Up' and was used by the first ship's company for a short while until the official Admiralty one was produced.

All major warships had their own unique badge. These badges were usually designed by a committee of specialists in heraldry from the College of Arms. "Cavalier's" official badge was accepted from the 'Clarenaux, King of Arms' on the 10th November 1944 by the Controller of the Navy Arthur Cochrane. Each ship's badge and motto was usually designed around its name. However because of the exigencies of war a badge had not been produced for her by the time she was ready for launching so unusually, on the 3rd August

1944 the builders, Whites had drawn and cast a badge for 'Cavalier' themselves, it was believed to have been designed by Lt. Cmdr McBarnett the first captain, who would have been 'standing by' the ship. It was based on the famous painting by Frans Hals of the well known 'Laughing Cavalier'.

The painters copy of the original drawing for the crest.

However the Admiralty committee vetoed the use of this one for various reasons, amongst them was the fact that Prince Rupert was a Bavarian and a Prince of the Rhine before coming to England in the early 1600's and, as HMS Cavalier was about to go off to fight the Germans it was considered to be somewhat inappropriate! Prince Rupert fought for the Royalist cause during the English civil war in the 17th century and was appointed head of the regiment of cavaliers, he became known as the 'Mad Cavalier' (There were more of these to come later!). The fact that he also later became the head of the Navy Royal, (now Royal Navy) made him ideal for the connection to 'Cavalier's' badge.

HMS CAVALIER's badge with motto.

This is the big badge you will see on the front of the ship's bridge. Made from bronze it weighs about 12 kilos. The gold is real gold leaf which lasts a lot longer in the salt laden air and severe weather encountered at sea.

Eventually the committee decided to use various details from Prince Rupert's family coat of arms; this would not have been so obviously German. They also had a say on what the wording would be for the ship's motto. Once again this would be based on the ship's name and the Musketeers motto of 'All for one and one for all'. What better motto then for 'HMS Cavalier' than 'OF ONE COMPANY'

By looking at the Admiralty badge and comparing it with Prince Rupert's family coat of arms below, you can see the various components that were used. The lion and the chequered pattern in the quarters of the Prince's coat of arms have been used indirectly within 'Cavalier's' badge. The Horseshoe and wings in 'Cavalier's' badge are believed to refer to the Cavalry and their horses being fleet of foot.

It is a strange co-incidence that Prince Rupert became head of the Cavalier's in November 1644 and 'HMS Cavalier' was completed in November 1944 exactly three hundred years almost to the day.

Prince Rupert's family coat of arms.

A large badge was produced for each ship and this went on the front of the bridge. Various smaller badges were produced either in the dockyards or onboard and these were placed at various places throughout the ship, such as on the gangway desk or lifebuoys. In countries all over the world they were often presented as mementos to VIPs and diplomatic representatives who visited the ship. The more important badges were made of brass or bronze and the smaller ones from cheaper materials.

The ship's basic dimensions.

For the technically minded a few of the basic details are appended below. Many more details appear in other publications and are not gone into here. Most of the measurements below varied over the years as she was refitted from time to time.

Builder:	J. S. White & Co Ltd, Cowes, Isle of Wight.
Length:	362' 5" over all
Beam:	35' 9" over all
Displacement:	Between 2,300 to 2,700 tons
Engines:	Developed 40,000 shaft hp
Speed:	Max, from new approx, 35 knots ahead, 20 knots astern
Fuel oil:	589 tons in ten tanks
Feed water:	(For boilers) 10 ½ tons
Fresh water:	74 tons in nine tanks
Radar:	Main set for surface and close air protection radar 293Q (The Big cheese). For close range and fleet work the type 974 and Type 944 IFF (Identification Friend or Foe) at the top of the mast. The 974 was replaced after 1966 refit by the improved 978.
Gun Director:	The highly accurate 275 directional radar.
Sub, gun director:	Could control 'Y' gun individually.

Main armament: 4 x 4.5" later 3 x 4.5" after 1956. They were open mountings not turrets. From eighteen to twenty two rounds could be fired per minute. They could elevate to 56 deg, for AA.

Max, range: 19,000 yards (9 ½ n. miles)

Close range guns: Varied during career ending with 2 x 40mm Bofors one either side of the bridge and a twin 40mm Bofors frwd of the Squid. Later replaced by a quadruple Seacat missile launcher 1966

Torpedoes: 2 x 4 sets 21" reduced to 1 set after 1956 then none after 1963.

Sonar: 492 transducer under the bow.

Depth charges: Three launchers for 38 carried. Replaced with 2 x 3 barrelled 'Squid' in 1956.

Magazines: Approx. 500 x 4.5" rounds for each gun and the cartridges to go with them.

Shells, types: H.E. Semi armour piercing and Timed fused. Radar nose fuse for AA . Star shell for illuminating surface targets and various types of practice rounds including radar echo producing a cloud of metal filings for calibrating radar.

Rum: 13 rum barrels plus 10 x 1 gallon jars held in the spirit room.

Crew: Varied but usually just under or sometimes just over 200. More specialists were carried in wartime or if running independently.

THE MEN

"Call the Hands, Call the Hands, Call the hands, wakey wakey rise and shine you've had yours now I'll have mine. Lash up and stow."

THE MEN

Training

It was 2200hrs when the Chief Petty Officer put the lights out and quietly said 'Pipe down' as he went to his room at the end of the wooden hut. The class of thirty five sailors under training turned in to sleep, however two carried on talking in whispers. A few moments later the lights came back on and there stood Chiefy fully booted and spurred and rolling a cigarette. He said in a quiet controlled voice; 'OK lads up you get and shift into No.8's on the double and fall in outside three deep'. When this was done they were ordered to double march around the perimeter of the parade ground, about half a mile. When they got back the chief calmly said; 'Inside and shift into No.3's'. Once again they had to double round the parade ground. 'Now change into No.1's' and again they went round. On returning this time somewhere around midnight the Chief quietly said 'OK lads turn in... and pipe down'. They turned in and all that could be heard was a bit of heavy breathing. No one dare say a thing for fear of summary justice being meted out by their shipmates or further punishment being inflicted.

There was nothing sadistic about the Chief's actions; it is the way the Royal Navy trained it's sailors to become self disciplined and to work together as one. It prepared them to live together in an overcrowded steel box called a ship. Shipboard life was a great leveller, factory workers, and farm labourers, 'Paddies', 'Taffs', 'Jocks', some colonials and the sons of the well to do and blue bloods were all brought down to the same level. Their training instilled in them a sense of pride which was reflected in their bearing as they walked ashore in their best serge uniforms. Until the IRA problems of the 1960's they were not allowed ashore in civilian clothing.

They were taught to curb their tongue and temper because the majority ruled in their overcrowded environment. In the early days many of the men came from broken homes, the slums of big cities, or were sent to join the RN rather than the alternative given by the juvenile courts, that of going to a remand home. Because of this many sailors considered the Navy and his oppo's as 'family', some ended up achieving high rank. Cleanliness, so important in a small ship, was rigorously emphasized. If an individual did not keep himself or his kit clean his shipmates would pick him up bodily and throw him fully clothed into the cold water of the fire tank (ashore), or hose him down with a salt water fire hose.

HMS Raleigh training school at Torpoint, the training ground is right of centre with a drill shed at either end. The accommodation was wooden huts with coke stoves in the middle of the highly polished floors. Although the amount of personnel was reduced after the war, in 1962 there were still 600 ships and 102,000 men were required to man them.

Apart from the occasional outbreak of 'crabs' or flu, and despite the overcrowding, disease and infections were rare because of this training in hygiene.

Sailors, from different branches went to different training establishments but all underwent similar training. In HMS Ganges, the boys training establishment at Shotley in Suffolk, and HMS St Vincent's at Gosport, the lads were ruled by a draconian regime that was even tougher than for the older trainees and they spent a year there. They all learned from wily old chiefs who had a wealth of experience in the ways of the sea and a chest full of medals from wars all over the world. Basic navigation, firefighting, first aid, knots and splices, anchors and cables, boat handling under oar and sail, signalling and many other skills that would see them through their naval career... and beyond. The boys underwent training in social skills with the padre and his family and they were taught to dance. They were schooled in the traditions of the Navy, many of which had not changed since Nelson's day.

Sunday Divisions, men under training at HMS Raleigh.

During breaks the old Chiefs would allow the men a crafty cigarette behind the drill shed whilst they regaled them with stories of their experiences in the mysterious Orient, the West Indies, the Middle East and Africa and about their encounters with the beautiful dusky maidens from faraway islands. Cross country running, ten mile forced marches and the assault course ensured they were kept fit. Visits were made to the dentist to get their teeth in good order; the last thing you wanted when several hundred miles from land and a dentist was a serious tooth ache. Each camp had its mascot; the one at HMS Raleigh was an old white Goat with a big beard which appeared on parade each Sunday dressed in his best coat with the ship's badge thereon. During the week he grazed on the lawn and was fed occasional cigarettes by the sailors! The regular staff kept a few pigs and fed them on scraps from the galley.

During the course of their training they were given numerous jabs against the types of disease they were likely to come into contact with in their travels throughout the world; Typhoid, Small Pox, Yellow Fever and many others, their arms ached and looked like pin cushions.

They were taught how to Dhoby (wash their clothing – from the Indian) their clothes in a bucket using 'pusser's' hard smelly soap (still in use from the 18th century) there were no laundries in small ships until sometime later. Persistent stains could be got rid of unofficially by towing the article on a rope over the ship's stern for an hour or two whilst she was under way at sea, making sure of course that you used the correct knot! There were no proper facilities for drying your washing although you may be able to dry them in the ship's boiler room if Chiefy let you but it had to be removed before 0900 each day. Each man was taught to iron and sew and was issued a 'hussif' or 'Housewife', this was a small blue folding cloth bag containing needles, buttons, cottons – white & blue, a small pair of scissors and a thimble and a wooden block with his name on for marking his kit. When ironed, each item of uniform had to be folded in a standard way because their small locker onboard ship had to hold the best part of a hundred pieces of kit.

A standard punishment for a minor misdemeanour, particularly relating to clothing was the dreaded 'kit muster'. If ordered to muster your kit it had to be done after your day's work, if anything was out of place or not up to scratch, then you did it all again the following day or until you got it right! And then you stuffed it all back into that little locker down in the mess.

ME Larry Nolan later of 'Cavalier's' 1961 commission mustering his kit on the quarter deck (Chiefy didn't like me!), notice the boots and shoes, every other one turned upside down to show that they were in good repair and insteps had been polished. Whites to the left blues to the right, kit bag and green case at the back. 2nd best hat is on his gas respirator. Pyjamas, 'hussif', enamelled mug and toilet gear in the centre on top of his small brown attaché case. Boot brushes and hair brush in front. To the left are his hammock, naval counterpane, and blanket, sheets, pillow and pillow cases.

Every morning in training they mustered on the parade ground and then marched off to the strains of 'Heart of Oak' (David Garrick

1759). After passing out of initial training they went off to other schools to be given specialist training in their chosen field, either gunnery, TAS – Torpedo and anti-submarine, or Radar. This would take several weeks or in some cases perhaps months. At the end of which they would eagerly await the list to be posted showing to which ship they were being drafted to.

Small arms' training was given to all men during their initial training, the .303 Lee Enfield rifle, .38 Webley revolvers, two inch mortars, hand grenades and the navy's own sub-machine gun the Lanchester. This was a dangerous weapon to be around. The safety catch on the Lanchester was just a slot to put the bolt in; if the gun was dropped or jolted it could release the safety catch and, if on auto would spray bullets all over the place! If you acquired your marksman's badge you got a few pence a day extra on your wages and were entitled to wear crossed rifles on your sleeve.

They were trained to work in armed sections ashore in case they were required to give aid to the civil powers in the colonies or in foreign countries or to restore order after a disaster such as an earthquake or typhoon. A destroyer such as 'Cavalier' would be expected to put at least one platoon ashore of about thirty eight men, it was made up of three sections of eleven men each with an Officer in charge, three Petty officers or Leading hands, a signalman and a marksman. If under attack they were trained to form a square, just like the Cowboys against the Indians! The normal procedure during riots was for the officer to indicate to the marksman by description, one of the ring leaders, the rioters would be warned by placards in five appropriate languages (Malay, Chinese, Arabic, French and German) not to cross a line, if they did the marksmen was to shoot the ring leader, and he wasn't trained to just wound! For people who have never had to stand on a riot line, you can be assured it is one of the most frightening things you can have to do. You are one of about thirty men facing a rampaging angry mob of perhaps thousands who may be wielding machetes, rocks, clubs and perhaps petrol bombs, you are disciplined and you cannot use any weapons unless ordered to. Many times in history troops on riot lines have opened fire and later been castigated for it, but the critics need to stand on the line before they make judgment.

Be afraid, the Navy is coming! A landing party from "Cavalier's" 1957 commission, they are marching to Stone Cutters Island in Hong Kong. There appears to be three sections (A platoon) in this picture. The officer has a Webley .38 service revolver. The ratings in the front rank have 9mm Lanchester sub machine guns slung over their shoulders and pouches for spare magazines. The rest of the platoon is carrying .303 rifles. One Bren gun and its tripod were carried by each section, the weight of that and a 2" Mortar and ammunition for them would be spread throughout the platoon. The radio operator with a radio pack on his back would take up the rear and be in touch with the ship. Water purifying tablets for water found ashore were also carried.

Life onboard ship

These sailors were obviously better off than their predecessors but life onboard small ships could still be very hard, hence their propensity for alcohol! Early destroyers were designed around the machinery and weapons and the crew then squeezed themselves in any spaces left! They usually ate cold food and washed in buckets of water. HMS Cavalier and her sister ships were some of the first small ships to be designed with crew accommodation, albeit very overcrowded for the two hundred men carried and for the first time proper bathrooms with showers. However in wartime 'Cavalier' would carry extra personnel and this could bring the number of crew to well over two hundred men. There would also be lots of extra equipment and spares stored in every available space.

Not much different from Nelson's day! A few hammocks slung on a mess deck, there is another row of bars staggered behind this one and the ropes of the next row would go between this set and another behind them. In rough weather they swung to and fro like bats. They slept top to tail and the wooden stretcher you can see held the 'nettles' open at the head end. Cigarettes and reading material was stowed on the cable trays above their heads. Some of the pipes above their heads were lagged with asbestos!

Even in peace time there were more men than hammock spaces. Before 'Cavalier's' refit in Gibraltar in the mid 1960's most men slept in hammocks, each hammock was allocated 18 inches of space (less than half a metre). You can imagine what this must have been like in an Arctic gale or in the tropics, or after a night out on the beer! You learnt to swing yourself into your hammock without waking your neighbour.

In the morning the hammocks had to be lashed up tightly in the correct way and stowed away; they could then if necessary be used by the damage control parties to block holes in the ship's side in action or collision. If they were not lashed up properly then you had to redo them. And to think in the event of your demise this could be your 'final resting place… accompanied by a shell to add weight to take you to the bottom'.

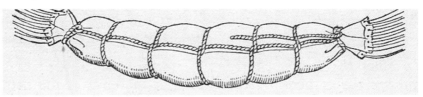

If you were going ashore you could not sling your hammock before you went because the rest of the men had to move around during the evening and when the duty officer of the watch did his evening 'rounds' (another left-over from the 18th Century when they made sure all naked flames had been extinguished), everything had to be ship shape for the coming night. Before going ashore you arranged with your 'Oppo' for him to sling your hammock for you after evening rounds which were usually about 2100hrs. For this favour he would probably get sippers or gulpers of your tot of rum the following day. Many found themselves sleeping on the tables and benches and in the passages on camp beds. Even today hammock hooks can be seen along the passageways and in other working compartments, including in the NAAFI canteen. When the main lights were turned off low red lights came on automatically so that you could still see, it was still difficult moving around the ship in the subdued lighting. Red lighting was used because it does not destroy your night vision. You had to walk in a crouched position to avoid banging into someone's hammock or tripping over a camp bed.

It was generally quite noisy on the mess; apart from the machinery humming away twenty four hours a day everything was on the move. Crockery, cutlery and anything else that wasn't actually fixed down was rattling away with the motion of the ship. In fact during storms the noise was horrendous. As the ship plunged into a wave the scuttles (portholes) looked like washing machines with the water swirling around and leaking through them. There were copper 'save alls' under the scuttles to catch some water but in rough weather they would be overwhelmed. It didn't matter how tight you hammered the deadlights (armoured covers) down they still leaked under the huge pressure they were subjected to by over two thousand tons of ship being pushed under the sea. After the Dunkirk evacuation, when many men died because they could not escape from the sinking destroyers, an escape hatch was fitted to all messdecks above the water line. However the scuttles spurted water through the seals like water fountains and soon you were paddling through several centimetres of water, as the ship rolled the water would be swilling around with bits of kit, shoes and hats floating in it. Three days in a typhoon left quite a mess to be cleaned up! And on top of that when you entered harbour you might be required on the jetty in your best bib and tucker in a guard for some visiting VIP. If your boots had been floating around in the salt water, you polished them, but within half an hour and before your eyes they turned white as the salt came out!

On arrival in harbour you may have to mount a guard for visiting foreign VIPs, author on right behind the gunnery officer.

In extreme weather it was impossible to do anything other than just move around. You automatically adjusted to the movement, as the ship rose on a large wave and paused before plunging down, anything from three, or more than twenty metres, you hung on to something as your legs would buckle as you hit bottom, you could then quickly move forward a few feet and hang on to something else for the next drop! Several days of this was very tiring as is later explained by one of the sailors from the first commission caught in a hurricane in the Arctic. In severe weather it was difficult to actually move at all and the cooks could not cook properly. They had two 28 gallon 'coppers' (Later three) in which they would throw every kind of savoury tinned food; this became known to sailors as 'Pot Mess'. The duty cook from each mess would take the mess fanny (see 'fanny' below) to the galley and ladle this conglomerate into it; he then took it to his mess deck and hung it on a hammock hook where it could swing away without spilling, anyone who felt like eating dipped their enamelled mug into it. One day in a typhoon off the Philippines when the author collected the pot mess from the galley he dipped the large ladle into the copper and caught a floor cloth that had fallen into it, it slowly slithered off and fell back in with a 'plop' to rejoin the meat and peas which were almost spilling over the side with the ship's movement!

Incidentally the word 'mess deck' originates from the Spanish Mesa meaning table i.e.; the deck with the tables. Many of Jack's words and sayings were borrowed from countries from all over the world, 'Banyan' from India which Jack used from the 16th century onwards to mean a 'Picnic' or party ashore. (Banya – Gujarati for merchants, they gathered in the shade of a type of fig tree to barter and others to picnic).

The Fanny

The fanny was an aluminium container with a handle and it held about half a gallon.

In the early part of the 19th century the Navy had just introduced tinned meat to ship's stores. They had a canning factory and depot at Deptford in London. The large meat tins after being emptied were found to be useful containers by the sailors. They smoothed the edges over and two holes were punched into the sides for a wire handle. At about this time there was a grisly murder which had occurred in London. A girl called Fanny Adams was murdered and her body cut up, most of it was never found. However parts of what was believed to her body were found in the Navy supply and canning depot in Deptford where the meat was canned and with typical sense of humour that sailors had, the meat became known as Fanny Adams and the tin eventually became known as the Fanny. The Navy recognized what useful containers they were and eventually manufactured something similar in aluminium, but it kept its name.

Incidentally the saying, to get 'Sweet Fanny Adams' meaning you received nothing also comes from the same source, because there was very little of her found.

Rum Issue

To make life a bit more bearable in the conditions in which they lived a tot of Pusser's rum, one eighth of a gill neat, or grog, two parts water which amounted to about a third of a pint, was issued every day to those over 20 years of age.

The fanny is being used here to hold the mess rum issue. Seen here are Ken Hickman (rum bosun) and Buck Ryan, both seamen from frwd seamen's messdeck from the 1960 commission, they are measuring out the rum in half pint glasses. The picture taken in the Far East shows them in just shorts because of the heat.

The rum became a currency, although illegal, you could get all sorts of favours, such as a swap of duty or to borrow money. Depending on the favour asked there was a range of measures that were offered. They ranged from a 'wet', 'sippers', 'gulpers', one finger, two fingers, half a tot or 'Sandy bottoms' (empty the glass), most of those speak for themselves. The rum was a mixture of Jamaican rums and became general issue by the early 1700's. The amount issued each day changed over the years; it was originally 'tow hole pnits a dya!'

The rum tub, made of oak and brass bound

Much of the rum was stored in stone jars, the tops sealed with wax. It was issued in the presence of the officer of the watch each day at 1150hrs and was very strictly controlled. The exact amount required for the days issue was tipped from the stone jars into a large oak, brass bound tub and the required amount of water was added to make it 'Grog', two to one, considering that when it arrived at Admiralty it was almost as thick as treacle it was still a potent drink. The reason for adding water to the rum was so that it would not keep and could not be stored up for one glorious drunken session. The tub had the words 'God bless the King/Queen' thereon in large brass letters. A representative from each mess, called the 'rum bosun' took the mess 'fanny' and collected the rum. Any leftover in the tub was poured away, watched by the officer. There were many ingenious ways employed to get more than their official issue. On one ship where the officer always poured excess rum into a sink, the waste pipe was diverted to catch it before it entered the sea. On another ship after a storm the Jack Dusty (Storeman) would break the bottom of a gallon rum jar over a container and catch the rum but leaving the wax seal intact. A small amount of rum was poured into the bilges to create a 'smell' so that when the office came for the official issue it was pointed out to him that one jar had been broken in the rough weather and had run into the bilge, he would then write it off, eight bottles of best Jamaican rum!

The rum bosun took his mess issue to his messdeck and carefully measured out each man's tot. The toast before downing their tot in one was 'The Queen, God bless her', it was naval traditional to do this sitting down. Any rum left over was called the 'Queen's' and was passed round and round to each member for a sip until it was all gone. The rum bosun had ways and means of fiddling the measures and each man watched very carefully as his tot was measured out. One way the measure was fiddled was by him putting his finger tips or thumb in the copper measure so that you ended up with short measure. It was traditional on a man's birthday to be given a sip of all his friend's tots, it was powerful stuff and more than a few died on their birthdays as a result. On the 31th July 1970 the Admiralty stopped the rum issue, it was decreed that rum had no place in today's technical navy. It had been a custom in the Royal Navy since 1655. It was a sad day for the old sailors who were used to their daily tot. The tradition of 'splicing the main brace' however is still carried out on special occasions.

Tobacco

Over the age of 18 years you were entitled to an issue of three hundred Blue Liner cigarettes a month at 2/ − (10p) per hundred or, three pound tins of rolling tobacco in lieu, this was very often referred to as camel dung and was widely believed to be the sweepings off the factory floor! A cabbage leaf would be placed in the tin to stop the tobacco drying out. The 'Blue Liner' cigarettes were just that, made especially for the Admiralty they had a blue line printed down the side of each cigarette and a huge RN printed on the front of the packet. They came un-tipped or later tipped.

The blue line made them readily identifiable by the dockyard police or Customs and Excise. Each packet contained twenty cigarettes but the allowance was twenty five per day of leave so it was easy to fall foul of regulations and take two packets with you. This tax free allowance was jealously guarded and it was made a serious offence to take ashore more than your allowance. Outside British territorial waters the issue went up to five hundred export size cigarettes a month for 1/ – per hundred (5p). These were export size and twenty five in a packet; they were recognized brands such as Senior Service, Players, Woodbines, or the more exotic Balkan Sobrani or Passing Cloud. On a foreign commission this allowance went up to six hundred per month.

Mail

Mail was very important to the sailors and of course to their families at home. After several days or weeks at sea the mail would be delivered by various means. In earlier days it was brought out to the ship by another ship and transferred by heaving line or 'Jackstay transfer'. Or it may be sent to the port of destination for collection on arrival. If at sea for several weeks, or even months, a Shackleton aircraft was often used to drop the mail into the sea in canisters to be picked up by boat or grappling hook. The author spent three months at sea without seeing land whilst on Fishery protection off Iceland, the relieving ship having broken down. The newspapers delivered with the mail were read to death… you tend to lose faith in a Horoscope in the newspaper that tells you to 'Get out and about and you will meet someone unexpected!'

In latter days helicopters have been used to deliver the mail. Incidentally the rotors that whizz round on top of the helicopter are there to keep the pilot cool… stop them and watch him sweat.

Men multi-tasking!

Everybody onboard had several jobs, depending on what the ship was doing at the time. Seamen, the executive branch, normally maintained and worked on the upper deck, they attended to the boats and wires and chipped and constantly painted the decks to combat salt erosion. After a serious storm the paint was sometimes stripped down to the bare metal by the force of the waves! They also acted as Quartermaster and steered the ship. At sea for twenty four hours a day two men were always on the bridge with binoculars acting as lookouts. A crew was detailed from the watch for the lifeboat (whaler), during the day they worked, at night they sat on the deck just inside the port passage (known as the Khyber Pass). Someone was always on the quarterdeck to act as 'lifebuoy ghost', this man watched over the stern of the ship for anyone who may have fallen overboard. If they did he had a lifebuoy with a light and smoke marker to throw over the side and an alarm button and telephone to contact the officer of the watch on the bridge. The officer of the watch would order at least seven blasts on the ship's whistle, which alerted the whole crew to the emergency and the boats crew to stand by to launch the boat. (Providing it wasn't too rough) He would then go through a procedure which in theory would steer the ship round to the position where the man went overboard. It did work as the author has seen, it was too rough to launch the boat but we found the man and pulled him in on the lifebelt. For obvious reasons to fall asleep when acting as Lifebuoy ghost was considered a very serious offence because he would be the last hope that a man had of surviving.

Apparently if you get excited and stutter it is said that it can be overcome by singing the words. One day a seaman ran to the captain on the bridge and started to stutter, several times he tried but failed to get the words out. Finally the captain said 'Sing it man, sing it', the seaman starting to sing... *'Should old acquaintance be forgot, and never brought to mind, the GI has fallen overboard and is now five miles behind'...* !

If a rating met an officer whilst moving around the ship he stood to one side to allow him to pass. In the early days there was very little social contact between the two. In fact on one ship that the author served on, when they posted a notice that a dance was to be held ashore in the village hall, there was a note on the bottom; Officers may bring their ladies, CPO's and PO's may bring their wives and Ratings may bring their women! Luckily by which time these extreme class attitudes had all but disappeared.

Cooks cooked, engineers operated the engines and boilers, the doc was in his sickbay, officers navigated or supervised their departments and everyone had their day job. During the night watches had to be kept, however when action stations sounded almost everyone had a different job. Officers went to their specialized tasks supervising the seamen who manned the guns, torpedoes, anti-submarine equipment and people like Cooks, Writers and spare stokers became ammunition handlers in magazines, damage control parties inside the ship or first aid parties. The damage control parties were trained to shore up holes in the ship's side and you can see in various places throughout the ship materials, baulks of wood and wedges for this purpose. As they went to their action stations all the water tight doors were clipped down to prevent serious flooding in the event of being damaged, the letters and numbers that can be seen on the doors indicating which ones could be left open in certain 'damage control conditions'. The electricians stood by to repair or bridge any damaged wiring, spare linking cables can be seen in the passages for this purpose. The wardroom would very quickly be converted to an operating theatre. All men were trained in basic first aid and firefighting and throughout the ship you will see first aid cabinets and fire hoses coiled up ready. Nearby are several buff coloured five gallon drums full of 'ox blood', this was fed into the salt water in the fire hoses and created foam for smothering fires. It was real ox blood, with other chemicals added. From continuous practice everyone knew exactly where everything was and how to use it.

As you will see later 'Cavalier' was involved in the Atomic and 'H' bomb tests at Christmas Island (Pacific). With the advent of these nuclear weapons new systems were developed to enable men to carry on fighting their ships. The idea being that the ship could steam through the area after an explosion and all the irradiated dust could be washed over the side. The crew in the meantime was closed down inside the 'citadel', which is formed by various compartments deep inside the ship with the air (and cigarette smoke!) being re-circulated. Afterwards special teams came out with radiac counters and special clothing and checked the weapons out so that they could be manned again…. that was the theory anyway!

Watch keeping at sea was very tiring. In peace time you were in three or four watches which weren't quite so bad, although having done your normal days work you then had to go on duty during the watches at night. You may also have been duty 'cooks of the mess', everyone took it in turns to get the food at mealtimes for their mess from the galley and dish it out, they then had to wash up afterwards. The 'gash bucket', an ordinary galvanized bucket, stood under the end of the messdeck table and all the waste food and tea leaves were thrown in this. It was emptied down the 'gash chute' over the stern of the ship after each meal by the cooks of the mess. At sea it fed the seagulls and fish, in Hong Kong the Chinese girls took it away (In war time it did not go over the side for security reasons). For captains rounds the bucket was brightly burnished.

At this point it may be as well to briefly explain the watch (Shift) system. Each day was split into four hourly watches, except between 1600 and 2000 which was split into two 2 hour 'Dog' watches (named after the Dog Star) so that it changed your watch pattern daily. The crew was split into three or four groups also known as watches. In times of high alert and wartime they would be in defence watches, which are constantly four on four off day and night at action stations, if you were on duty at midnight to 0400 in the morning one day you would be 0400 to 0800 the following day. In this way you can see that you never got more than three and a half hours sleep on any day at sea and this may go on for weeks. This probably explains why Jack made the most of it when he did get ashore.

Engine and Boiler (A&B) rooms

These three compartments comprise almost a third of the length of the ship. They push two and a half thousand tons of ship through the water at up to 33 knots and sometimes faster.

Each boiler room contains a huge three drum boiler which produces superheated steam at 450 pound per square inch. The fuel for heating this was a thick black crude oil (FFO) which was sprayed into the furnace and ignited. The whole boiler room operated under pressure, therefore to get into and out of the room there were airlocks to negotiate. Failure to operate the airlock properly was very dangerous because a sudden loss of pressure caused a back draught and flames could engulf the operators or cause a serious fire. There is a small glass peep hole in the doors so that no two doors were opened at the same time.

The 'Cavalier' carried some three hundred tons of FFO stored in several tanks situated in the lower parts of the ship. These tanks under normal circumstances were not allowed to go below about 60 per cent capacity; this was so that she was always ready to steam off to any emergency anywhere at a moment's notice, it also acted as ballast.

Refuelling:

Most refuelling was done at sea (RAS or Replenishment At Sea) from any of the Royal fleet Auxiliary oil tankers or she could take oil from any other ship, usually but not necessarily bigger than her. Some of the fuel tanks are situated under the after crews messes which caused a disaster on many occasion. The fuel was pumped under pressure from the ship doing the pumping; communication between the two ships was usually done by flags or by sound powered telephone. A misunderstanding, particularly with a foreign vessel about when to stop pumping meant that fuel overflowed into the mess decks. The biggest problem of all was that this thick black highly toxic smelly oil had to be 'bailed' out of the mess and everything had to be scrubbed and repainted to make it habitable again. This could take some time and in the meantime they had to borrow clothes and double up in already overcrowded messes to sleep. Worse things happen at sea they say!

Roger Hunt LME

The engine room housed two huge Parsons Turbines, each one had an astern, ahead and a cruising element, and between them they could produce 40,000HP (To give you some idea of what sort of power that is the average family car at the time she was built was rated around 8 to 10HP.). All this power was passed through a gear room and transferred to the twin shafts and propellers. Both of the propellers were made of solid bronze, were about ten feet in diameter and weighed several tons. The ship's electricity was also produced in the engine room from two steam turbine electricity generators. In emergences ashore, such as earthquakes or other disasters, ships had been known to provide electricity to run hospitals or to a town, this type of exercise was practiced from time to time.

On either side of the engine room were two evaporators that took in salt water and distilled it for use in the boilers. They also produced all the fresh water used by the crew. Under normal circumstances this was fine except if one or other of the evaporators broke down the boilers took priority on the fresh water, the crew then had to go on severe water rationing. If this happened in the tropics it made life doubly difficult.

Above the gear room was an engineer's workshop which included a lathe and a stock of spare metals and materials. Using this workshop the engineers and some gunners were trained to make spare parts for the engines and gunnery equipment from scratch, when halfway across the Pacific and a thousand miles from land you couldn't just pop down the shop and get a couple of extractors, shells for the removal of!

Cooks and the Galley

There were three galleys onboard, four if you count the wardroom galley. The main one was situated amidships just below the mast, this was the main crews galley and was in the most stable part of the ship in bad weather. Nobody envied the cooks who worked this galley in the tropics when temperatures could go off the scale. Down aft were two emergency galleys, one the Chiefs and petty officers and the other for ratings. These came into use if it was too dangerous in rough weather to get forward to the main galley. The main galley did a sterling job producing food for nearly two hundred men four times a day. One commission worked out that the main galley had supplied a quarter of a million meals in what was a typical eighteen month commission. The cooks of the mess for that day would go to the galley and fetch breakfast in trays, stagger up the passageway bouncing off the bulkheads as he went and hoping not to drop anything. It could be yellow peril (smoked haddock), train smash (tinned tomatoes) on fried bread, bacon and egg, Shit on a raft (see recipe under glossary) or Spithead pheasant (kippers). Lunch time it could be baby's heads (Individual steak and kidney puddings), or if it was rough perhaps chips with custard over them! By the time he got back all bedding would be stowed away and the men would have been to the bathroom for a wash and shave. With the men sitting eight or ten to a table, the cooks would start dishing out the breakfast on china plates. After breakfast the cooks washed up and cleaned the mess whilst the rest 'turned to'. Having left the mess you would not normally be allowed back in until the official 'Stand Easy' at 1030hrs. The Royal Navy at the time was one of the only navies in the world to use china crockery and metal knives and forks. (They had a personal enamelled mug each for emergencies). I remember on one ship tomatoes had no middles, only tops and bottoms, whilst mushrooms only had stalks, no tops. The middles of the tomatoes and the tops of the mushrooms went to a senior rates mess.

Punishment

Punishments depended on the seriousness of the misdemeanour.

Death penalty: For treason, murder or arson to dockyards. This was reduced to life imprisonment when the death penalty was abolished in December 1960.
Detention in cells: basically prison, for striking an officer or continued absenting from leave.
No 9's: Stoppage of leave and extra hours of work, start work early, only half hour an hour for meals and working two extra hours in the evenings.
No 11's: Stoppage of pay for so many days, dictated by the captain, stoppage of leave up to thirty days and muster with men under punishment but no extra work.
No 14's: Muster with men under punishment every time but only two hours extra work.

All these punishments were to be avoided because you had very little sleep in the first place and you still had your washing, ironing and other jobs to keep up, otherwise you ended up with more punishment.

Ship's Routine

The time varied depending on where you were but the Tannoy would burst into life as the first pipe of the day was broadcast by the Quartermaster in a very loud voice. *'Call the Hands, Call the Hands, Call the hands, wakey wakey rise and shine you've had yours now I'll have mine. Lash up and stow.'* There were other not repeatable versions to this call. Men under punishment would have been called at 0500 with a personal shake and put to work early.

If you had stood the middle watch (The graveyard watch) you would have only been in your pit or mick (hammock), on the table or on the seats wherever you slept, since 0400hrs, but everyone had to get up because the tables were needed for breakfast! If you were not out quick enough you would be helped out and if you got out late your foot might end up in someone's breakfast! Having stood the Middle Watch you were given a 'Make and Mend' and were given the afternoon off from working. That is of course if there was not an exercise on. It was intended for you to catch up on making or mending your clothes. However in practice it meant that you could get your head down for a couple of hours.

The Bosun's Call: All messages passed over the Tannoy were preceded by the shrill whistle from the Bosun's call, (The general call see below). This drew the attention to everybody that a message was being broadcast. There were other calls which everybody understood and did not need an explanation. Whistling onboard was discouraged so as not to be confused with the Bosun's call.

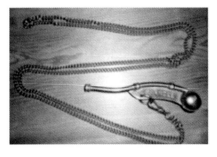

Bosun's call, the quartermaster's badge of office which was worn round his neck by its chain.

Ship's daily routine at sea

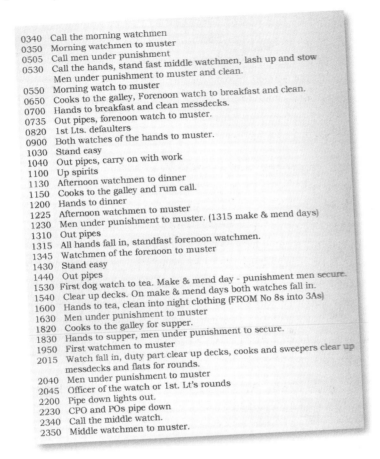

```
0340   Call the morning watchmen
0350   Morning watchmen to muster
0505   Call men under punishment
0530   Call the hands, stand fast middle watchmen, lash up and stow
       Men under punishment to muster and clean.
0550   Morning watch to muster
0650   Cooks to the galley, Forenoon watch to breakfast and clean.
0700   Hands to breakfast and clean messdecks.
0735   Out pipes, forenoon watch to muster.
0820   1st Lts. defaulters
0900   Both watches of the hands to muster.
1030   Stand easy
1040   Out pipes, carry on with work
1100   Up spirits
1130   Afternoon watchmen to dinner
1150   Cooks to the galley and rum call.
1200   Hands to dinner
1225   Afternoon watchmen to muster
1230   Men under punishment to muster. (1315 make & mend days)
1310   Out pipes
1315   All hands fall in, standfast forenoon watchmen.
1345   Watchmen of the forenoon to muster
1430   Stand easy
1440   Out pipes
1530   First dog watch to tea. Make & mend day - punishment men secure.
1540   Clear up decks. On make & mend days both watches fall in.
1600   Hands to tea, clean into night clothing (FROM No 8s into 3As)
1630   Men under punishment to muster
1820   Cooks to the galley for supper.
1830   Hands to supper, men under punishment to secure.
1950   First watchmen to muster
2015   Watch fall in, duty part clear up decks, cooks and sweepers clear up
       messdecks and flats for rounds.
2040   Men under punishment to muster
2045   Officer of the watch or 1st. Lt's rounds
2200   Pipe down lights out.
2230   CPO and POs pipe down
2340   Call the middle watch.
2350   Middle watchmen to muster.
```

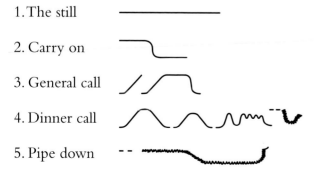

1. The still

2. Carry on

3. General call

4. Dinner call

5. Pipe down

Some other calls, the fine wiggly lines indicate the trill.

Entertainment

Films: The navy had its own Fleet Film Unit and regularly sent films out to the various ships away from home. In a flotilla of destroyers there may be several films available, some of them new releases. After they had been shown on one ship to both watches they would be passed to the other ships in company by a 'heaving line' or 'Jack Stay' transfer. Films could be either shown in one of the larger messes with half the crew crammed in there to watch, with some behind the screen watching it in reverse, or on the upper deck in good weather or in harbour. The trained projectionist was usually an electrician.

Quizzes: On long voyages inter mess or inter ship quizzes would be held in the evenings after work. The questions would be sent over the radio and broadcast over the Tannoys of the ships of the flotilla; the first back with the answer received the points. It was amazing that with approximately eight hundred men in four ships there was always some bright spark with the answer… whatever the question.

Uckers: This game is played with two large dice; about four inches (200mm) square, and has a giant board similar to the civilian Ludo. The teams dress up, usually as pirates or similar. The rules are quite complicated, with 'blobs' and 'Mixy blobs' and 'snake eyes' (double one). Some of the strange rules… *rule 16 Royal Marines may have a helper to count the spots on the dice. And; 17, Submariners must wash before entering the playing area. 18, Hairy fairies must have served 24 hours on the ship.* Both teams try to cheat and that becomes a part of the fun!

Cockroach racing: It was said that the cockroaches that were caught around the warmth of the galley in the tropics were so big they could race a taxi. It was not unknown for a group of the lads whilst in Hong Kong to number them with white paint and race them along the jetty.

Tombola: This had been a popular game played in the navy long before it gained popularity ashore as 'Bingo'. Although gambling as such was against regulations, a blind eye was turned against a few pence spent on Tombola.

SODS Operas: Sailors Operatic and Drama Society. Many ships staged their own shows either on board or ashore. With long periods at sea the men would gather together anybody with talent; singers, comedians, actors and musicians and organize a show. The show would be played out either on the ship or when the fleet met up after exercises. Some of these shows could rival the best to be found in the West End of London and in fact many of the participants ended up on stage when they left the service.

Costumes for SODS operas were made from anything they could find or make onboard or pick up in port. (Mmmm good acting).

Songs: Wherever a group of matelots got together ashore they inevitably ended up singing their drinking songs and ditties. One of the many has been adopted by the public, particularly sports teams and that is the Oggy Song. It originated in the West Country, a Janner being a Devonian (Jagger being Cornish born and bred). The oggy (or Oggie) is the Cornish pasty.

The Oggie Song

Where be going to Janner?
I be going to Looe,
Cor bugger Janner
I be goin there too.

Chorus:

Oh 'ow 'appy us will be
When us gets to the West countree,
Where the oggies grow on trees
Cor bugger Janner.

Half a pound of flour and marge
Makes lovely clacker★
Just enough for me and you
Cor bugger Janner.

Chorus; 'oh 'ow happy us will be etc.

You make fast, I'll make fast
Make fast the dinghy
You make fast, kiss my arse
Make fast the dinghy
And we'll all go back to oggy land
to oggy land to oggy land
And we'll all go back to oggy land
Where they don't know sugar from,
Tissue paper, Tissue paper Marmalade or jam.

All shout: *Oggy Oggy Oggy*
Singer: *Oggy*
All: *Oggy Oggy Oggy.*
'*Oi! Oi! Oi!*' was sometimes added at the end.

*A 'clacker' was a pastry, it got the name from the fact that the chef was said to crimp the edge of pastries using his false teeth... clack, clack, clack!

My Jenny WREN bride
A sailor's song

I've just got back from a wedding
I laughed till I could have cried
I'll never forget – the people I met
When I married my Jenny WREN bride.

Her father he worked in the dockyard,
Her brother in the Marine store
And as for habits – why talk about rabbits
They had half the dockyard ashore.

So – I asked her father for a dowry
He gave me a drum of soft soap,
Some cleaning paste, a bale of waste
And thirty two fathoms of rope.

We decked out the churchyard with bunting
And painted the archway with flattening,
And on her head – a deck cloth was spread,
With a spud net in front for a veil.

Her knickers were made of black hessian,
Her petticoat was made of green baize,
And as for suspenders – two motor boat fenders
And two Pusser's gaiters for stays.

The vicar who stood by the alter,
Said 'Who gives this woman away'?
Then Jack off the Hood – said 'Cor blimey – I could,
But let every dog have his day.

And now I'm off on my honeymoon,
I don't know what to do tonight,
But I know quite a few – who reckon they do,
As they say she's a bit of alright.

Welfare:

In all naval towns, at home and abroad there were always many young ladies… and some not quite so young, who attended to the young sailor's physical and mental welfare, particularly if they had testosterone problems! Some of these girls did this work for nothing, whilst others were paid for their work! In Portsmouth there were several girls who became legends within their lifetime within the naval community; Pompey Lil, No Nose Nora, Slack Alice, Geordie Joyce and Big Sylvie amongst others. Big Sylvie usually frequented the 'Hotel de Leenox' (The Lennox pub), she used to sit on top of the Juke Box and sing her own words, (unprintable) to modern pop songs. She was entertaining, kind hearted and very often loaned money to sailors who were broke. But woe betide anyone who upset her… she had a hefty left hook. Other pubs frequented by some of the girls were the 'Albany', the 'Fleece', 'The Great Western' and the 'Yorkshire Grey' most of which have long since been demolished. In Devonport there was 'Straddling Madeline', in Chatham 'Nickerless Nora', in Weymouth 'Suck back Sally', Porto Rica 'Rico Rita' – all the ports had their favourites. Sometimes, especially abroad, the sailors would get something they never bargained for, this they called 'Catching the boat up' and as a result they would lose their rum issue until they had finished a course of treatment in 'Rose Cottage' for their ailment. The sailors in some foreign ports had to be very careful as to who they were associating with, particularly in places like parts of the Far East and South America where some young men dressed as women. In Singapore they were known as 'Kyties' and mainly frequented a place called Booghie Street (I am told!), in the Philippines they were 'Binni Boys'. Some of these 'girls' were as attractive as the real thing and it was not realized who was who until a 'toggle and two' or 'meat and two veg' were discovered!

Spiritual wellbeing, Divisions and Church:

Most Sunday mornings, on the dockside in harbour or if convenient on deck at sea, 'Sunday Divisions' were held, that is every man on board had to dress in his best uniform and fall in by divisions for inspection by the captain. This originated in the 18th century when they realized that clean clothes made for a better life in the confined space of a ship. The captain inspected them to make sure everyone was complying with his order that working clothes should be changed twice a week, Thursdays and Sundays. The saying, 'One good turn deserves another' comes from a time when sailors wore their clothes till they were dirty and then turned them inside out to do another good turn. After Divisions a compulsory Church of England church service was held for those whose documentation showed their religion as C of E, minority religions were excused or held theirs separately. A padre, the 'Sin Bosun', 'The Bish' or the 'God botherer' was not normally carried by individual ships so the Captain took the service. There was usually one Padre to each part of the fleet or squadron. If a man died in action at sea he was sewn up into his hammock, the last stitch was put through his nose, if he didn't complain, it confirmed he had 'crossed the bar' (had died). A burial service by the captain with the crew was held before the body was committed to the deep. A practice shell for weight was put in one end. With modern refrigeration this does not happen as frequently as it did.

Lower Deck 'Buzz'

The rumour system that operated onboard was known as the buzz. The crew was very often kept in the dark, especially in war time as to where the ship was going and what she was to get involved in. They could not risk alcohol loosening Jacks tongue in the bars ashore! However the 'buzz' would travel throughout the ship as quick as war drums and was usually pretty accurate. During the war the issue of special arctic clothing for instance was bit of a giveaway about your next destination! Very often people ashore had more of an idea than 'Jack' did, they provided stores and provisions and rumours would very often be spot on. It was not unknown for the girls in the bars to tell Jack where he was going to next.

Aid to civil power

Small arms and weapons carried on board Cavalier:

.303 Lee Enfield rifles, sixty.
.303 Bren guns, four.
.38 Webley service revolvers, thirty.
2" mortars, HE or smoke.
Hand grenades, 8 seconds. (You were supposed to count to six before throwing them but Jack to be on the safe side counted 2… 6 and lobbed it! This then became the standard chant instead of 1… 2…. 3 when coordinating effort it was 2… 6 heave).
Bayonets, working (pig stickers) and ceremonial (knife blades) for attachment to the .303 rifles.
1 lb scare charges for use against divers in foreign ports: If the ship was in a hostile port, men patrolled the upper deck and threw the charges over the side every so often to keep divers away from placing limpet mines or spying on our underwater equipment. The resultant underwater explosion was enough to kill a man if he came too near. They were also used very effectively for fishing when it became necessary!

Another anti diver tactic was to operate the asdic which would not do his hearing any favours!

Hogging and sagging

Ships bend up and down in rough seas; this is called 'hogging' and 'sagging'. This picture of 'Cavalier' illustrates well the 'sagging' as the weight of the centre of the ship is not supported by the sea and it sags. As she goes over the next wave the front and back ends are not supported and they bend down, this is 'hogging'. The whole ship would be shuddering as she rode the waves. They are of course designed to withstand this constant movement and just below the mast, at what is called the break of the forecastle, there is a metal deck plate that is not bolted or welded, in rough weather this can be seen to be sliding to and fro as the deck bends. The guard rails can also be seen to be tightening and slacking as the whole ship bends up and down.

'Cavalier' sagging, the weight in the centre is not supported properly. This picture also illustrates why the upper decks are no go areas in anything but reasonable weather.

Storm lines were rigged on the upper deck to hang onto, a bit like the underground train hanging straps but they slid along the wire and had a 'monkeys fist' knot on the end.

When it really got bad and the sea was going over the superstructure then the upper decks were out of bounds altogether. Because of the engine and boiler rooms being amidships there is no way of getting aft on the inside of the ship therefore the men down aft were fed from the emergency galley.

A Chinese 'Dhobey whalla' hanging on to a storm line, fanny in hand, makes his way to the galley in rough weather. On the right is the fresh vegetable screen, this did not take long to empty after a few days at sea. The motor boat has a 'tingle' on her side (a repair patch).

Work up

You will see 'Work up' mentioned throughout this book. After commissioning and the equipment and crew were onboard, all ships underwent a training period. No one really looked forward to it; it was usually a period of two to three weeks of intensive and nonstop training, training, and training, night and day, night and day under war conditions. A team of experts from FOST (Fleet Officer Ships Training) would come aboard to put the crew through vigorous exercises designed to mould them into an efficient fighting unit. They would be at action stations, firing weapons, fighting fires, damage control, first aid, hunting a submarine and being attacked by aircraft. Close the ship down for atomic fall out and clean the radiation hot spots on the weapons to get her back into action, this was a particular problem for 'Cavalier' because she still had an open bridge. During action when the wardroom becomes an operating theatre, the special lighting, stowed in lockers under the seats is erected and a curtain pulls across to isolate the operating table. The bathrooms became air locked decontamination areas, with rails for plastic curtains around the doors. No department escaped rigorous testing, electricians repairing shell damaged cables, the cooks in the galley would be told the galley had taken a hit and they would have to improvise and prepare cold food for nearly two hundred men. Engine and boiler room staff would be told steam or oil pipes were ruptured and they had to find alternatives to keep the ship under way. First aid parties (during action the cooks and miscellaneous trades) treated men for all sorts of injuries and practiced getting a man out of the small hatch of a compartment using the 'Neil Robertson' stretcher, a canvas and cane affair with straps, placed in strategic places throughout the ship. Very little sleep was had by anyone for days on end; they were pushed to the limit. At the end of it all they were either pronounced fit to go on to the world stage... or not. If they failed they did it again until it they were proficient. Sometimes key personnel were changed to get the team right. Sometimes it meant the ship returning to the dockyard to correct some fault in equipment (As in the 1961 commission with the guns). When it was all over, your messdeck, your lounge if you can imagine it, was cleared of the fire fighting foam and hoses, black out curtains, bits of timber shoring and ropes and water mopped up. All the PVC curtains used to darken ship and air lock the bathrooms had to be taken down and stowed away and the day to day equipment, cutlery and crockery was brought back out of lockers to resume 'normal routine'.

HMS CAVALIER - DAILY ORDERS.
THURSDAY 9TH DECEMBER.

///

OOD....................	MID WILKIE	IMEA...............	MEA BOND
D. SEN W/E..............	OEA THOMPSON	DUTY PO...........	PO MOODY
DUTY LEM................	LREM ADAMS	DUTY SA...........	SA COWLING
NBCD STATE..............	3X	D. SRE OP..........	CEM WYATT
DUTY PART..............	1ST STBD		
DRESS; No 8's 1800 NC			

///

DAILY SEA ROUTINE.

0700	Mail closes onboard.
0740	Helo transfer Party to muster. Dress 50W and Rig Gemini.
0755	SSD, ME's Fuelling Party close up. White Watch Seamen close up, Rig Boots DMS, Lifejackets and lights. Assume DC State 3Y Down all deadlights Port Side.
0800	R/V with Wave Chief, Helo Transfer with Lossie, OFF ASWO, Records, Mail. ON One Mid McKENZIE Ex Wasperton, Mail.
0815	Commence RAS with Wave Chief, Our Port Side Fwd.
1200	All Weekly books to Wardroom Flat.
2015	Fwd JR's Around the World under the Sea.
2100	CPO's CINCINATTI KID.

Daily orders

At the top NBCD.............. 3X refers to the damage control state for water tight doors to be at.
Duty part............... 1st STBD means the 1st of starboard watch is 'duty watch'
Dress No8's is the rig of the day and 1800 NC means to change into Night Clothing, No3A's at 6pm
D. SRE OP means the duty Ships Recording Equipment operator (ships entertainment system)
Helo (helicopter) transfer
0800 R/v with Royal Fleet Auxiliary oil tanker 'Wave Chief' for refuelling and mail transfer.
2015 film 'Around the World under the sea' showing in junior rates mess
2100 film 'Cincinnati kid' showing in the CPO's mess, Chiefs only!

Uniforms numbered

Daily orders were posted on the notice board each day; they would give the daily routine and what 'rig of the day' was to be at certain times. To be out of the rig of the day was an offence. One of the punishments meted out was the 'Kit muster'.

No 6A's, Singapore. In the background the 'Belfast' and 'Alert', the C in C's yacht. To the right an RFA.

No 1's	Best bell bottom blues, gold wire badges
No 2's	No 1's minus jacket, collar and silk
No 3's	Second best rough blue (itchy) serge, red cotton badges
No 3 A's	No 3's without the jacket, collar, or silk
No 6's	Best white uniform, white shoes, blue collar, Medals.
No 6 A's	above but without jacket, collar and silk and medals.
No 7's	Full whites but without medals.
No 8's	Working denim type trousers and blue shirt, black shoes
No 10's	White front and shorts black stockings and shoes.
No 10 A's	Blue shirt, blue shorts, sandals or black shoes and stockings.
Footwear	Two pairs of boots (without studs so as not to damage the deck). Two pairs of black shoes (and knee length socks). One pair white leather/canvas shoes. One pair of brown 'Jesus' sandals. Gym shoes and Civilian clothes for walking out in certain counties abroad.

Bell bottoms were folded, not to represent the seven seas as is popularly thought but in order that they would stow away in a locker. They were wide so that in the early days they rolled up easily to scrub decks and were easily removed if needs be if you for example fell into the water.

Added to the above would be other specialist equipment depending on which branch you belonged to. Everyone had a gas respirator and anti-flash hood and gloves. Seamen who worked the upper decks also had extra kit in the form of Sow'esters and oilskin coats for foul weather and Stokers and electricians had boiler suits.

For fighting fires there were asbestos suits stowed at strategic places around the ship, these had hose pipes for breathing air through (made of asbestos!).

Special clothing was issued for other activities when required such as jungle warfare or if you were going ashore as an armed unit in 'support of the civil power' gaiters, webbing, helmets and small arms

Watch Keeping System

1200 – 1600 afternoon watch
1600 – 1800 *first dog*
1800 – 2000 *second dog*
2000 – 2359 first
2359 – 0400 middle
0400 – 0800 morning
0800 – 1200 forenoon

The two hour dog watches (named after the Dog Star) were designed so that you did not do the same watches every day; it had the effect of shifting you a watch each day and also allowed everyone to have their tea at a reasonable time.

The crew was generally divided into four 'watches', Red and green, parts one and two.

When in harbour some would be on duty to look after the ship whilst the other watches went ashore. They would then change over. At home one watch would cover the whole weekend and then swap over the following weekend. Each man had a station card showing his duties.

Mick Davies' station card (Found onboard during the ship's restoration). It shows him to be the 'first' part of the 'port' watch and of Church of England religion. His Next of Kin is his wife and her address is shown.

There were different variations to this system depending on which ship you were on or the circumstance you found yourself in.

You will now have some idea of what made a sailor and understand why he was the way he was when he got ashore. They were off to explore the world and be paid for doing so… an AB got the princely sum of £3.10.0 a week (£3.50) juniors considerably less.

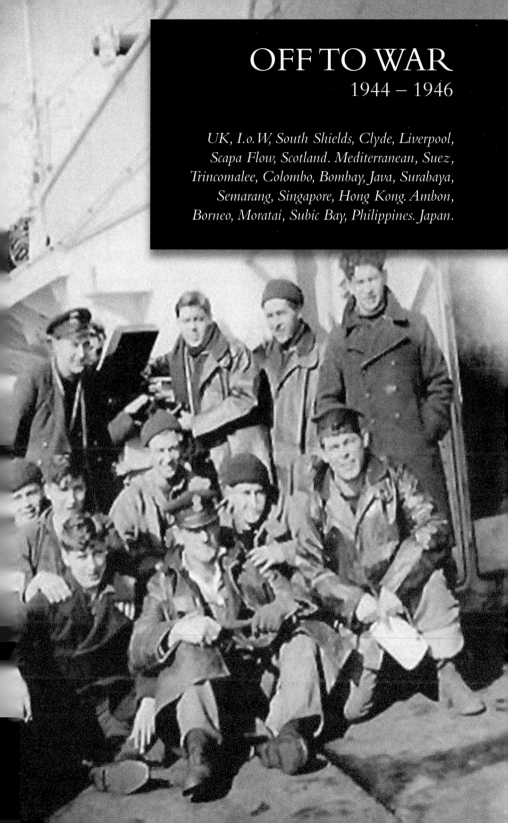

OFF TO WAR
1944 – 1946

*UK, I.o.W, South Shields, Clyde, Liverpool,
Scapa Flow, Scotland. Mediterranean, Suez,
Trincomalee, Colombo, Bombay, Java, Surabaya,
Semarang, Singapore, Hong Kong. Ambon,
Borneo, Moratai, Subic Bay, Philippines. Japan.*

OFF TO WAR
1944 – 1946

Lt Cdr Donald T. McBarnett DSC RN
(Ship's first commission)

Prior to commanding 'Cavalier' Lt Cdr McBarnett distinguished himself at the Battle of the River Plate, with his expertise in damage control he helped to save the cruiser 'Exeter', then using only a boats compass from the emergency conning position, navigated her to the Falkland Islands for repairs. For this he was mentioned in dispatches and, many years later, was mentioned in the film made about the battle. In 1940 during the Dunkirk evacuation, he was awarded the DSC for his part in rescuing nearly a thousand men under fire from the beaches using a Dutch Schuit (barge). He served on several destroyers and was well qualified to take command of the new large fleet destroyer 'Cavalier'. Having said all that he apparently got command of 'Cavalier' because he'd blown the stern off his last ship, the destroyer 'Wizard'! It was through a misunderstanding in communication. At 0216hrs 10th June 1944 after 'Wizard' had been circling the battleships 'Anson' and 'Duke of York' and dropping depth charges to deter attacks by U-Boats; she was ordered to go to anchor. As she approached the anchorage the Captain ordered 'Let go' meaning for the anchor to be slipped, however the Depth Charge party down aft also heard the order and 'let go' a Depth charge before someone could stop them. Because the ship was going astern to set her anchor it exploded underneath her doing serious damage, killing at least five men and injuring another twenty five. All communication is now carefully worded to avoid such mistakes; For instance when a gun's crew is told to fire their gun they are told to 'shoot' not 'Fire', otherwise the fire parties rush into action!

In hindsight we know that 'Cavalier' survived the war as did most of her crew, some of whom were very young when they joined her. The life expectancy of the average destroyer was about two years and many men were being killed every day. They knew by now that they were probably winning the war but it was still a dangerous world out there!

As 'Cavalier' took shape on the slips and became recognizable as a ship, some of her key personnel would be sent to lodgings nearby and work onboard to familiarize themselves with the equipment they would be working with.

Frank Toop, AB: 'I joined the ship on the 8th September 1944 at Cowes, at that stage she had no engines or guns mounted. At the first muster the first LT asked if anyone had any experience of handling boats, I immediately put my hand up and was appointed coxswain of the motorboat. Actually I had never handled a boat before but I soon learnt and I had the job until I left her in Singapore in 1946. The fact was that I was always seasick in any sort of sea but the extreme cold never bothered me in the slightest'.

Finally on completion of trials she was officially accepted into the Royal Navy. The full crew arrived and commissioned her on the

22nd September 1944; they changed the Red Duster for the White Ensign and left Whites yard as R73 and with her hull painted an unusual shade of pale grey green.

The first crew shortly after commissioning, the capstans and cables have had very little if any use. It's not known if the list she appears to have is the photographers fault or the slight list she sometimes suffered from during much of her career. CDR McBarnett front centre is holding a small dog. (Dennis Packham AB)

Special Sea Duty men: Whenever entering or leaving harbour everybody stood by their special stations. The captain, navigator and other key personnel were on the bridge. One man would be down in the cable locker to make sure the cables ran out if needed (He was locked in and in the event of a collision could not be released until the water tight integrity had been checked!) The Cox was on the wheel, an engineer was in the tiller flat to make sure the steering gear was operating properly whilst manoeuvring, fire and damage control parties were stood by. Seamen were at their upper deck stations to handle wires and fenders as required by the bridge.

'Procedure Alfa':

Bridge broadcast: *'Special sea duty men close up, assume damage control state 3, hands fall in for leaving harbour'*

Bridge to Engine room; *'Obey telegraphs'*

Engine room to Bridge; *'Main Engines ready Sir'*

Bridge; *'Remove gangway, single up fore and aft'*

Bridge; *'Let go forward, let go aft'*, then *'Let go springs'*.

Bridge to wheelhouse; *'Half ahead starboard'*, *'Half ahead Port, six zero revolutions, steer 090 degrees'*.

Coxswain (on the wheel, repeating everything for clarification); *'Half ahead starboard'*, *'Half ahead port, six zero revolutions on sir, steer 090 degrees'*.

As she moved forward the men would fall in either side of the fo'c'sle and quarter deck until they had cleared the harbour. Then the berthing wires were stowed away on the reels and the men would go back to their allotted work places. She was under way and this routine with variations would be repeated for perhaps a thousand times in the next twenty eight years.

Anthony 'Dusty' Millar AB: 'The skipper being a Scot adopted the tune 'The bonnets of bonnie Dundee' for the ship and this was played loudly over the Tannoy on entering or leaving harbour. On occasion he could be seen doing a Scottish jig to it'.

Victor Rolt CPO Tel, joined 'Cavalier' and 'stood by her' from mid-1944, whilst she was under construction. He took a great deal of interest in the new radio and electronic equipment being installed and all the associated generators and alternators, these would become his responsibility. He was amazed at the advanced technology of most of the equipment, much of it American. Having a good look around the ship he realized how lucky he was to be a part of the crew of a ship that was being built with some creature comforts for her ship's company in mind. He had never before seen anything like it in the old ships he had served on. There were small electric heaters in all the living and working spaces and even air conditioning in the Transmitting Station, the fighting heart of the ship. There were bathrooms with rows of stainless steel sinks and even privacy curtains round the showers, what luxury. When commissioning day came, the full signals staff joined and comprised of one PO radio/radar mechanic, one leading Telegraphist, five ordinary Telegraphists, and three coders, they soon settled in and made a good team'.

The skipper being an expert in damage control made sure they were well trained, he also swapped some specialist crew from the frwd and after mess decks so that there was a cross section of expertise available at both ends of the ship in an emergency, something that later became standard practice. 'Cavalier' immediately sailed North to join the 6th Destroyer Flotilla at Scapa Flow. This Flotilla consisted of all eight of the 'C&A' class destroyers; 'Cavalier', 'Caesar', 'Carron', Caprice', 'Cambrian', 'Cavendish', 'Carysfort' and 'Cassandra'.

They made for Tobermory off the Isle of Mull for their workup under Commodore Stephenson of the Western Approaches command.

They were soon involved in the war proper. She and the destroyers 'Cavendish' and 'Zebra' were due to go on the outward bound Arctic convoy JW64 (3rd Feb) but were then detailed for an operation to evacuate five hundred men, women and children from Soroy, the island at the entrance to Stjern Sound in Norway (Late lair of the German Navy's battleship Tirpitz). However this operation was cancelled at the last minute (It was later reinstated as operation 'Open Door').

Between the 12th and 14th February '45 she was part of the escort for operation 'Selenium'. This group was split into two forces, 'Cavalier' being a part of Force 2 escorting the aircraft carriers 'Premier' and 'Puncher' along with the cruiser 'Devonshire', her sister 'Cavendish' and the destroyers 'Scourge' and 'Zebra'. This operation, which was successful, was to launch a sortie of Barracuda and Avenger aircraft to lay mines off Skatestraumen in Norway.

A few days later in early February they were involved in the operations 'Shred' and 'Groundsheet', this group was designated as Force 4 and consisted of again the carriers 'Premier' and 'Puncher', the cruiser 'Dido' and destroyers 'Myngs' and 'Scorpion'. The first part, 'Shred' was a run through a German minefield off Stavanger with the 10th Minesweeping Flotilla consisting of the sweepers 'Courier', 'Jewel', 'Serene', 'Wave', 'Hare' and 'Golden Fleece'. They went on from there to carry out the second part, operation 'Groundsheet', which entailed the aircraft from the carriers laying mines in the Karmoy channel. At one stage they escorted the fast minelayer HMS Manxman into the Fiords of Norway to lay mines. They left before daylight, with everything rattling and shaking, they were said to be doing 38 knots. The 'Manxman', and her sisters were, at that time long held to be the fastest ships in the Navy and passed them doing 45 knots. In fact 'Manxman' very often sailed alone after dark to lay mines on an enemy coast and by morning would be back in her berth, most people would not have known that she had ever left.

The 'Woolworth' aircraft carrier 'Premier' one of forty converted from merchant ships. She had been an American merchant ship which after the war reverted back to being the 'Rhodesia Star'.

John Downie: 'When entering Scapa one day we received a message to say we had been allocated the buoy No40, these buoys were huge. As buoy jumper I, with an Oppo were put onto the buoy by boat. We were wearing normal boiler suits, gym shoes, wooly hats and lifejackets, it was well below freezing and the snow and sleet was coming down almost horizontal in the wind, as it very often did up there. We waited and waited until we were almost hypothermic then a motor boat appeared and told us we had been put on the wrong buoy! It took us to another buoy and we got the ship's heavy chain cable secured how I don't know because we couldn't feel our fingers which were blue and swollen like sausages. We were helped below to our mess and then suddenly a messenger from the Gods arrived... with a large glass of rum each... all was forgiven!'

Back at Scapa they hardly had time to refuel when they were ordered to go to the assistance of the returning Arctic convoy that they would originally have been escorting, RA64. In the earlier convoy RA62 on 11th December '44, her sister ship 'Cassandra' had been torpedoed and had her bow blown off back to 'B' gun, they saved the ship but had lost 62 men killed.

A poor picture of 'Cassandra' minus her bow back to 'B' gun, being towed backwards into Murmansk, (Graham Latter, origins unknown).

Convoy RA64 was now in serious trouble. Owing to bad weather in the Orkneys the outbound convoy had been delayed sailing and consequently JW64 had sailed close behind. The Germans realizing the prize that was being presented to them in a double convoy sent as many U-boats to cross their route as they could muster. It is known there were at least ten that had previously been withdrawn from the Atlantic lying in wait. The second convoy was being hit badly and the escort was running desperately short of ammunition and depth charges. The escort from the first convoy which had only just arrived in Murmansk was ordered out even though they had not had time to replenish their stores. The returning convoy, RA64 had left the Kola Inlet on the 17th February with the temperature at -40°c and with ice flows on the sea. It consisted of thirty three ships and they found themselves in serious trouble in the Barents Sea. They had already lost one escort; 'Lark' and a merchant ship, the Thomas Scott. Later the little escort 'Bluebell' was torpedoed and sunk with all hands bar one. They desperately needed help. 'Cavalier' sailed immediately from the UK end along with two other large modern destroyers, the 'Myngs' and 'Scorpion', this was named operation 'Hotbed'. They could not have chosen a worse time to be going into the Arctic. The Meteorological office records show that it was some of the worst weather ever recorded in the Arctic; Sir Winston Churchill said he thought… 'It was the worst journey in the world'. For the next five days the wind force ranged from force 8 to 10 then rising to 12 which is the beginning of hurricane force on the Beaufort scale (70 mph winds plus). To give you some idea of the size of the waves encountered, the Aircraft carrier had waves constantly washing along the flight deck and was rolling to almost 45 degrees. The men lived and slept in their hammocks fully clothed with lifebelts and sea boots on. When not on watch they could only wedge themselves in a corner and hang on.

One of the surviving merchant ships escorted by 'Cavalier', shown here on convoy RA64. To end up in this ice laden sea with -40°c degrees temperature meant almost certain death. (Paul Kemp, Convoy)

The rendezvous with RA64 on the 23rd February 1945 was just in time, two of the original escorts were running very low on fuel and four others; the destroyers 'Zambesi', 'Zest', 'Zealous' and 'Sioux' had already been detached for the new operation to evacuate the civilians from Soroy. It was believed they may be held hostage by the Germans so they were taken to Russia for safety.

Due to the weather, serious damage and shifting cargoes the convoy was scattered over a wide area and had to be rounded up more than once. They were attacked several times by groups of nineteen to twenty five JU88 aircraft at a time but these were fought off by the escorts. Fighting the frwd guns in these seas was a dangerous business. One further ship, the 'Henry bacon' was lost when it dropped astern of the convoy. The convoy was finally brought back without further loss to Loch Ewe and then into the Clyde on the 1st March.

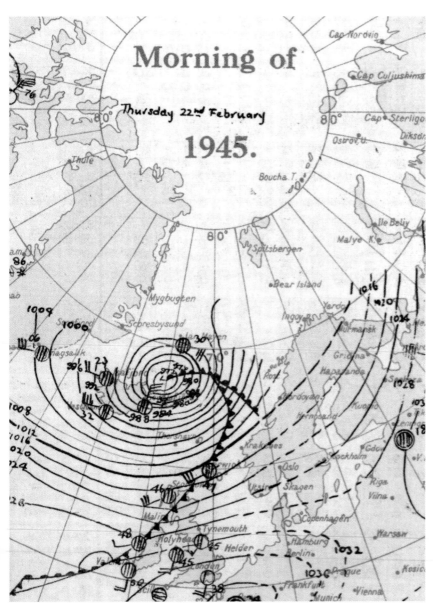

Detail from a weather chart for 22nd Feb. 1945, showing a severe
depression off the east coast of Iceland, this moved N.E. across the path of
convoy RA64. The Kola Inlet is to the top right of this chart and Britain
is bottom centre. (National Meteorological Library & Archive)

HMS Nairana on convoy RA64, all of her 161 meters long hull was being thrown around like a toy. Her aircraft (here stowed below) brought down several attacking JU 88 torpedo bombers and damaged more before the weather closed in and prevented both sides from flying. The names of the other ships in the picture are not known but one could very well have been 'Cavalier'. If you were standing on her deck (and not hanging on) you would probably have run the 100 yards sprint in record time! (Paul Kemp, Convoy)

All of "Cavalier's" boats had been smashed to pieces, her life rafts were washed away and much of her superstructure and guardrails had been damaged, had she been sunk there would have been great loss of life, it is bad enough to have to abandon ship in these waters but without lifeboats there was no chance of surviving. She had well earned her battle honour of ARCTIC 1945.

Charlie Melling: (Arctic Convoy RA64) 'We met up with the merchant ships and started the return trip in bloody awful weather. It is only the rare mammoth of a wave breaking like surf that holds danger for a well-founded ship. But it is the sound and the fury, and the violent motion of the ship, hour after hour, day in and day out, that is exhausting. Anywhere between decks, especially forward becomes soaking wet with water sloshing about across the decks and dripping from every bulkhead in an atmosphere of 100 percent

'Cavalier' Battle Honours board

humidity. The thought of being pitched out, with the loss of one's ship in action, into that screaming inferno of near freezing water did not bear thinking of. Our motor boat and both whalers were torn from their davits (During this period 'Cavalier' carried two whalers). My skimming dish (small fast boat) and its cradle were torn from the deck and washed overboard. The fore part of the deck house under 'X' gun had a huge dent in it which put the after galley out of action, so no hot food for the lads down aft. It took us twenty four hours to get up there and more to get back… it was supposed to be a fast convoy! We got a new motor boat and whaler at Scapa and proceeded to the Clyde for repairs and another whaler and skimming dish.'

Ivor Robinson Telegraphist: 'My abiding memory is of having to climb to the top of the mast to rig an emergency radio aerial. That's a long way up there with the ship rolling and no safety harness, just a bit of rope tied round your middle when you get up there'.

They had survived all that the Arctic and the enemy could throw at them. AB Reg Linley 2nd from right seated, photograph taken on the fo'c'sle behind 'A' gun. They are wearing an assortment of oilskins and watch keeper's coats and woollen hats (Force's comforters knitted by the women from home); this then was their arctic clothing.

Derek Wood PMX/672543, O CK: (You never forget your official number, without it you got no pay and it stays in your memory for the rest of your life) I joined as an ordinary cook and left 'Cavalier' as a Leading hand. All our photographs taken onboard and all letters sent home had to be passed by the censor.

The censor's stamp on the back of one of Derek's photos.

The Monsters: After being repaired at Rosyth she was attached to the Home Fleet Western Approaches Command and was based in the Clyde. From there she would be escorting the 'Monsters', the nickname for the huge liners *Queen Mary, Queen Elizabeth, Mauritania, Aquitania, Louis Pasteur* and others bringing in the American troops that were being poured into Europe. These liners were relatively safe travelling alone in the open sea because of their ability to zigzag at speed. However when they came nearer to the areas covered by the U-Boats they became more vulnerable so two of the fast C & A's would rendezvous with them in the North Atlantic and escort them into the Western Approaches. Now although 'Cavalier' had a good turn of speed she would find it difficult in rough weather to keep up with these liners that dwarfed her. On one escort 'Cavalier' whilst going as fast as she could prudently do in rough weather dived into a huge wave and 'A' gun, which weighs many tons was lifted out of the deck. On arrival in harbour it was removed altogether and for some of the time escorting the 'Monsters' she ran without it. Early in April whilst escorting the *Queen Mary* it was so rough that half of *Queen Mary's* bottom could be seen when she heaved out of a wave. 'Cavalier' made a contact on her ASDIC's with a suspected U-Boat, *Queen Mary* went off zig zagging at speed whilst 'Cavalier' spent some time dropping several depth charge patterns over it, although they saw some wreckage there was not enough evidence to confirm a 'kill'.

A rare wartime photograph of 'Cavalier' escorting the Monsters into the Western Approaches. This picture was taken on 6th April 1945 by pilot, Bruce Mackie, 179 Squadron Coastal Command flying a Warwick aircraft. Paint has peeled off her sides showing the hard running she was doing. At this stage she still had 'A' gun. (Bruce Mackie)

Derek Brooks Signalman: I joined 'Cavalier' at Scapa Flow in December 1944 and went on the convoy RA64. We encountered very severe weather lost our boats and suffered a lot of damage. We went to Rosyth for repairs and had a huge crockery bill! After that we went over to America and met and escorted the *Queen Mary* over to the UK loaded with troops. We detected a U-Boat in the Atlantic and kept it down whilst the *Queen Mary* steamed away at high speed. Later we spent the rest of the day trying to catch up with her. On entering Liverpool we had a destroyer ahead of us which slowed down, we slowed and the *Queen Mary* which was right behind and towering over us almost ran up our a★★se end!

One of the Monsters that dwarfed the destroyers, the *Queen Elizabeth*.

Frank Toop, LS: During the phase of escorting the liners I had asked my fiancé to marry me and, knowing that our next 'boiler clean' was to be in Liverpool on the 9th April 1945 I requested leave. Leave was granted and I sent a telegram to my intended to arrange for the wedding on the 10th. Back at sea Admiralty changed the plans, I learnt that we were now to escort a ship to Northern Ireland and then escort another liner from there into Liverpool… putting us two days behind! I was in despair, all my attempts to hurry things along with the 'Jimmy' having failed I resigned myself to thoughts of my loved one waiting at the altar.

A proud Frank and his new bride Florence, he is wearing the traditional white ribbon when marrying in uniform. The anchor on his arm indicates Leading Seaman and the one stripe four years of service with good conduct, or as Jack says 'Four years of undetected crime'!

Fortunately there is a God in Heaven who looks after poor sailors and after two days at sea we were ordered into Falmouth to oil before picking up the second ship. I requested to see the 'Jimmy' who spoke to Captain McBarnett who granted me seven days leave starting from Falmouth. So there I was at midday on the 9th and due to get married at 2pm on the 10th in Manchester. I arrived at Truro station and was explaining my predicament to a lady porter (So who else do you tell your troubles to?) She said if you get over to the other platform quick you may just catch the Cornish express which goes direct to Manchester. I just managed to catch the express and started the 'slow' journey north; we stopped several times for air raids. We arrived at 0500hrs and I made my way straight to the KGV club in London Road for breakfast then on the first bus to home. I spent most of that morning going round the town looking to buy a pair of pyjamas… well this was a long time ago and we wore them then! This was the start of our fifty four years of happy marriage.

'Cavalier' leaving Liverpool in April 1945 on another escort duty.

Vic Rolt CPO Tel: We were secured alongside the Cunard troopship Mauritania in Gladstone Dock in Liverpool and because it was 'classified information,' only the skipper, the signals officer and I knew that we were to escort her to Gibraltar. She was to load RAF personnel from the dispersal base at West Kirby, Cheshire. I knew that my sister, a WAAF Sergeant would be among them, she had volunteered for overseas service and was being posted to Ismalia on the Suez Canal. On the day before sailing I visited her at her base but because of the official secrets act I could not tell her what I knew. Imagine her surprise the next day when I met her lorry on the jetty and carried her bags aboard Mauritania and introduced her to the first radio operator. I had another surprise for her; because of radio silence at sea I had arranged that each day at 0900 I would communicate with her through their signalman using Morse code by Aldis lamps. This worked well till the last day when Mauritania left us behind in rough weather and she was handed over to the Mediterranean fleet destroyers'.

'Cavalier', R73 in Gladstone Dock Liverpool, she has just returned from escorting the Monsters and her 'A' gun is missing. Outboard of her is an American destroyer escort. (IWM)

1945, 'Cavalier' in the Atlantic, escorting a surrendered U-Boat, 'B' and 'X' gun are trained on the submarine. The U-Boat is flying the black flag that they had been ordered to do on surrendering. A Sunderland flying boat of Coastal Command can just be seen circling overhead. Picture taken from her sister ship 'Caprice'. (Caprice Association)

When on the 8th May 1945 the war in Europe officially came to an end, Germany surrendered and 'Cavalier' was at sea in the Western Approaches escorting the MS Ile de France into the Clyde at the time, so under the circumstances all they could do in celebration was to 'Splice the main brace'. However the convoy escorts were to continue on a war footing as it was suspected that fanatical Nazi U-Boat commanders may continue attacking convoys. One U-Boat surfaced and surrendered to her and her sister ship 'Caprice'. In the photograph below both 'Cavalier' and 'Caprice' are in a position where the submarine cannot immediately fire a torpedo at them. 'Cavalier's' 'B' gun can also be seen trained on the U-Boat and no doubt the other weapons as well. The Admiralty ordered them to instruct the intercepted U-Boats to remain where they were and other ships would be sent to escort them to Lough Foyle in

Londonderry. The last convoy was brought in on the 3rd of June and the European war finally ended for the escorts on the 7th.

Reg Lindley AB: To most of us our skipper was superb, he knew what he wanted and he knew how to get the best out of his men. The 8th May 1945 found us some 200 miles west of Ireland having seen a troop ship on its way clear of U-Boats. We were ordered to do sweeps of the area to round up any U-Boats, which had been ordered to surface from the 5th May. We then went up to Scapa Flow to await further orders, eventually being told to prepare for the Far East, the Japanese were still fighting. We practiced torpedo firing in June 1945. The practice entailed firing dummy torpedoes set deep so that they ran under the target ship to show whether it would have been a hit or not. Having fired two torpedoes ourselves, one of which did a porpoise; that is it leaped up and down out of the water instead of zig sagging from side to side. We chased it like a dog chasing a rabbit at thirty knots and several miles later eventually recovered it (They were expensive!).

The other ship then fired at us, I'm not sure which ship it was so I'll 'darken ship'. I've no doubt there is someone somewhere still trying to settle his slop chit! The incoming torpedo was picked up on our Asdic and we did some dodging and speed adjustment to avoid it. Suddenly there was an almighty bang and a terrible scream of grinding metal and vibrations from 'Y' gun to the depth charges on the stern. The stern of the ship became airborne; it lifted out of the water then settled and we just wallowed in the sea. Soot flew out of the funnel and persons appeared on deck that we had not met before! Stokers were holding their heads and eardrums with expressions that meant 'exactly what was that'. The engineering officer resplendent in his white overalls, followed by many other officers, CPO's and PO's all headed down aft. The Captain and the Jimmy waited on the bridge to find out the problem and solution. Words were spoken which Nelson had never heard. Everyone on deck was covered in soot and rusted paint flecks. The Gunner, Mr.

Baker appeared in a diving suit and face mask. Suitably roped up he was lowered over the side adjacent to the port side screw protection pad and was lowered into the hog wash, he disappeared in bubbles and a couple of minutes later (Long enough in these temperatures) he reappeared. He was hoisted onboard and was surrounded by the EO and his staff, his report was lucid and short; the port 'A' bracket was broken and the propeller blades were bent over. A tug was called for and a short tow to Scapa arranged. Messages crossed the air waves, passing pleasantries and comments on paternal issues and requests for details for the supply and accountants branch'.

In June they proceeded to Rosyth on one screw with a tug in attendance. Reg went down into the dry dock later to see the damage, they had been told that the air vessel on a torpedo was bored from solid steel for strength and they weighed one ton, they were right!

Meanwhile the decks were opened up in order to replace both shafts and gearboxes. Oerlikons were replaced by the more powerful single pom poms in preparation for the East. Despite secret coding being used, the Japanese had heard about 'Cavalier's preparations for the Far East and decided on the 14th August 1945 to surrender. The fact that the Americans had dropped a couple of big bombs on Hiroshima, 6th August and Nagasaki on the 9th August may also have had something to do with it as well! 'Cavalier' was actually alongside the ammunition jetty at the time.

After the repairs they sailed to South Shields on Tyneside arriving on the 25th August 1945 for an official three day visit. This was 'their' adopted city and although this adoption took place in January 1945 this was their first chance to visit the town. It had been suggested by the crew that there should be a competition to find a pin-up to represent the ship and subsequently a competition was organized by the South Shields Savings Committee. There were more than seventy entrants, Miss Audrey Bryant from Talbot Road

South Shields was chosen and was duly crowned. On arrival, there was an official reception laid on by the lord mayor, Alderman J. Mitchell and the council who laid on a very enjoyable program for the crew. They marched through the city and past the Mayor and his entourage who took the salute from the town hall steps. Later that day a reception and dinner was laid on for a hundred and sixty of the crew plus their pin up Audrey Bryant. In the evening a dance was laid on in the Bolingbroke Drill Hall. A football match against South Shields AFC at Cleadon Park was organized, it is not recorded who won but celebrations after the game at the Transport Social Club were enjoyed by all. 'Cavalier's' left back on the team, George Hunter was from South Shields and had formerly played for the town. Two other members of the crew were 'Geordies' from South Shields, Stanley Carr and Mike Donaldson and both made the most of the visit. The crew were given free Corporation transport, access to the local swimming baths and the cinemas.

Young Audrey Bryant winner of the 'Cavalier' Pin Up competition 26th August 1945. To her right and just behind her is Frank Toop, she is wearing his cap.

The ship was then thrown open to the public and the crew proudly showed them round. Amongst the visitors was Mary Rutter, born in South Shields, she remembered the day well, it was her twenty first birthday and the sailors made it a memorable one for her.

Mary Rutter in 1945

After their visit to South Shields they were instructed to boiler clean and give a few days overseas leave to half the ship's company at a time. Before leaving for the Far East two ratings who were experts in Japanese codes joined the ship.

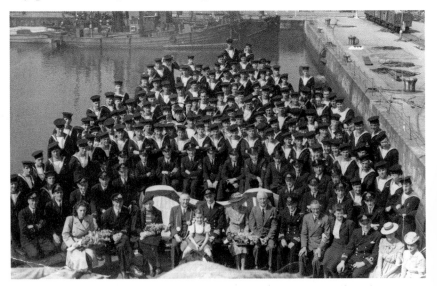

LT CDR McBarnett and his crew with sitting next to him the Mayor of South Shields, also Lady Glyn and the young girl and her mother from the launching. This was taken at South Shields on the ship's official three day visit 26th August 1945, she had been adopted by the city earlier but this was the first chance to visit. Derek Brooks is the fourth man back on the right with his hat at a 'jaunty' angle.

Along with 'Cavalier' part of the 6th DF consisting of 'Carron', 'Cavendish', and 'Caprice' sailed from the Tyne at 0830 one August morning to join the Pacific fleet. They were still needed to clear up the mess that was the Far East, some Japanese were still holding out. The only brief stops they had were at Gibraltar, Malta, through the Suez Canal and again at Aden for refuelling.

They joined the fleet at Colombo then went through to Trincomalee which was the base for ships intending to liberate Malaya. However after the surrender of Japan, Malaya was taken without a fight. In November they were enroute to Australia to give leave when they received the following urgent message, a rebellion had broken out in Java. Java (Indonesia) had been a Dutch colony before the war and until they had re-established themselves there the British would be looking after their interests and restore the status quo.

Dennis Packham AB, sitting in the aimer's seat of the starboard Pom Pom. The picture is probably taken somewhere east of Suez.

The message received by 'Cavalier':

Headquarters S.E. Command 2nd November 1945

From Supreme Commander S.E. Asia

To G.O.C. Imperial Forces. Re directive ASD4743S

You are instructed to proceed with all speed to the island of Java in the East Indies to accept the surrender of Japanese Imperial Forces on that island, and to release Allied prisoners of war and civilian internees. In keeping with the provisions of the Yalta Conference you will re-establish civilian rule and return the colony to the Dutch administration, when it is in a position to maintain services. The main landing will be by the British Indian Army, 5th Division, who have shown themselves to be most reliable since the battle of El Alamein. Intelligence reports indicate that the landing should take place at Surabaya, a location that affords a deep anchorage and repair facilities. As you are no doubt aware the local natives have declared a republic, but we are bound to maintain the status quo that existed before the Japanese invasion. I wish you God speed and a successful campaign.

Mountbatten

Vice Admiral

Supreme Command S.E. Asia.

Until 1941 Surabaya had been the Dutch naval base before the Japanese invasion and where they kept a flotilla of eleven submarines based.

Derek Brooks, signalman: 'We were at church service in Singapore one day; we had the church pennant flying, when we received an urgent message to proceed to Java, we immediately prepared the ship for action and sailed'.

The Royal Navy's church pennant hoisted when a service is in progress.

On the 2nd November '45 the destroyers 'Cavalier', 'Carron' and 'Caesar' of 6th Destroyer Flotilla with the cruiser 'Sussex' left for Java, with them went the Tank Landing craft 3001, 302, 413, and 327, the Landing Craft Troops 1161, 1195, 1060 and 1055. Added to these were the three Landing Ships Infantry; the 'Glenroy', 'Waveny' and 'Princess Beatrice' and the merchant ships *Bappeta, Pulasti, Malika,* and *Floristan*. Between them they carried the 5th Indian Army Division, the 2nd West Yorkshire Regiment, the 3/4th Gurkha Rifles, the 3/9 Gurkha Rifles and the 1st Burma Regiment. This would not be the last time in her long career that she would carry Gurkhas into a war zone. On arrival at Surabaya (Dutch *Soerabaja*) 'Cavalier' with others commenced a rolling bombardment ahead of the landed troops. A RAF Mosquito aircraft spotted the fall of shot for them on the grid system. Behind these troops were landed a party of Royal Marines and Naval radio operators (Naval Party 2482) who set up a radio communications base in the harbour area. The harbour was full of masts and funnels of ships that had been sunk during the earlier Japanese attacks. The recent troubles had been sparked off with the massacre of twenty three British soldiers who were on a plane that had crash landed nearby. The Officer commanding the 49th Indian Brigade, Brigadier A. Mallaby had also been shot dead by the rebels. It is a little known fact that the British later re armed the Japanese on the island to assist in its defence. They were heavily criticized by the international community for it but it worked and helped to ease the situation.

16th November 1945 'Cavalier's 'A'
gun bombarding at Surabaya. It was
hot work in the tropics in full anti
flash gear and helmets. (IWM)

They fired 57 rounds of 4.5" shells at the government offices and army headquarters which were being used by the insurgents… with the desired effect! The effect of one 4.5" shell would probably demolish a house; they were feared by troops ashore. When the crew fired a round from these guns the shock wave could be felt on their whole body, the barrel and breach block recoiled half a metre and the heavy brass cartridge case ejected into the safety net and fell to the deck with a huge 'bong', like a large dinner gong!

The Gurkhas along with Indian and British troops soon had the town under their control.

Whenever the ship anchored outside the harbour 'Big Bertha', as they nicknamed it used to fire at her. This was a large gun on a railway carriage which the rebels kept in a tunnel during the day and brought out at night. Their fall of shot was usually not very accurate and it was considered just a nuisance with a big bang.

However one evening a request was put in to the skipper for permission to be allowed to show a film to the crew on the fo'c'sle using the 35mm projector, it would be cooler. He gave permission, but reluctantly because of 'Big Bertha'. The CO's caution was justified because a huge explosion nearby was far too close for comfort and the film was brought to an abrupt end! Shortly after that the Gurkhas brought 'Big Bertha's' activities to a permanent end!

'Cavalier's' 4.5" guns bombarding the government offices at Surabaya. In the foreground appear to be the boats gripes which were probably strung there for painting! (IWM)

Des Gannon PO, Buffer: 'We were anchored off Surabaya one evening and a film was being shown in the open air on the fo'c'sle. It hadn't been on long when a whistling noise was heard and a huge explosion occurred not far off our bow. It wasn't near enough to worry us too much but the next one might do if they got our range. The film was stopped immediately; it was attracting shells like moths to a flame'!

4.5" shells, weight approx. 24 kilos. L: high explosive, R: star shell for illuminating a target, a 'P' under the star indicates parachute. The copper ring at the base is the driving band that causes the shell to rotate in the barrels rifling which arms the fuse. A red band at the top indicates 'explosive'. The nose contained a timed fuse that could be set for range by hand or automatically. (BK)

97

On the 10th December they moved up the coast to Semarang to bombard an airfield that was in rebel hands. By about the 29th the British Army along with the Indians and the Gurkhas had the situation ashore under control.

Percy Newell AB 'Caprice': 'I recall that 'Cavalier' off Java was in disgrace. Several men had gone ashore from her to set up a radio and communications centre in Surabaya and had found a spirit store… and got drunk. That wasn't too much of a problem but when they started shooting at their own Royal Marines and British soldiers somebody was not too happy. Luckily they didn't hit anyone! A signal was received in 'Cavalier' from the C in C saying: 'Your ship is a disgrace to the Royal Navy; you will go to sea and will steam at 3 knots for five days'! (It is hard work steering a ship at very slow speed, especially with a sea running)

As soon as they were able there was a combined Army and Navy operation to evacuate the mainly Dutch nationals who had been interned by the Japanese and had now been freed. Those that had survived had suffered five years of brutal treatment during the Japanese occupation, many had died from starvation and torture; the sight of 'Cavalier' and the other allied vessels must have been beyond their wildest dreams after the years of captivity. Although the journey across the equator to Singapore would not be a long one the crew knew they would be overloaded, with roughly twenty adults to the ton, two hundred people added a further ten tons top weight to the ship, so most were put below. It would be difficult for the Doc to attend to any pregnant women if they were in a crowded mess deck below, so the Doc, SURG LT Holt, detailed Yeoman Mackenzie and CPO Rolt to place all the pregnant women into the wardroom. The idea being that it would be more convenient to deal with them if they went into labour. The crew from the messes concerned would have to sleep on the upper deck.

Des Gannon CPO: Before leaving Java we loaded many Dutch nationals onboard who had been prisoners of the Japanese. Most of them were women and children. The Doc ordered that all pregnant women should be put into the ship's wardroom, which in action doubled as an operating theatre. This was in case they went into labour on the voyage to Singapore. Nearly all the women were directed to the wardroom until there was no room left. The problem was finally sorted out when they found a Dutch interpreter; he explained that in fact only a few were pregnant; all of them had bloated stomachs because they had eaten nothing but rice for so long'!

Derek Brooks: 'After our arrival back at Singapore to disembark the POWs someone noticed we 'were still flying the church pennant' that we had hoisted at church parade before leaving'!

Top Left: PO Des Gannon, first commission 'Buffer' supervising some of his men, they are wearing tropical rig.

They joined what they called the 'triangle run', Singapore, Hong Kong and Subic Bay in the Philippines. They arranged for Japanese POWs to be evacuated by the Kaiser built Liberty ships to POW camps and escorted some of the Liberty ships being returned to the Americans in Subic Bay (Philippines). Every item on these ships had to be accounted for except on one occasion the generous Americans gave them a refrigerator to share between the Chiefs and officers; this was very welcome in the tropics as at that time she did not have her own refrigerators.

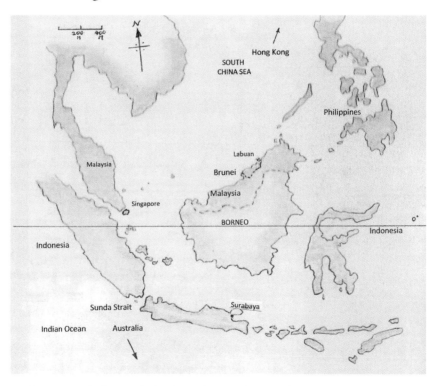

Surabaya is roughly five hundred miles to the east of the Sunda Straits and two hundred to the west of Bali. The normal route from Singapore to Australia was via the Sunda Straits.

On returning to Singapore they visited the Jahore Straits on the North of the Island. Many of them were suffering from tropical ringworm and had to be treated by the medics of the Indian Field

Army unit, who were accustomed to dealing with this malady. Some of them also contracted Malaria. The RAF 230 Transport squadron supplied them with transport and chauffeurs for runs ashore and took them to see the infamous Changi Jail.

When working with the USN they were sometimes supplied from their very efficient fleet train, they looked forward to this because some of their stores were fresh, but otherwise it was canned food only. Occasionally they were able to land on some of the islands and collect yams, coconuts and green bananas. The green bananas proved to be a good substitute for chips or as roast potatoes.

LME Charlie Ross, showing the No 6 uniform as worn in the tropics. The cap would have been whitened with Blanco. Back home the white cap was worn in the summer and a black one in winter. The practice of tying the bow almost to the front was later frowned upon.

Later the CO, CDR McBarnett assumed the title of Senior British Naval Officer of the Moluccas and Celebes group of Islands. The communications staff were kept very busy during this period because apart from the normal radio traffic they had to keep in touch with all the Army and Air Force units on the islands using a variety of methods, Walkie Talkie, Field Radio, Radio Telephone, Morse and visual signals. They were lucky they were carrying the specialist signals staff with them and the 1st LT/Signals Officer LT

Peter Moens and Yeoman John Mackenzie backed them up with the coding. They visited most of the NEI Islands including Bali, Kau and Kei Islands, Kei Manado, Ambonia, New Guinea and Borneo. On one of the islands they were able to resupply a unit of Australian troops who were running short of stores and to let them know that there were still 11,000 Japanese troops on the nearby Kei Island. During the night off Stilu Island they literally ran into three native wooden fishing boats, one quite substantial boat was sliced in half. Not one of the boats was carrying a light of any sort. Using the 20 inch Aldis lamps they spent some time recovering the fishermen from the sea, in their pigeon English they were able to confirm they were all accounted for (The sharks hadn't got any of them).

AB Gunner Joe Morris manning a single Pom Pom anti-aircraft gun. 'Cavalier's' Pom Poms were later replaced by the 40mm Bofors guns which had a heavier hitting shell.

If 'Cavalier' visited an Island with a sizeable town the crew was given plenty of Japanese occupation money to spend, this was still legal tender and it meant they did not have to spend any British Sterling.

In February 1946 they were dispatched to Trincomalee, Ceylon, (now Sri Lanka) and then at high speed to Bombay, India where a part of the Royal Indian Navy had mutinied. Two cruisers, a carrier HMS Patroller and other destroyers were also on their way. Rioting was taking place in the town in support of the mutineers. After several hours of fighting with British troops at the Castle Barracks the occupants surrendered. Vice Admiral Sir John Godfrey, head of the Indian Navy threatened to 'blow them out of the water' if they refused to surrender. 'Cavalier' and other ships were stood to, ready to engage. The RAF flew over low and other troops were on standby. Rioters attempted to steal arms from the HMIS Hindustan and were fired on by that ship using her 4" guns. One man was killed and several injured. More and more Indian ships flew the 'black flag' which indicated they were not taking part in the mutiny and eventually the mutiny petered out. They returned to Trincomalee (Ceylon) where the skipper decided that the crew needed a rest, they had had no leave for a long time. There was very little at Trinco and it was said to be similar to Scapa Flow as far as amenities were concerned. However half the ship's company at a time was bussed to a camp up a tortuous road in the cool mountain air at Diyatalawa. Every 'man jack' of them was waited on hand and foot by native servants, they were able to play golf, with caddy service, or go cycling or hiking. They were given a tour of a tea plantation and watched the elephants hauling teak logs and later saw them in a traditional parade of the elephants at Kandy (the Esala Perahera). In early '46 'Cavalier' returned to Jahore Straits off Singapore and came under the jurisdiction of the shore base HMS Terror. In May they escorted some lend lease mine sweepers back to Subic Bay and returned with seventy naval personnel to Singapore who had crewed LST's and LCQ's on a previous trip. From there the ship was ordered back home and sailed on the 11th May '46. However for some it was a bitter disappointment as they were drafted from 'Cavalier' to other ships before she sailed. The same thing happened when they reached Trinco and everyone wondered whether they would be next 'not to return home'. They called at Aden and Gibraltar and luckily nobody else was drafted off. Knowing that strict rationing was still in force in the UK, they bought a lot of goodies in Gibraltar, including salad stuff for the mess parties at home, 984 nautical miles away. On arrival off Plymouth customs men were ferried out to join them, this was in order that by the time they reached Portsmouth they would have saved time and 'cleared customs'.

On a cloudy day on 16th June 1946 'Cavalier' finally entered her home port of Portsmouth for the very first time. She was playing the 'Bonnets of Dundee' on her Tannoy system and it was audible for miles! She was flying the yellow flag of quarantine and a huge 'Paying off pennant' which trailed from the forward mast into the water astern, ably supported by a couple of blown up items donated by the Sick Bay! (The length of a Paying off pennant was calculated as the length of the ship plus a foot for every month in commission)

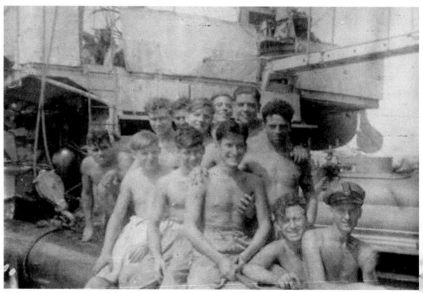

Some of them, not much more than kids are seen here in their shorts in the Mediterranean and on their way home in 1946. Sitting on a live torpedo are Reg Linley, centre, AB Stan Carr, AB Coe, Don Stevens and their PO (with cap). Top right is the back of the starboard Pom Pom. The 'catwalk' top right was used in rough weather to avoid seas washing over the torpedo deck.

The mess parties were a huge success for those lucky enough to have their families there. The rest were given immediate 'Overseas Service leave'. After all they had been through together as shipmates they bid farewell to each other, after their Foreign Service leave many of the 'hostilities only' personnel would be demobbed back to Civvy Street. Many would find it difficult to re adjust to an austere bombed out Britain still under rationing; they had led an exciting life of extremes, seen strange people with strange customs and languages, Gharry carts, sampans and dghajsa (Diso) and beautiful foreign maidens. The rest of the men would return to barracks and later be drafted to other ships. Some key personnel were retained onboard and along with a new slightly smaller crew under the command of LT CDR Winder would sail for Gibraltar for repairs to her propeller shafts and gear box. She had a vibration in them which according to some of the first crew she had had from her earliest trials; it only occurred for a short spell at dead on 28 knots, she was afflicted with this for the rest of her service. This had the added bonus of keeping the still huge post war navy men busy as well as giving Gibraltar dockyard work.

Returning to Portsmouth flying her paying off pennant in 1946

Patrick Quin, AB RP3: I was languishing in the shore base HMS Victory at Portsmouth when I received a draft to the destroyer 'Cavalier', R73 lying in Portsmouth yard. I was part of a short crew that was to take her to Gibraltar for a refit. I joined her with others on the 1st October 1947. We sailed at 1100hrs on the 29th November, a bitterly cold but calm day at sea. Although that didn't last long because the Bay of Biscay living up to its name was very rough and quite a few of the men were on the upper deck calling for 'Bill' (Being seasick). We arrived in Gibraltar at 0930hrs on Sunday the 2nd November and prepared her for docking. By the 22nd November I had been drafted off 'Cavalier' to bring her sister ship 'Carysfort', R25, home. Before leaving we did engine trials and achieved a speed of 33.5 knots. On arrival home with me being 'hostilities only', I was demobbed into Civvy Street.

Ken Mower AB G: Whilst in dry dock in Gib a lighter blew up in the dock next to us, we were lucky because we were low down in the dry dock and the blast went over the top of us, I think we suffered a small amount of damage to our superstructure but nothing much and luckily no one was injured. A LS and an AB went ashore one pay day whilst we were there. They got drunk and took a boat and rowed to the Spanish mainland for a 'run ashore', there they were picked up by the Spanish police and were only returned by the intervention of the British Consul. They were both court marshalled and sentenced to 56 days detention. They were sent to the army prison as the navy did not have cells on the Rock. On returning to the UK we went on the 'Trot' (A row of buoys) in Porchester Creek along with many other frigates and destroyers, most awaiting the axe. I remember the officers onboard serving us our Christmas dinner and shortly after that I and many others were discharged from war service'.

Up the creek at Fareham she was 'mothballed', this was the term given to the process of cocooning all her guns and other sensitive equipment in fibreglass with air conditioning machinery to control the humidity; she was now in a state of deep reserve. Ships thus treated could, in emergency be brought to readiness within a very short time. The ships were constantly monitored by a small group of men.

Terry 'Lightning' Motson, PJX823316. 'I was in a team that lived on 'Cavalier' in Porchester Creek; we were mothballing and monitoring a line of destroyers on the Trot. We had a good thing going with a tobacconist from Gosport; he used to come out to the ship in a Kayak and pay us 15/– for each tin of Tickler (rolling tobacco) that we could lay our hands on. We always did the deal through the porthole never up on deck in case we were seen. We finally mothballed 'Cavalier' and moved on to her sister ship 'Caprice' on 1 July 1948.'

Derek Brooks, the signalman mentioned earlier, was an unusual character; he served in all three services. He joined the Royal Warwickshire Regiment in 1942 but after a year applied and was accepted in the Royal Navy and served in 'Cavalier'. His neighbours at home questioned his parents as to what he was up to because he left home in Army uniform but came back in a navy uniform. 'Cavalier' was his only ship; he never slept in a hammock or drew a tot of rum and he never learnt to swim. He has the Russian Convoy medal but missed getting the Atlantic Star by one week. He left the Navy after the war and then in 1951 applied to join the RAF; he served in Sunderland flying boats as a signaller before finally being demobbed in 1970. Official No's: Army 14426914, Royal Navy P/JX617179, RAF 4080063. He appears in the crew photograph on the fo'c'sle of 'Cavalier' in 1945 at South Shields, he is fourth sailor back on the right wearing his cap at a jaunty angle. At the time of writing he still lives in Warwickshire.

This could have been the end of 'Cavalier' but there were problems on the horizon, the 'Cold War' with the Eastern Block and the spread of communism in the East. The Soviets were building so many submarines that in the event of this war going 'hot' NATO would need all the anti-submarine escorts they could lay their hands on to keep the supply lines open. 'Cavalier' was amongst many that were to be modernized and brought back into service. In 1955, eight years after being laid up she was taken to Thornycroft's yard at Woolston near Southampton.

1955, 'Cavalier' undergoing conversion in Thornycroft's yard in Southampton.

They completely rebuilt her bridge superstructure along the lines of the latest 'Daring' class destroyers. It was still an open bridge and was to remain so for the rest of her service, she was in fact the last major RN ship to retain an open bridge. The radar and weapons systems were upgraded, one set of torpedo tubes was removed and more importantly she was fitted with the new 'Squid' anti-submarine system that she still has today. At the back of the operations room there is a small compartment that even most sailors onboard were not allowed to enter. This was the Electronic Warfare and Electronic Counter Measures office. This is where the IFF (Identification Friend or foe) equipment was located; it worked in conjunction with the 293Q radar and was a very sophisticated piece of kit. The 944 radar sent out a pulse which would trigger a transponder on the friendly ship, or aircraft to indicate he was a friend. No pulse and the fur would start flying!

On 15th July 1957 she was ready to be brought back into service.

Letter from mother

Dear Son.

Just a few lines to let you know that I am still alive. I am writing this slowly because I know you can't read very fast. You won't know the house when you come home, we've moved.

About your father, he has got a lovely new job working for the corporation. He has five hundred men under him; he's cutting the grass at the cemetery.

Your sister Mary had a baby this morning. I haven't found out yet whether it's a boy or a girl so I don't know if you are an Aunt or an Uncle.

I went to the doctors on Thursday and your father came with me. The doctor put a tube in my mouth and told me not to say anything for ten minutes. Your father offered to buy it from him.

Your Uncle Patrick drowned last week in a vat of whiskey at the Dublin brewery. Some of his workmates tried to pull him out but he fought them off bravely. They cremated him last week and it took three days for the fire to go out. It only rained twice this week, the first time for three days and the second time for four.

We've had a letter from the undertaker; they said that if they don't receive the last payment on your gran's plot in seven days… up she comes.

Your loving mum.

PS: I was going to put £5 in with this letter for you but I've already sealed the envelope.

1944 Crew list

Anderson W	AB
Baker C	Gunner T
Barnard F	
Barton N	Civ. App
Bedford D	ME
Birnie W	AB RP2
Borrett C	AB
Bowers A	AB S
Broadhead G	
Brookes D	Signals
Buckle G	
Burns J	Signals
Bush S	
Byard T	ME
Cairns R	AB R
Carr Stanley	
Carter P	
Champion W	
Coburn M	JS
Coe J	AB T
Costar E	AB
Cottingham J	AD AS
Cottrell G	SPO
Crawley G	
Cripps D	OD
Cross J	
Culley R	ME1
Dawson J	AB
Dickinson	AB
Donaldson Mike	
Dowling E	
Downey J	
Dowson G	
Dutton F	

Dyso L	
Elliott F	AB
Evans E	
Finch R	
Franks K	
Gannon Des	PO buffer
Garbett R	
George P	AB T
Glaver H MBE	LT E
Gregory Fred	OS
Gooding 'Gerry'	
Grosmann J	EMS
Gutteridge J	AB
Hamblin S	PO STWD
Hamer E	
Harold L	LS
Hawthorne J	
Hay F	
Hewlett J	
Higgins R	AB RC3
Hockey J	Signals
Horrigan T	
Howe J	
Hudson H	
Humby R	
Humphries D	
Hunter 'Geordie'	
Hussell D	LT RNVR
Ivory H	LS
Johnson R	
Johnson J	
Johnson C	AB G
Kelly J	AB G1c
Knowles	AB
Krall	AB

Latham N		Ross C	LME
Linley Reg	AB ST	Self N	
Lowe P		Skelton T	
Martin H	AB T	Smith F	ME1c
Mayne R	LT	Smith R	LEM
McBarnett D (DSC) LT CDR CO.		Spiers P	ME1
		Spurgeon J	
Melling C	AB	Stanley R	LT
Meons P	LT	Stevens D	AB ST
Mercer J	Civ App	Stubbs B	AB
Millar A	AB	Summerson J	
Millwood R		Taggart D	
Morris J	AB	Taylor G	A PO
Moss C		Taylor H	
Mower K	AB G	Tindall L	
Nelson J		Toop F	
Norcliffe-Roberts J		Tope E	AB AA2
O'Brian A		Towell R	
Packham D	AB G	Trench D	LT
Page R		Tuck N	
Parsons C		Tydeman K	RO
Porter F		Vickers E	
Prescott H		Watson J	
Price H		Wells J	AB
Puttick R	AB AA3	Wheeler D	ME
Puttock B	AB	Whiting E	AB RC3
Quin Patrick	AB RP	Winjberg M	LT
Rand	AB	Wildish H	AB
Raven P	AB	Williams S	STWD
Redhead J	AB	Witt R	ME
Richardson E	ME1	Witts A	AB QA
Robinson I MBE	TEL	Wood D	O CK
Rolt V	CPO TEL		
Rose N	AB R		
Rose R	ME		

LT CDR Winder was the CO for the Trip to Gibraltar in October 1947

HMS Cavalier - Torpedoed!

R A Linley

HMS CAVALIER 1944

Despite some recent publications indicating that HMS CAVALIER was despatched to the Clyde area post war along with other Ca class destroyers, my memory bank, which is still on recall after leaving the ship in Trincomalee, Ceylon (Sri Lanka) in May 1946 some 50 years on, disagrees with these articles.

8th May 1945 found CAVALIER some 200 miles west of Ireland having seen a troop ship on its way clear of possible U boat interference. There then followed signals to carry out 'sweeps' for any surrendering U boats, who had been ordered to surface from May 5th.

We returned to the Scapa Flow anchorage to await further orders about the middle of May and actioned preparations for Far East activities. Boiler cleans, dickey refits, more 'Ack Ack' fire power were reviewed, torpedo firing and drills were to be done efficiently! There had been one exercise of torpedo firing in which the single torpedo fired from each set of tubes had been a 50% success. The first firing went off well, on course and under the opposing destroyer target. The other torpedo, due to gyro controls being out of sync, produced a 'porpoise' which means, instead of maintaining a preset zigzag to target, the torpedo kept appearing and shooting out of the 'oggin' as it headed roughly towards the target, which is missed, thank goodness! CAVALIER was in full chase like a dog chasing a rabbit at 30 kts. The renegade torpedo, having blown itself out, was retrieved by one of the whalers and torpedomen. There followed an inquisition as to 'who, what and how' the 'fish' went wrong! It was CAVALIER's turn to be the target for a torpedo fired from the other Ca Class destroyer (as I am not positive which ship it was, I will 'darken ship'). I have no doubt that there is still someone trying to settle his slop chit account! The ship's normal draught aft towards stern and screws would be approximately 14ft. There was much adjustment of our course and speed in the process of dodging the incoming torpedo which was detected by the Asdic devices aboard. Speed was worked up and smoked emitted from the funnel. Special lookouts were posted, then suddenly there was an almighty bang! A terrible scream of metal grinding, followed by vibrations from Y gun to the depth charges on the stern. At the same time CAVALIER seemed to become airborne. However her stern did lift out of the sea and then she slowly hove to and wallowed on the sea. Hatches opened, persons appeared on deck whom I had never seen before! Stokers holding their heads and ear drums, many expressions which meant 'exactly what was that' were emitted by all and sundry. The Engineer Officer, resplendent in white overalls, appeared with the Chief ERA and Chief Stoker and a selection of ERAs and Stoker POs and the Buffer! All headed down to the stern quarters. The Captain and 'Jimmy' waited up top for messages as to the problem and solution. Words were spoken but Nelson had never heard. They were short, very descriptive and dirty, as everyone on deck at the time was covered in soot and

rusted paint flecks. The Gunner TI, Mr Baker, appeared in a diving suit and face mask. Did he know something we didn't'? Suitably roped up he was lowered over the side adjacent to the port side screw protection pad where we had 8ft of free board and then into the 'hog wash'! He disappeared in bubbles and a couple of minutes later (long enough in those water temperatures) re-appeared. Hoisted in board, he was surrounded by the engineering staff, and tiffies. His assessment was lucid and short. The propeller and A bracket were useless, the starboard prop bracket were showing serious damage and its blades were bent over.

Signals were sent off, and eventually a tug appeared from Scapa, not a long tow. I do not recall the other destroyer appearing close by - no doubt the air waves to and from CAVALIER were somewhat busy with pleasantries and comments on paternal issues, including rank and file name and number so that payments due to cause and damage could be adjusted to the satisfaction of the supply branch and accountants.

On inspection by a Naval Survey Diver at Scapa it was found necessary to dry dock CAVALIER. Rosyth was the location selected and early in June 1945 No 1 boiler was flashed up and the starboard prop and shaft tested. It was decided that CAVALIER could make way ahead at 5 kts with a tug in attendance. We headed for Rosyth. The buzzes were by now coming thick and fast. As the ship entered dry dock, the crew knew that there were draft chits ready for some, Foreign Service leave for others. Before going on leave I was able to go below into the dock and observe the damage to the port side shaft, propeller and 'A' bracket. Recalling the instructors comments at HMS VERNON's Torpedo Training Base, that the air vessel on these torpedoes are bored out of the strongest steel possible, I reflected that this has been proved right, as had the designers. Meanwhile the decks were being opened up to remove and replace the gearing and shafts to both engines. Oerlikons were replaced by single pom pom guns (more powerful) and preparations made for the Far East. Despite secret coding being used, the Japanese heard about CAVALIER's refit and refurbishments, and decided on 16 August 1945 to surrender. CAVALIER

was then alongside the ammunition jetty at Rosyth. We sailed to South Shields on the 25th. This was CAVALIER's adopted town. There were many greetings, celebrations and social events over our four days there. We sailed off down the Tyne at 0830 on the 30 August for Gibraltar, and beyond and a lot of 'post war activities'

The First Commission was under the command of Lieutenant Commander Donald T McBarnett DSC. To the majority of those onboard he was a superb skipper. He knew what he wanted and how to get the best out of his officers and men. His experience was vast and it was evident that Damage Control Parties aboard and all crew members would be changed round regularly so that both forward and aft messdecks had a cross section of expertise available in the event of any emergency. We had learnt this from his involvement as the damage control officer in HMS EXETER during the action with the GRAF SPEE at the River Plate in December 1939. In that action he had to extricate the ship from the River Plate to the Falkland Isles, where she underwent emergency repairs prior to sailing home. His team steered the ship from the after control position using the engines and damaged rudder and plugged the leaks below the water line to get the ship there and back to the UK for refit. He was mentioned in despatches.

Following that, in May 1940, he was in command of a Dutch ship commissioned into RN service. The Schuit DOGGER BANK was involved in the rescue of approximately 1000 men off the Dunkirk Beaches where he won his DSC. Later, in 1941, he was the First Lieutenant of the Hunt class destroyer TYNEDALE. He moved on to JAGUAR as 1st Lieutenant during Mediterranean operations and Malta convoys. NUBIAN was his next ship, and in 1943 he took command of HMS EXMOOR a Hunt class destroyer. He was again mentioned in Despatches for actions aboard in the landings in Sicily and Salerno. He was undoubtedly a destroyer captain with vast experience and considered of his officers and men, he had a 'happy ship'. Problems were sorted firmly and positively, there were no doubts. His ship's company aboard CAVALIER for entering and lea

ROYAL NAVY

BACK TO THE ORIENT
1957 – 1959

UK, Gibraltar, Malta, Port Said, Suez, Aden, Trincomalee, Singapore, Sandakan, Hong Kong, Saigon, Kudat, Jesselton, Australia, Freemantle, Melbourne, Hobart, New Zealand, Auckland, Fiji Islands, Suva, Christmas Island, Ocean Island, Bahrain, Thailand, Bangkok.

BACK TO THE ORIENT
1957 – 1959

Cdr. J. D. Cartwright RN
(Second commission)

Cavalier commissioned on 16th July 1957 at Portsmouth and proceeded to work up. During this they tested some of the newly fitted equipment and weapons. The Squid Mortar anti-submarine weapons that had been fitted had been developed in 1942/3 and replaced the depth charge system. They were so successful that they were still in use up until the early 1970's. They can still be seen on 'Cavalier' today. Two 40mm Bofors guns had also been fitted on sponsons on either side of the bridge to replace the pom poms.

Having worked up and now sporting the number D73 to conform to the new NATO system and with a large No. 8 on her funnel she sailed for the Far East to join the 8th Destroyer Squadron. They would be sailing into what had been virtually a war zone in Malaya. Between 1949 and the late fifties the 'Malayan Emergency' was at its height. For twelve years there was a vicious confrontation with on the one hand the British and the Malay Sultans against on the other hand the Communist insurgents. Hundreds of people were being murdered yearly, consequently there were some 10,000 British forces stationed in 'forts' in the jungle all over Malaya to combat them. The Navy was to prevent insurgents and weapons being smuggled in by sea. By the late fifties it had got a great deal better but there were still many terrorists hiding out in the jungle into the early 1960's.

A pattern of six Squid bombs exploding; they were fired over the mast and up to 250yrds ahead of the ship, in this way the operator did not lose asdic contact with the sub which he did if running over it to drop depth charges. They were designed to land in a diamond pattern and at different depths thereby bracketing the sub. In this picture the deeper ones have not yet exploded. There were several hairy moments when a weak charge allowed a bomb to fall short and close to the bows!

Each bomb was twelve inches in diameter and weighed some 400 lbs

David 'Granny' Grantham AB: I was due to be married to my girlfriend Phyllis in July 1957; she was not a happy bunny when Naval Drafting decided that the Country and 'Cavalier' in particular needed me more! So with our wedding advanced a month to June we duly got wed. The day we returned from our honeymoon I was rushed into Stonehouse Hospital with glandular fever. Having recovered I managed to get two weeks leave before joining 'Cavalier' in the August. You can imagine how we both felt! However, luckily for me anyway 'Cavalier' worked her magic and was to be the best ship I ever served on in my twenty three years service'.

As they sailed towards the Bay of Biscay they took their last look at the UK on the 31st August, the ship herself would not see a home port again for another six years. All her boxed spare parts would follow her to the base in Singapore. For some of the crew it was their first foreign draft and the first port of call was Gibraltar where they enjoyed the pleasures that it is well known for, the Stroppy Vicar (Angry Friar!), the Donkeys flip flop (The Horseshoe!) and the London Bar.

The next port of call was Malta, known to many as the place of Hells, Bells and smells, not because the place smells but if you drank the beer and then went to 'pump your bilges'… you would smell! (It was known as Malta Dog). The bells referred to the church bells which rang three or four times a day. They experienced Strada Stretta (Straight Street) known to Jack as 'The Gut', a street full of Bars, with all sorts of entertainment and restaurants on a hill with steps every few yards. Most matelots started at the top and worked their way down during the evening, at the bottom was usually stood a very large Maltese policeman called 'Tiny'. To get back to the ship meant either a long trip around the point by road or going down the shaky old Barracca Lift and then catching a dghajsa (Diso), a Maltese water taxi similar to the Venetian gondola.

Opposite: The old Barracca lift with a warship lying in the harbour.

The Barracca lift stopped running after 2100hrs and the odd drunken matelot was known to have climbed down the outside metal frame… all 197 feet of it! (It was closed in 1973 and was later demolished.) They stayed there for four weeks and sailed east on the 9th October for a much needed 'rest'!

More ports were visited on their journey: They transited the Suez Canal on 12th – 13th October and the Gilly Gilly man (Egyptian Magician) came onboard to do tricks with chicks and cigarettes that he would 'borrow' … and make them disappear!

Maltese dghajsa

The ship was followed through the canal by tankers, merchant ships and with Dhows in between. It was a strange sight to see a camel train trotting alongside the ship! By the 18th October they had arrived in Aden, then still a British colony.

A few days in Aden and then on to Trincomalee on the 26th October, by this time they had acquired a suitable tan. After leaving Trinco it was decided to hold a SODS opera, Whacker Payne was detailed as Entertainments Officer! After much badgering of various people he finally got a show together and as it was calm it was held on the fo'c'sle. A stage was set up and the 'Old Man of the sea', Pony Moore opened with a rendition on his 'squeeze box', the audience was somewhat disappointed that he didn't catch his shonk (nose) in the bellows of his accordion. He was accompanied by Granny Grantham on guitar, Humph Humphries on Drums and a group of juniors pretending to be the Luton Girls choir.

Eddie Thirkettle AB with youngsters in Aden.

Leading Coder Julian Eldridge did a monologue about Albert and the Lion. Next, three luscious forms glided on stage singing to a record and taking off the Andrews sisters. Alfie Lomax, Tony Parsons and Buster Brown after miming to 'Rum and Coca Cola' could not keep a straight face, or live it down. In the second half Alfie was playing the bride, Tony playing guitar and Buster was taking off Spike Jones singing 'I went to your wedding' and although the audience was curled up he never grinned once! AB's Wakeford, Anderton, Willshire and Peppiatt sang a song they had written about the ship and her company to the tune of 'Much Binding in the Marsh'. Sir 'Ric' Peppiatt then played a couple of tunes on the harmonica. The wardroom contributed with three females, the Jimmy as Cleopatra, 'Shirley' Eaton as Lady Godiva and 'Whacker' as Mae West. They were anything but seductive; in fact they were quite ugly! REA Monk and EA Richards in smart toppers and tails did an impersonation of the

Western Brothers. Their song was again about the ship's company, including 'Ginge' himself (The Captain).

They finally arrived where they were meant to be, Singapore, on the 31st October. They did not get to enjoy the delights of Singapore straight away, they were ordered out to convey the South Wales Borderers to Sandakan. They were exercised constantly by Captain 'D' enroute and landed them on the 11th November.

They returned to Singapore to exercise with the French aircraft carrier FS La Confiance for a week, more training, gunnery, manoeuvres and flying off and on. They then sailed back to Sandakan to pick up the brown jobs and return them to Singapore.

'Cavalier' sailed with the cruiser 'Newcastle' for their Island in the sun, Hong Kong.

A transfer between 'Cavalier and the cruiser 'Newcastle'
enroute to Hong Kong, December 1957.

They were there from the 12th December till the 31st January. 'Honkers' was all it was said to be and more, an evening in Wanchai was worth five elsewhere and the pound went a long way. Although war time rationing had finished back home it was still a time of austerity there. The island of Victoria and the town of Kowloon never slept, all night long the clatter of tiles from the Ma Jong games being played, the Chinese are inveterate gamblers, and the tailors working on their sewing machines in small rooms above shops never ceased. The people still wore their traditional dress, conical straw hats with black baggy type pyjamas. In the fields in the New Territories some women wore the straw hats with a black fringe around them, these were the Hakka women, sworn to celibacy. On the open air stalls there were strange foods, raw meat from indeterminate origins, horses heads, skinned with their eyes still in, pickled ducks, frogs, lizards and although illegal in the colony black dog was also popular. The Chinese ate everything living and most things that weren't. There were still hundreds of red and green rickshaws pulled by Chinese men, many of whom were opium addicts. Very few spoke English, although the girls in the bars and tradesmen picked it up very quickly by necessity. The matelots also picked up useful bits of Chinese; 'Yat, yee, sam, sei, ng, lok (One, two, three, four, five, six). Huge junks still plied the waterways and hundreds of sampans, twelve or fifteen feet long with whole families living on them were crammed in every bay. New born babies were very often to be seen floating past the ship, there was room only for so many children on these small boats. There were cardboard 'cities' on the hills outside the town where the poor lived, life was cheap. The 'forbidden walled city' in Kowloon was a no go area. It was said to be ruled by the Triad gangs and was a dangerous place for Europeans to enter, it was not administered by either the British or Chinese, occasionally some foolhardy matloes would enter the area… because it was out of bounds! Many Chinese appeared to be very bow legged, this was caused by them being carried on their mother's backs when they were children and when not on mum's back they slept with their legs wrapped around a bolster as a sort of comforter.

Hong Kong, work hard play hard!

Pissy Willy and the custard: Pissy Willy was the nickname given to the domestic steam cooler; it cooled used steam from the low pressure steam range in the ship's galley back into feed water for the main boilers. The ship had tied up alongside in Hong Kong and Pissy Willie had been shut down, as it cooled it caused a vacuum inside. A steam lance was provided in the galley with low pressure steam that could be used for heating up liquids. The duty Chinese chef mixed up a large container of custard ready for dinner, put the steam lance in to gently boil the custard, opened the stop cock and was amazed to hear a loud sluurrrp and witnessed all the custard disappearing up the pipe, his Cantonese/English expression being something like 'WERRA BLURRY CUSTAR GO'? The boiler room stoker was equally surprised to see his glass gauge half full of custard! After much joviality, a bit of swearing and sweating the clear up job was done before tot time with no ill effect to anyone.

John Hughes LEM, sabotage: 'It may be that someone was enjoying Hong Kong a bit too much and was not in a hurry to leave:

One of my jobs before leaving harbour was to check the lubrication on the steering motors in the tiller flat because the bearings run hot when in use. On checking them just before leaving Hong Kong I discovered that someone had attempted to sabotage them. They had placed aluminium cartridges, used for starting motors, in on top of the bearings and replaced the covers. I climbed out of the hatch, grabbed the nearest rating to me and told him to stand guard over the hatch and not to let anyone, even the captain in there. I went to my boss, the electrical officer, who then went to the engineering officer, who called the captain. They all trooped down to the quarter deck and the captain asked the rating to open the hatch, he obeying my order told the captain that he could not let him in there 'Sir'… until he saw I was taking up the rear and gave him the nod. CID was called in to investigate but the culprit was never discovered. Not that many years ago this offence would have carried the death penalty! This was not the only attempt at sabotage in Hong Kong. One day 'Y' gun breach mechanism had been stripped down for maintenance and whilst the men were away on a 'stand easy' someone threw the breach block over the side. The skipper cleared the lower deck and went 'ape', once again the culprit was never discovered. Luckily these incidents were very few and far between'.

The rugby team's proudest moment, January 1958 winning the 8th DS Championship.

The football team did well when 'sea time' did not interfere. Games were played at Sandakan and the local inhabitants applauded (and laughed) in the appropriate places and then extended their wonderful hospitality at their social club.

In Singers (Singapore) on their way to play at Krangi the Indian taxi driver took them to Changi instead, forty miles out of the way. The sports officer tried to explain to him in Pidgin Hindu, but it took one of the team using a few expletives and gesticulations to get them on their way. On arrival the other team had given them up and gone home, so not to be outdone they played a six aside in torrential monsoon rain and almost darkness.

The football team
Back row: ME Thomas, ME Petch, AB Wilsher, S LT Lafferty, ME Hodge, LTO Mottishead, LME Langthorpe, CPO Roose. Front row: RO2 Bolton, LEM Elliott, LRO Ginns, AB Pickersgill, AB Englishby

Hong Kong should always be followed by a long rest… it wasn't, they went straight to Saigon for a continuation of the same! A short stay back in Singapore and then off again to North Borneo, Kudat and Jesselton. Here they were entertained with various activities including the Jesselton races! A week of strenuous exercises followed in an exercise named 'Belson' with the fleet off Pulau Tioman from the 24th February.

Pulau Tioman (Pulau – Malay for island, was pronounced by 'Jack' as Paula) was a beautiful virtually deserted tropical island about sixty miles off the east coast of Malaya. Coconuts and bananas grew wild there and the occasional giant Iguana lizard could be seen, it was like a throwback to the period of the dinosaurs. There was only one family on the island in a Kampong (wooden hut on stilts). The Royal Navy ships anchored in Juara Bay and used the island to give rest and relaxation to crews of ships that had perhaps been at sea for two or three weeks.

Eddie Thirkettle AB and Oppo skylarking on the beach at Pulau Tioman.

At 0345hrs on the 1st March 'Cavalier' was detached along with 'Cheviot' and 'Cossack' to proceed to Australia. The visit to Australia was the start of some of the best months of their lives. Enroute a SODS opera was held and was relayed to the other ships in company. Frankie, Schoolie and Doc did a hilarious sketch on Salesmanship. 'Navy' recited 'The Green eye of the little yellow God,' whilst Wally, dressed as an ancient Indian Colonel made numerous remarks which brought the house down. LT Vallings, ably assisted by Broph and Ken Meads, organized an inter-part quiz and twenty questions over 'Radio Cavalier' which went down well. Roy Ginns and Motts Mottershead did a well polished comedy act and the Three Krowns, led by Granny Grantham on guitar, Tony Parsons on Drums and Buster Brown plucking away at his 'tea chest' bass!

A native Kampong on Pulau Tioman, it was occupied by a Malay couple and their three children. They scratched a living from coconut products and selling them to the sailors.

At 0620hrs on the 3rd March '58 they passed three quarters of a mile N.E. of Christmas Island (Indian Ocean). At 0720hrs they were piped to 'Air bedding' on the upper deck. At 2345hrs on the 4th March they advanced the clocks by half an hour. On the 6th

126

they did a jackstay transfer with 'Cheviot' and LT CDR Haines joined them. By the 7th they entered Fremantle and joined HMAS Melbourne (Australian aircraft carrier) 'Swan', and 'Fremantle'. The frigate HMAS Quiberon berthed alongside them on No.8 berth. They were immediately put at one hours notice for steam and were on standby as guard ship for the Queen Mother's flight which was leaving from Perth. After being stood down they opened the ship to visitors for two hours each day. They went to the races and had good times with the girls and the locals in the bars. There were their big jugs and little glasses of very cold beer which gave you hiccups. Because the bars closed early, (some states closed the pubs at 1830 or 1900hrs) matelots would get a bottle in and go 'up homers' with local families.

Up to this stage in the commission, No.6 warrant was read! These are read to the whole ship's company outlining the offence with which a sailor had been charged with.

On the 18th they left for Melbourne, during this trip they advanced the clocks by one hour and they experienced problems with their AGMC (Compass) which broke down. On the 21st they passed and spoke to the Swedish tanker 'Nanny' which was enroute from Melbourne to the Persian Gulf. They crossed the 'Bite', notorious for bad weather, a bit like our Bay of Biscay, the temperature dropped and for a short while they shifted into 'blues'. On arrival at Melbourne they went to North Wharf, No.4 berth. Some of the crew were invited to live with families in the bush for a few days… a never to be forgotten experience rounding up and shearing sheep. They left Melbourne and crossed the Tasman Sea for Hobart they could see Mount Wellington. In Hobart they berthed on the Queen Elizabeth pier and held an official cocktail party for the great and good of the city and opened the ship to visitors between the 27th and the 29th.

The Australian Bite, like our Bay of Biscay has a reputation of getting a bit 'lumpy'

Another thousand miles and they were in New Zealand the land of the Maoris, to Rotorua where they toured the Maori village and visited the hot pools. Then to Auckland Harbour on 2nd April where they stayed until the 9th.

Now forget the fun, they were at Christmas Island (Pacific) for the atomic bomb tests, 'Operation Grapple'; Serious stuff now with Orange flashes, damage states 'A' and 'B', Roentgens and Dosimeters, monitors and slide rules and protective clothing. It didn't seem real to some. From March to May 1958 'Cavalier' acted as weather and guard ship for some of the tests. She watched and warned shipping to stay away from the test area and gathered and relayed data on the weather. The crew was ranged on the upper deck; they heard the roar of a distant Valiant bomber and saw its contrails.

The Vickers Valiant bomber used to drop 'A' and 'H' bombs at Christmas Island in the Pacific. The tests in April 1958 yielded 10 times more power than previous tests.

'Make sure your neck is covered and adjust each other's goggles correctly'. Forty seconds to go; 'Sit with your back to the blast and do not turn round until you are told'. This was all so unreal, the countdown started three, two, one zero – then one, two, three, four… nothing, some didn't feel the blast, and they wondered what had happened. 'Open your eyes and turn around' and there was this great awesome inferno in the sky, black and red and growing, evil yet beautiful, growing into a white and red monstrous fungus reaching thousands of feet high. Some men faced the blast others put their backs to it. Later, anchored off Christmas Island they were warned not to eat the fish or swim in the sea.

An awesome sight, don't eat the
fish or swim in the water!

The captain was waiting for the big bang!

In July she visited the Persian Gulf (to top up the tan) and then returned to Singapore for refit.

Singapore and Captain 'D's' inspection, he is followed by the skipper and his minions. Everyone has had the regulation haircut and their uniforms are spotlessly clean and pressed. If anyone was not up to standard they would probably be awarded a 'kit muster'. The older officers as you can see are wearing their many WWII medals.

Shortly after this refit eight men were going to sail the whaler to Pulau Tioman from the naval base, a journey of about one hundred and twenty miles, it would be but nothing to these intrepid experienced sailors... would it? It was another exercise in navigation and survival and a bit of relaxation from the ship, which would meet them there. They stocked up with food and 'bubbly' (rum) and took a radio, and two lifejackets each! Right from the start there was absolutely no wind, so the motor boat towed them several miles down the river almost to Changi. The wind suddenly got up with a vengeance and the monsoon poured from the heavens. Sitting in bathing trunks and hats, like you do, they even had to take in a reef and were soon bounding along. The wind and rain stopped and they sat becalmed under a beautiful night sky with shimmering stars, it was a balmy

June night, the night sky there has to be seen to be believed. Of the provisions the beer seemed to be most popular during the evening! Daybreak the following day brought a sizzling sun and they did not seem to have moved very far. Three men took a dip and were not bothered by the tiger snakes and sharks, which luckily did not appear. At midday the wind increased so much it almost capsized the boat before they could reduce the sails. It got cold and rained again. They picked up the ship on radio and shortly afterwards she appeared over the horizon. They were a bit crestfallen to find that they still had forty miles to go. Did they wish to be taken in? No, they would soon get there with this wind blowing. With that they surged ahead... under the flare of the ship's bow, the mast caught something and parts of the rigging snapped with a resounding twang, dragged the boat over and she filled with water. The crew were covered in wet flapping sails and found it hard work pulling her with oars. Yes thank you they would take up the offer to go onboard!

Do you want to come aboard? Whalers do not sail very well full of water.

Heard outside the sickbay in the queue one day;

Rating; *'What is the best way to prevent itches caused through biting insects Doc?'*

Doc; *'Don't bite the insects'.*

An expert was our Doc!

Sharp shooters, the 1957 rifle team at the Fleet Rifle meeting Hong Kong. Winners of the Small Ships Team cup and 300 yards snap cup. AB Kemp won the individual Pistol cup and AB Taylor 3rd in the 600yrd event.

It was a sunny afternoon during a pleasant cruise to Hong Kong when 'Cavalier' was ordered to haul out of the line. She had been detailed to investigate an apparently derelict Chinese drifter which was eagerly watched by the remainder of the fleet. Gunnery Officer; *'The last bloke I knew that had to board a derelict junk suddenly had the fright of his life when an irate Jap appeared and took a ruddy great swipe with a ruddy great sword that fortunately only lopped off one of his ears'!*

That pleasant thought flashed through Frankie's mind as his 'Harry Tate' very slick boarding party were to board for their very first time.

Cries of *'Ahoy there'* on the loud hailer evoked no response. Try it in Chinese, send for a Chinese Steward. The language for hailing derelicts is apparently universal and *'Hoy'* from the steward had no better results. Frankie and his 'Harry Tate's' boarding party boarded her and confirmed the drifter abandoned. The C in C made a signal,

'Act in accordance with Q.R.'s and A.I.'s.' (Queen's Regulations and Admiralty Instructions)

Intelligent and intensive research in the matter disclosed they were to sink the cause that spoilt their afternoon.

Captain; *'How will you do it guns?'*

'HE from 'B' gun sir'

'How many rounds?'

'Bout ten Sir'

TAS Officer; *'If he doesn't Sir, can I have a go with the Squid?'*

'How long to get ready?'

No answer.

Guns very much on his dignity and ears burning; *'Close up normal 'B' guns crew, Captain of the of the mounting, sight setter, Layer, Mr. Francis. Trainer G.I. Officer of Quarters, Gunnery Officer. Remainder loading'.*

Half an hour and twenty four shells later it sunk!

Chinese junks were very often found with no crew onboard they having lost their crews during a typhoon. These were sunk by the RN as they were a danger to navigation.

Gunnery Officer; Stonecutters Island Hong Kong; 'I have to admit to being impressed by the ferocious bayonet charge on the butts at Stonecutters and seeing you all trying your utmost to become one with Mother Earth as you crawled to your objective

'Well dun 'B' gun! – Anything off th bottom shelf!

under withering live Bren gun fire. I also have to hand it to 'Pincher' Martin for winning the beer by reaching his objective unseen... through the brilliant expedient of commandeering a bus, including all the Chinese passengers, embussing his section and riding there!

Winter in Hong Kong and the crew, in blue uniforms hold Sunday divisions on the dockside. Top right can just be seen one of the Kowloon 'Star' ferries.

In February they left Hong Kong for Australia, here as usual they were warmly welcomed by the population. Many were invited 'up homers' to stay with ex-pats who wanted to catch up with the news from home. It seemed to all go so quickly and then they were headed north towards the sun! They arrived at Fiji and they were entertained by soldiers playing their guitars and singing like Harry Belafonte. Next stop Suva where it rained. The policemen there made a strange sight with their great mops of black fuzzy hair... and grass skirts. They turned east across the date line (two Wednesdays that week!), then to Hong Kong

Wherever the ship was secured to a buoy the ship's motor boat was used as a liberty boat. If it was carrying officers they sat in the front on padded seats and the ratings sat in the rear part alongside the engine. Sometimes the whaler was also used to transfer men ashore. The boats would be run on a time table and woe betide you if you missed the last boat. (From whence the saying comes of 'Missing the boat').

CDR Cartwright boarding the ship's motor boat to return onboard. The ship can be seen in the background lying to a buoy.

They sailed for the base at Singapore for the last time and on the 1st January 1959, having been away for 18 months, they flew home leaving the ship there for a new crew.

The animals will be alright Jack but she will have to go into quarantine

All the nice girls love a sailor
All the nice girls love a tar
For there's something about a sailor
Well you know what sailors are
Bright and breezy, free and easy
He's a lady's pride and joy
He falls in love with Kate and Jane
Then he's off to sea again
Ship ahoy, sailor boy

DID YOU KNOW?
(End of commission facts)

- They had steamed 63,299 miles
- 21,500 letters had been sent home
- 6 tons of 'rabbits' (presents) had been sent home
- They had drunk 56,064 tots of rum
- Smoked 2,315,820 cigarettes & used 47,040 boxes of matches lighting them.
- Drunk 51,960 cans of beer.
- Eaten 85 tons of spuds
- Consumed 298,000 tins of milk
- A quarter of a million meals were cooked in the galley
- Their electricity bill was £25,000 (cash preferred please)
- The props had revolved 33,782,000 times
- 2,926 tins of metal polish had been used
- They spent £89,212 .10s.0d on oil fuel
- They kept themselves clean with 11,316 bars of soap
- And their clothes with 5,364 packets of Dhobey dust
- They ate 17,745 ice creams.

Ammo Humping;

The gunner's party got involved in the great sport of 'Ammo humping', They fired 2,160 rounds of 4.5" ammunition and this all had to be brought up, and sometimes back down if the target plane was 'unserviceable'. Add in the 3,800 rounds of 40/60 Bofor ammo and 17,000 rounds of small arms and the Gunner's party was not the bed of roses some people thought!

Crew List 1957 – 9

Adair J	RS
Anderton W	LS
Anderton V	LS
Andrews P	ERA2
Anscomb P	OA3
Arnold P	LS
Backhouse K	TO2
Bainbridge B	AB
Bell J	
POME	
Bettam H	AB
Bilham N	RO3
Black G	ME2
Blears E	CY
Bliss T	SHPRT3
Bosley H	PO
Bowditch F	AB
Bowers R	AB
Bramley N	LRO
Brice R	ME1
Brinton R	OS
Brock J	ME1
Broome J	CK S
Brophy M	S LT
Brown D	AB
Budd K	AB UC3
Bumsted A	AB
Butcher D	LME
Burne G	AB
Carden E	EA2
Cartwright J	CDR CO
Chapman D	LS
Chowler P	AB
Clarke V	
Cleaver G	S LT RNVR
Coburn M	OS
Collyer R	PO
Cook A	OS
Critchley I	ME2
Culley J	AB
Daniel D	ERA3
Darrock D	AB
Davison G	OS G
Dawson J	LS
Dimond R	OS
Donno A	POME
Douglas E	OA4
Dreyer J	LT
Durling N	AB
Dutton V	AB
Eaton K	S LT
Eldridge J	L CODER
Elliott D	LEM
Englishby P	AB
Etheridge D	LME
Eva J	AB
Farrow N	AB
Fisher F	AB
Francis H	S LT SD
Franks T	PO
Fraser G	
Gavin C	TO3
Gibson M	AB
Gillespie D	
Ginns R	LRO
Godfrey D	POME

Golledge M	ME1	Kemp M	AB
Goodwin J	LME	Kendrick G	LEM
Gosden E	PO	Kersey J	S LT
Gough H	L CK S	Kilby E	OS
Graham T	ME1	Kirkland T	C ERA
Grantham D	AB	Kirkman D	AB
Graves L	LEM	Lafferty C	L ST
Gunner J		Landon W	LT INSTR
Haisman K	PO	Langthorpe S	LME
Hales W	ME1	Law Sung	STWD
Hall G	AB	Le Poidevin E	ME1
Har Wing	CK S	Lee Ching	L CK S
Haverty M	AB	Leese M	ME1
Hendy L	AB	Leung Ching	STWD
Hering W	ME1	Lewis B	REM1
Hipkins T	LT SD	Lomax A	OS
Ho Tin	CK O	Looker G	COA
Hodge A	ME1	Lovell F	C CK S
Hodkinson R	OS	Mansfield D	ME1
Holdbrook G	EM1	Mapp P	TO2
Holgate J	PO	Martin R	PO EL
Holland B	EA4	Martin W	LS
Holman M	AB	Mason M	OS
Horne J	AB	McDermott T	TO2
Hughes J	LEM	McDonald P	AB
Humphries A	SA S	McDonnell R	TO2
Hunt H	AB	McKinley J	LME
Jenkinson R	AB	McLellen W	RO2
Jenner P	AB	Meads R	LT SD
Jones R	SURG LT	Meakin F	LME
Jones R	LME	Meluish T	S LT
Jones M	TO3	Millar I	PO EL
Joy R	AB	Miller M	LME
Joyce J	OS	Miller K	ME1

Monk R	REA3	Smith A	
Moor C	EM1	SmithP	CPO
Morrow A	AB	Smith R	OS
Mottershead B	LTO	Smith R	EM1
Murray D	SPO V	Snow A	POME
Neil D	ME1	Somers C	LS
Newdick W	CEA	Stallard J	LME
Newman A	OS	Staveley W★★	LT CDR
Parker 'Fez'	REM1	Steel L	ERA3
Parry G	EM1	Stephenson R	COA
Parsons A	AB	Stracey D	ERA4
Payne R	LT CDR	Stubbs S	OS
Perry R	LME	Swann D	AB
Petch P	ME1	Tatters J	CK S
Pickersgill B	AB	Taylor R	LME
Platt D	ME1	Taylor G	AB
Pogson J	PO EL	Tebb H	POME
Pollock H	L WRTR	Thirkettle E	AB QA2
Pratt M	LS QA2	Thomas R	PO EL
Puckett K	AB	Thomas C	ME1
Quinn J	OS	Thornton W	AB RP
Randall S	SA V	Toop C	LS
Rathbone C	LME	Tung Shun	L STWRD
Read C	PO R EL	Turner W	AB
Rees W	S CPO S	Vallings G★	LT
Rhodes J	ME1	Vanneck J	ME1
Rice J	AB	Vollbrecht W	AB
Richards W	EA3	Wakeford P	AB
Ritchie M	AB	Walker W	POME
Robertson W	REM1	Walker W	AB QA2
Roose R	CPO	Walsh P	LS
Scoates J	ME1	Warren W	AB
Shand 'Jimmy'	LT CDR	Watson L	
Shaw V	CPO ME	Weeks A	PO

Willsher M	AB
Wong Chung	L STWD
Wood D	LSBA
Wood E	AB
Wright L	CPO EL
Wright A	EM1
Yeaman C	AB QA3
Yee Sing Jee	CK S
Yung Feng	PO STWD

★   Later Admiral Sir George
     Vallings KCB

★★ Later Admiral of the Fleet
     Sir William Staveley GCB

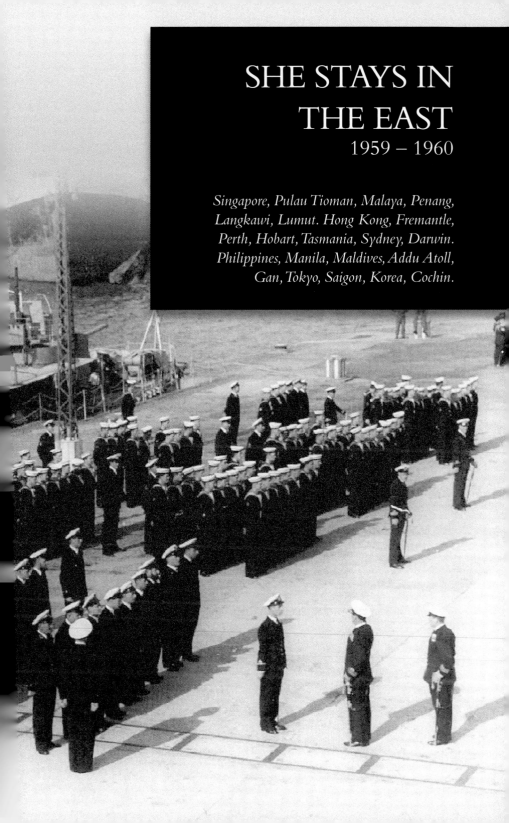

SHE STAYS IN THE EAST
1959 – 1960

Singapore, Pulau Tioman, Malaya, Penang, Langkawi, Lumut. Hong Kong, Fremantle, Perth, Hobart, Tasmania, Sydney, Darwin. Philippines, Manila, Maldives, Addu Atoll, Gan, Tokyo, Saigon, Korea, Cochin.

SHE STAYS IN THE EAST
1959 – 1960

Cdr J.D. Hope
(Third commission)

CDR Hope was later promoted to the rank of Captain. His daughter Emma was Christened onboard and her name was inscribed on the inside of the ship's best bell.

Pat Grotrian LT CDR, 1st LT: An advance party of the Buffer, the gunner Frank Tricky and a few others formed a group that left the UK on 30th December 1958, the rest of the crew arrived in Singapore just before the 9th January '59. I don't think many people nowadays have any concept of what an eighteen month 'Married *Un*accompanied' foreign commission means. The only wife out there at the time was the captain's and she had got there under her own steam, I think she worked out there as a journalist. Later during our visit to Hong Kong in December 1959 the E.O. John Nelson, got married and at the same time got his other half stripe and was made CDR.'

144

Gwen Hollamby, wife of Mike Hollamby POME: 'Oh how I missed my big beautiful hairy hunk of a matelot...' *er Mike this is Gwen's story...!*

'My life as a naval wife was full of ups and downs. Very sad days when ships sailed out of Pompey Harbour but joy of joys when they returned, the children ecstatic, not sure if it was seeing their daddy again or the rabbits (presents) he would bring. Having married in the 1950's we had no phone so relied entirely on letters, our only way of communicating. Sad when no letters arrived for several weeks then two or three would arrive together and that brought a smile to my face. It was disappointing when our daughter was born as husband Mike could not even get a couple of hours off to see us, he was in Gosport and I was only across the water in Southsea. I suppose the RN thought he was too important to be let off for a couple of hours! Again when I was expecting our son he was given a draft four weeks before he was born, the RN could certainly be awkward at times. My naval allotment was just £3 per week, and our mortgage had to come out of that! Friends and neighbours played an important part of my life; I knew I could call for help when in difficulties. I think being a naval wife you have to be of good temperament to put up with being apart eighteen months at a time, sometimes a lonely life. I have shed many tears in sadness and happiness. Would I do it all again...? Yes, with the same man beside me. We have made lots of friends from our Navy days, especially from HMS Cavalier, and our naval friends all stay loyal and keep in touch'.

They commissioned on the 9th January 1959 in Singapore Dockyard and sailed on the 20th for 'Work Up' off the island of Pulau Tioman, this is situated about sixty miles off Pahang State on the east coast of Malaya and was used for rest and relaxation by most warships after exercises. The island had white sandy beaches overhung with palms and coconuts and bananas. It was not unknown for some of the sailors to bring back onboard some beautiful parrots, usually against the Captains orders. These parrots mainly a brilliant red were caught and sold by the natives. On the days of the Captain's inspection of the ship they would have to be moved around to avoid detection. Having worked up to peak efficiency they were off to Hong Kong (Chinese 'Fragrant Harbour') for a few days rest and recuperation before returning to Singapore.

Hong Kong was relaxing but not what you would call restful!

One of the hundreds of bars in Hong Kong, these tickets were handed out around the ships and usually enticed men by offering the second drink free. (Don't know how this one got its name but a cherry boy was one that had yet to lose his virginity!)

The frwd seamen's mess deck celebrating Christmas 1959 in Hong Kong.

Ray 'Scribes' Ingram, L WRT: 'Nobody remembers a writers Christian name… because we were universally known as 'Scribes'. Part of our job was to deal with the ship's administration and issue of pay for the crew. When the ship's future programme was known the correspondence officer or squadron supply officer if he was carried, would take on sufficient foreign currency for the countries to be visited. This was got from the shore base at HMS Terror (Singapore) or HMS Tamar (Hong Kong). So at any one time we could be carrying British pounds, Japanese Yen, Hong Kong and Singapore dollars and Australian pounds altogether in the ship's safe. Whilst on passage a pipe would be made over the Tannoy that currency changing would be carried out at the ship's office between certain times. We also ran a Post Office savings business for the crew, and we had very few complaints'.

Some celebrated ashore in the China Fleet Club, Hong Kong 1959. Clockwise from left corner: LT Peter Honniball, POME Sullivan, REM Vickerstaff, SIG Faloon, LSBA Dobson unknown, unknown and Surgeon LT Bob Telfer, making a rude gesture (Hope he washed his hands!) LS Dear, PO Mat Harrison, REM Wallace (with glass) EM McIlvenny and ME1 Lupton.

On the 19th February they sailed for operation 'Rolex', escorting the Royal Yacht Britannia. They joined up with the gun cruiser HMS Ceylon, the destroyer 'Cheviot' and frigates 'Chichester', and the Australian 'Queenborough' and 'Quiberon' and exercised for the coming manoeuvres. On the 21st February they met the 'Britannia' half way up the Malacca Straits. HRH the Duke of Edinburgh waved to them as they steamed past at speed, they fired a salute and manned the side and cheered. Before taking up station to escort her into Singapore Harbour, they passed some mail to her by jackstay transfer which they had collected for her from Singapore. Then she was off to Penang and from there to another one of Jack's paradise Islands, Pulau Langkawi, this one being on the west coast of Malaya almost on the border with Thailand.

A few days later they again met up with her and escorted her out of the area and she continued on to Borneo. They detached from the fleet refuelled and went on to Penang on the west coast of Malaya. There they picked up a Malayan Naval training class before proceeding to Langkawi Island to the north for a banyan. At 0300hrs the next day they travelled to Lumut up the Dindings River. Here they saw a Malayan village untouched by time; it was like going back to the middle ages, a unique experience. They spent some time in Penang and several of the men returned to the ship with shaved heads. Their shipmates had to endure

In the Malacca Straits, Royal Yacht 'Britannia' left of centre. Cruiser 'Ceylon' Top right: followed by 'Quiberon', 'Quickmatch', 'Cheviot' and 'Cavalier' bottom right.

the sight of their progression from Easter Eggs to gooseberries and from gooseberries to lavatory brushes!

The 6" cruiser 'Ceylon' entering Singapore via the Jahore Straits, followed by destroyers 'Cavalier', 'Tobruk' and 'Solebay'

As always in these waters flying fish could be seen, particularly at night whilst escaping predators and attracted by the lights they would fly inboard. They were about eight inches long; the Chinese loved them and at dawn would search the upper deck for them. During calm days huge manta rays with up to twelve feet (4 metres) wingspan could be seen occasionally coming up out of the water then crashing down with a splash to knock lice off their bellies, some were believed to weigh half a ton. These were not dangerous but off Singapore every few hundred yards 'tiger' snakes, which had been washed down from the rivers were seen swimming by, these could give a nasty bite; they had black and yellow ring markings hence the name. During the monsoon season here you could almost set your watch by the arrival of the torrential rain which lasted for about an hour or so with an inch of water running everywhere. It then stopped and steam arose in the heat of the sun like steam from a boiling kettle.

Stores basin Singapore naval dockyard. The dry dock was to the left and the C in C's house to the right on the hill.

On March 10th they started a long refit with the ship docked down at Singapore; the crew was billeted in the shore base, HMS Terror, half a mile away from the Dockyard.

This was a time for a group from the crew to go off on an expedition to Malacca (FEXPED: Far Eastern Expedition Training). They took Two Motor fishing vessels with them, MFV715 and MFV742, two dinghies… and one rubber duck!

HMS Terror showing some of the accommodation blocks the canteen and parade ground.

FEXPED, MFV's and intrepid crew

They got dirty looks from a Shell Super Tanker whilst negotiating Singapore (civilian) Harbour, 'Well we had the right of way'! Later they anchored off Pulau Kukup and for supper they had Pot Mess, cooked by 'Reg', washed down with Carlsberg. The following day was taken up entirely of signposting. It was quite an exacting task, laying marker posts about every few hundred yards. These markers are brightly coloured cylindrical objects; they are designed to reflect the rays of the sun. Inscribed on them are words of encouragement to other seafarers like; Guinness, Carlsberg and Alsop's. They prided themselves on doing the job well. That evening they anchored by the beautiful Water Islands just outside Malacca. The following morning the sunrise was something never to be forgotten and they bathed in the sea that was until Cpt. 'F' started to describe a shark that was swimming around MFV 715. After a light snack of two eggs, fried bread, bangers, bacon, tomatoes, beans, wedges and a mug of tea they 'upped hook' and ceremoniously entered Malacca harbour. Their senior officer then paid official calls on the manageress of the Sky Ballroom and Excelsior bar to drink Knickerbocker Glories (if you haven't had a Knickerbocker Glory Superior with two bananas sticking out the top you haven't lived). They then spent three days touring the town and generally living a luxurious lifestyle that befits men having returned from the perils of the deep. All too soon it was all over and it was back to work refitting 'Cavalier'.

The ship came out of refit at the end of June and they left the comforts of the shore base. Due to technical difficulties they didn't actually sail until July 20th.

Olympic sized swimming pool at the shore base HMS Terror, one of the accommodation blocks can be seen in the background they were light and airy with balconies shaded by overhanging eaves to keep off the tropical sun and monsoon rain.

The ship's cricket team, being in refit gave some of the men time to enjoy their sports.

They made up for their relaxed time in port when they sailed for operation 'Jet'; they took a week to cross the Bay of Bengal where they joined up with the destroyer 'Cheviot' and the Indian Fleet. It was nonstop and the pace was fast. During these exercises violent manoeuvres are practiced which can be as bad as being in rough weather!

The ship will be under wheel for the next thirty minutes… and it usually coincided with meal times!

They re-entered port a week later but there was not a great deal to go ashore for. That didn't last long as they unexpectedly received orders to sail, destination unknown. It wasn't until they had left harbour they were told their destination was the Addu Atoll (Maldives) where the 'natives were becoming restless'. They steamed at high speed for twenty four hours and were to prepare landing parties. Weapons were assembled, radios checked, boots, gaiters and tin helmets made ready. On arrival all was quiet and the first landing party to go ashore was on a Banyan! The natives were actually very friendly people. The only attraction ashore was a bar set up by Costain's, the British company that was building an airport there.

A lot of fishing was done, the biggest one being landed was an eight foot shark caught by JS Crawford.

A bit of fresh shark fin soup is on the menu.

On the 29th August 'Cavalier' was relieved by 'Caprice'; when they arrived they had quite a shock, they were attacked by a war canoe full of fierce looking natives… from 'Cavalier's' wardroom! (Boys will be boys)

On returning to Singapore from Ceylon they passed and said goodbye to their old friend 'Cheviot' as she sailed for home, she had been in the Far East for several years.

A week's maintenance in Singapore and they were off again, this time to Saigon. They all enjoyed their time there and were struck by the friendliness and goodwill of the Vietnamese people. The pace ashore was fast and the Vietnamese apparently thought they were Albinos because as well as being white skinned they had red eyes!

Back to Hong Kong and as everyone was about to go ashore an urgent recall order was received, they were to sail immediately. A merchant ship, the 'Taichungshan' was being shelled by the army of the People's Republic of China off Amoy (Also known as Xiamen off the south coast of mainland China). They met up with her and luckily she was not seriously damaged and none of the crew was injured. They escorted her back to Hong Kong under the safety of the White Ensign and then remained there as Duty Guard ship. Being Guard ship restricted their leave somewhat. There was always a contingency plan for the Duty Guard ship, in the event of the Chinese overrunning the colony, to evacuate the Governor and other VIPs and their families. The ship was also affiliated to the current army regiment, which at that time was the Lancashire's. The ship very often took parties from the regiment to sea with them when they were exercising and the regiment hosted groups from the ship's crew and took them on exercises with them. 'Cavalier' took some of them on a trip to Tokyo with her, despite the seasickness en-route a good time was had by all. The prime reason for these visits was as a flag showing exercise, but they were also relaxing for the crew.

On 13th October 'Cavalier' along with the carrier 'Centaur', the destroyer 'Lagos' and the Australian 'Anzac' and 'Tobruk', joined the U.S. 6th fleet off the West coast of the Philippines for exercises. Whilst acting as Plane guard for 'Centaur' a huge crack developed in 'Cavalier's' port side from which fuel oil was escaping.

Mike Hollamby POME: 'Friday the 16th October I was on the morning watch (0400 – 0800) it was a bit rough but we were steady steaming. Lofty Hulks and Ginger Basterfield were on watch in 'B' boiler room, they were sucking Fuel oil from No9 and 10 tanks when the flames started to go out, there was much spluttering and spitting in the furnace indicating water is at the sprayers instead of oil. Boiler steam pressure started to drop and machinery slowed down. Quick thinking on the part of the boiler room crew managed to keep everything running. They closed the valves in the after bulkhead and opened the frwd bulkhead valves. Daylight revealed that we were trailing a huge oil slick astern back to the horizon; we were leaking oil from No 9 tank'.

She made her way back through some rough weather to Hong Kong, where having de-ammunitioned and emptied her fuel tanks she was put into the Whampoa commercial dry dock in Kowloon, there they pumped out 280 tons of water from the damaged fuel tank.

Whampoa dry dock Kowloon; Chinese dockyard workers replace the split plating in the port side amidships. A fire hose can be seen coming out of the second scuttle from the left… just in case.

Three days later the repairs having been completed and having re-stored the ammunition and refuelled she was back in Hong Kong again alongside her old running mate 'Caprice'. The crew could sample the delights of a run ashore. Because of the cheap labour in

Hong Kong a new suit or handmade shirts or shoes could be had for a few dollars. You could be measured for a shirt on Sunday morning and it would be ready to wear out in the evening. It was a reasonably priced evening to go to the floating restaurant in Aberdeen and have a top class meal, you could pick out the seafood you wanted whilst it still swum around in a tank. There were thousands of Chinese living on sampans in the harbour, which was not too bad in the summer but Hong Kong could still get cold in the winter and a typhoon could devastate their boats. On the hills behind the city was a cardboard and tin town of thousands more Chinese. After a torrential down pour in the monsoon or in a typhoon there would be reports of landslides and many deaths.

Mike Hollamby: 'On the 28th October they decided to flash up the 'Spanner' boiler which was complicated and unreliable, that's why we didn't normally use it. It was designed to provide steam when the main boilers were shut down. It was supposed to be more economical and cut down on watch keeping at the same time. At 1030hrs the Chief Engine room Artificer applied a spark to the mixture of warm diesel fuel and hot air... which resulted in a loud but muffled explosion! Fortunately the boiler had a spring loaded explosion door on the front which saved anybody from injury. The boiler room filled with soot and smoke and blew off the two foot diameter quarter inch steel plate on the funnel... this was hurled into the air like a cartwheel and landed on the awning of 'Caprice' alongside. The boiler room crew came up out of the boiler room hatch looking like the Black and White minstrel show. The whole episode was treated with great hilarity and the Spanner boiler was left to rot away unused in the starboard corner of the frwd boiler room.'

The men that make her go and look after the fuel and water – the engineering branch. It's winter in Hong Kong and they are wearing their blue serge No 1 uniforms. Front row Left is POME Mike Hollamby, in centre front with his sword is the engineering officer. Many of these men had served during WWII and the Korean War and had the 'fruit salad' (colourful medal ribbons) to show for it.

She was off and on her way to Tokyo again. Having passed Mount Fujiyama and the wooden houses with their upturned roofs they berthed on the Shibaura Pier, it was disappointing to see how Tokyo was becoming westernised. The crew enjoyed the Ginza stores and played with all the toys... in the evening their pockets were painlessly emptied by the lovely topless hostesses in the numerous night clubs and bars!

Mike Hollamby: '30th October found us in the Ginza bar in Tokyo, a barn of a place with cubicles of four seats, two occupied by topless Japanese girls and two by you know who and company! There was music belting out at 400 decibels and at the end of each record the girls would move up to the next table, quite a novel idea. They of course were drinking 'sticky greens'. (A bright green sugary water bought by the sailors for the girls, this was how they were paid for

Aberdeen harbour Hong Kong, tens of thousands of Chinese lived on sampans, whole families on each one. It was not unusual to see unwanted just born babies floating past the ship simply because there was no room for any more children, nature at its basic. Just to the right of this picture was the famous floating fish restaurant.

the 'entertainment') We of course were drinking Saki and ended up yaffling (eating) octopus and sushi and all the sauces.'

Mount Fujiyama

By the 2nd November they were back at sea refuelling from the RFA tanker 'Tidesurge'. They passed Okinawa and got some fresh bread from the carrier 'Centaur'. They watched 'Centaur's' planes bombing and rocket firing and refuelled again from 'Tidesurge' using two positions at the same time, there was a slight mishap at the aft position (mess flooded yet again with oil!)

9th November saw them in Junk Bay Hong Kong for a fleet regatta. Despite being able to get little practice the 'Cavalier's cleared the table! The Boys cup, Littleton & Galgrace cup, Davey cup, Fleet cup, the Club cup and all the 8th DS trophies.

Reports were coming in that typhoon Emma was coming their way so instead of enjoying the celebrations they had to leave early to avoid a rough passage to Singapore. They did however leave their rifle team behind to take part in the Port Rifle Meeting. Typhoon were annual events; they were given female names starting at the beginning of the year with 'A' for the first one and then working through the alphabet, so Emma was the fifth typhoon that year.

They cleaned up in all the races including the wardroom team winning the officers race. CDR Hope centre, sitting with the winning teams and their cockerel. The whaler oars were 20 feet long.

Having arrived in Singapore they entered dry dock for the fourth time for a self-refit, they were billeted with the 13/18th Hussars at the Sembawang Air Station (Sembawang village was just south of the naval base). The food wasn't particularly good but the mosquitoes enjoyed their stay.

The rifle team was left behind in Hong Kong

Bob Osborne AB: 'My time on 'Cavalier' was the happiest time of my service. Unfortunately my time on her came to an abrupt end ten months before the commission ended. The ship received a message that my father at home was seriously ill. We were on passage between Sydney and Darwin at the time and were exercising with the Australian Navy. I and my kit were transferred by jackstay transfer to the aircraft carrier HMAS Melbourne and from there by Gannet aircraft to Darwin; there I was put aboard a Quantas airlines 707 to London. Thanks to both navies and Australian airlines I was home within thirty six hours and able to see Dad before he died. My one regret was that I was not to be returned to 'Cavalier' where I still have abiding memories of runs ashore with John Dinnewell and other good friends I had made'.

1959 crossing the line certificate.

Each time they went to Australia they crossed the equator, the first crossing if time permitted, they had the time honoured crossing the line ceremony. The bears brought the uninitiated before King Neptune who read out the rules of his oceans before they were given a pill, made from flower dough. They were then shaved with some horrible gunk and a large wooden razor before being pushed backwards into the salt water pool.

The ship's 27ft whaler was known as a 'three in one', it could be pulled by oars or sailed but it also had an engine.

The 27ft whaler was a general purpose boat and could be dropped at sea whilst they were under way. It was heavy (approx. 1½ tons) and ruggedly built. Here it is under motor power but you can see the keel box and the rowlocks for the oars. On the bow can be seen the ship's crest, this was in order that she could be identified when coming alongside another ship. The coxswain was a leading hand, the bow man an AB and a stoker (ME) operated the engine.

The motor boat had two compartments; the frwd one had cushioned seats. When the ship laid to a buoy this was the main means of ferrying the crew to and from the ship.

In December they carried out firings of live torpedoes at the Ninepin Islands off Hong Kong and then entered HK for Christmas. The messes were decorated and the traditional swapping of ranks and uniforms took place. The youngest in the crew becomes the Captain for the day and various senior officers swap with some of the CPO's. The brown jobs, the Lancashire's treated them to a concert party and then lent them their band to play at Sunday divisions. Hong Kong was changing rapidly; land was being claimed from the sea all the time, the mode of dress of the people was changing to more westernised styles, the villages in the New Territories (Guangdong Province) were growing larger and noisier, they wondered would they recognize it on their return?

On 26th April 1960 they were on passage to Manila and exercise 'Sea lion', a SEATO exercise. In company were 'Belfast' (FO2) and her sister ships 'Cavendish' (D8) and 'Caprice'. The weather on leaving Hong Kong was ominous with tropical storm 'Carron' brewing causing havoc in the Philippines.

CDR Hope at a meeting in the wardroom with his officers prior to Operation 'Sea Lion'. L to R: LT CDR Pat Grotrian – the 1st LT. LT Hugh Murray, Gunner. LT CDR John Nelson, EO. CDR Hope and the back of the EL OFF, LT Peter Mallison.

The Americans were in charge of this exercise and at the wind up the US Commander sent the following message:

```
DISTD STAFF X LOGS.
ACTION...GO8.
- - - - - - - - - - - - - - - - - - - - - -
DTG.....050335Z.              DEFERRED.
FROM....CTU 313.2.4.          UNCLASSIFIED.
TO......CAVEND SH.
INFO....CAVALIER.
- - - - - - - - - - - - - - - - - - - - - -
        UPON TERMINATION AS A TASK UNIT COMMANDER OF
WHICH CAVALIER WAS A PART. MAY I EXPRESS MY PLEASURE
AT HAVING SO SMART A SHIP TO WORK WITH. EXCELLENCE
IN GUNNERY ENVOKED THE ADMIRATION OF ALL.

              DTG.....050335Z.
```

Pat Grotrian LT CDR: My specialization was as a gunnery officer. In their day the 'C' class had a state of the art Fire control system in the 'Flyplane 5' which was fitted in the 1950's modernizations. The above message from the American Commander speaks for itself.

You wouldn't think so when you read the following notice which appeared under the gunnery section in their commission book...

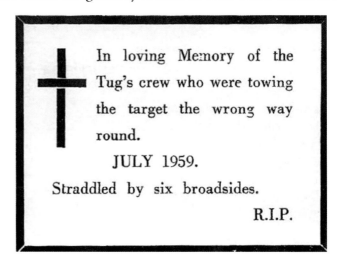

In loving Memory of the Tug's crew who were towing the target the wrong way round.

JULY 1959.

Straddled by six broadsides.

R.I.P.

Tinned salmon was very often on the menu for tea. A seaman asked 'Why was it that the salmon we get is marked up as 'grade three'? The leading seaman of the mess replied; 'Because there is no grade four'!

They had another trip to Australia and Tasmania exercising between times and then returning finally to Singapore. On the 13th May 1960 they flew home and left the ship for the next crew, they also posted the advertisement on the following page (for the next crew).

Crew list 1959 – 60

Adlam E	LS PTI
Akrigg W	ME1
Anderson H	AB
Angove J	AB
Angus K	OD
Ansell D	AB
Ash J	RO2
Baldwin R	ERA
Balfour D	LT
Ball R	LT S
Barnett S	RO1
Bass R	OD
Basterfield R	ERA
Beaney R	ME1
Berry W	LS
Bicknell C	LME
Bird A	ME1
Booy P	AB
Bourne C	LRO
Braithwaite B	CPO ME
Braund E	LME
Broadhead R	POME
Brookes F	AB
Burgess J	AB
Chaplin C	ME1
Clanfield C	JTO
Clarke D	SCPO S
Cleaver L Buffer	CPO GA
Collins C	AB
Connolly T	PO EL
Cooke R	PO CK
Cowen R	LS
Courtie P	CK
Cox M	AB
Crawford K	OD
Crickmore P	SPWT
Curry T	AB
Dack M	OA
Dassow D	OD
Dassow R	OD
Davies K	LME
Davies L	AB
Davis W	AB
Dear V	LS
Dennison J	LT
Dinnewell J	AB
Dixon D	SPO V
Elton L	ME1
Etherington R	RELM
Evans C	CPO ME
Evans D	AB
Evans R	PO
Falloon W	TO2
Farrant K	AB
Fielding G	S LT
Forbes J	LME
Fordham R	AB
Foster M	AB
Fransham J	OD
Fraser G	ME1
Friend J	AB
Garrity T	AB
Gigg R	REM
Gould K	EA
Graham M	LME
Green R	ME1

Griffin P	AB	Lazero K	LME
Grotrian P	LTCDR 1st LT	Lever D	ME1
Hamilton W	ME1	Long B	AB
Hanley D	ME1	Lott W	PO
Harding B	OD	Loveday J	TO2
Hardington W	CK S	Lupton R	ME1
Harries D	LME	MacDonald I	CEA
Harris R	CPO	MacDonald J	LME
Harrison C	CPO TASI	McDermot B	EM
Harrison J	S LT	McIlvenny J	EM
Haydon C	JS	Maggs C	L CODER
Henri M	OD	Mallison M	LT EL
Hogg D	AB RP2	Martin V	AB
Hollamby M	POME	Medley D	AB
Honniball P	LT	Mills J	EA3
Hope JD	CDR CO	Mooney M	POME
Horridge A	LEM	Munro J	ME1
Hoskins A	OD	Murphy M	CY
Howell R	OD	Murray H	LT G
Hulks A	POME	Mynheer R	ME1
Hunt A	AB	Neall H	ME2
Ingram R	L WRT	Neave J	AB
Jackson J	EM	Nelson J	LT CDR E
Jackson S	LS	Newstead M	AB
James J	OD	Nicholas R	POME
Jeffries G	AB	Osborne R	AB G
Johnson K	LME	Page D	AB
Johnston A		Paine J	LEM
Jones D	OD	Parker R	AB
Keegan T	A LEM	Pasco K	ME1
Kennett F	RS	Paul A	OA
Kuttan C	S LT RMN	Pearson R	ME
Latham A	PORE	Perrett N	S LT
Lavery J	L CK S	Pickergill H	AB

Potter F	AB	Thirwell R	AB
Poyton T	RO2	Thompson W	OD
Pratt J	CPO ME	Tomkinson E	CEA
Preston J	LS	Traer E	RO3
Reid J	ERA4	Tricky F	LT GO
Richardson S	AB RP	Veal P	OA3
Rigby W	AB	Vernon H	ME
Robinson A	AB	Vickerstaff B	REM 2
Robson G	LSBA	Wall D	ERA5
Robson M	PO	Wallace A	REM2
Ross A	TO3	Ward F	LS
Routley R	LS	Ward K	AB
Rowell G	PO EL	Warriner D	CK S
Rundle A	AB	Watson I	
Sandford R	JS RP3	Whaites D	CPO OA
Sewell A	REM 2	Whalen D	ME1
Shaw C	A LTO	Wheeler F	EM2
Sims A	ME1	Whitford L	ME1
Skeels G	AB	Willocks S	CPO EL
Smith K	EA5	Willson P	RO2
Soutar S	AB	Williams M	SURG LT
Spalging R	EM1	Wilshaw M	LREM
Sprules J	AB	Winn G	ERA
Stevens F	OD	Winter D	AB
Stevens M	AB	Withchell L	CPO EL
Stuart C	RO2	Woodward H	PO GI
Sullivan J	POME	Wright K	AB
Surman R	SA V	Yates D	ERA
Sydenham G	AB		
Taylor D	AB GA2	**Chinese Cooks and Stewards:**	
Telfer R	LT G	Har Wing	CK S
Temperly J	CPO EL	Kan Up Pui	
Thear B	SA S	Law Sung	STWD
Theil S	ME1	Lee Cheung	L CK O

She stays in the East 1959 – 1960

Lin Poi Chin
Mak Sau Wah   STWD
Tung Shun Cheng L STWD
Yee Sing Jee   L STWD
Yue Yan Ngar   STWD

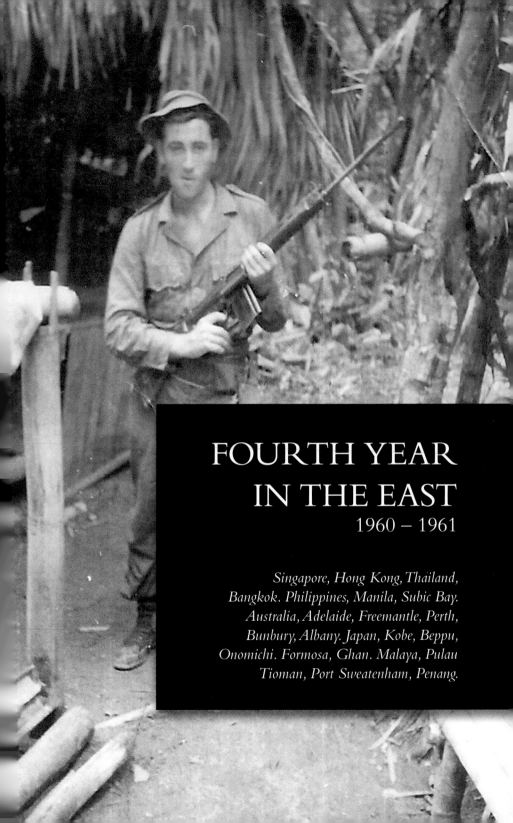

FOURTH YEAR
IN THE EAST
1960 – 1961

*Singapore, Hong Kong, Thailand,
Bangkok. Philippines, Manila, Subic Bay.
Australia, Adelaide, Freemantle, Perth,
Bunbury, Albany. Japan, Kobe, Beppu,
Onomichi. Formosa, Ghan. Malaya, Pulau
Tioman, Port Sweatenham, Penang.*

FOURTH YEAR IN THE EAST
1960 – 1961

CDR Gwynedd Idris Pritchard RN
(Fourth commission)

CDR Pritchard joined the Royal Navy as a volunteer in 1942 as 'Hostilities Only' ordinary seamen. He went to the training establishment HMS Ganges in Suffolk. He served for two years on the destroyer 'Ferndale' when she took part in Operation Torch (N. Africa) and the landings in Sicily. He spent time in the Atlantic and Russian convoys and ended the war as Gunnery Officer in the destroyer 'Zealous'. He became a LT and obtained his first command, the MTB 2017. He spent a short time with the Fleet Air Arm at the shore base 'Gamecock' and on the Aircraft carrier 'Indomitable'. In 1952, during the Korean War, he had command of the mine sweeper 1786 based in Hong Kong. In the late fifties he was 1st LT of the destroyer 'Contest' during the Icelandic 'cod war'. He was promoted CDR and took command of 'Cavalier' for the 1960/61 commission.

He later commanded a frigate squadron on the frigates 'Phoebe' and 'Charybdis'. In '68 he was with Defence Intelligence (Soviet Navy section) and in the 70's he became Director of Naval Operations and Trade at the Admiralty. In '73 he transformed 'Dryad' into the school of Maritime Operations rising to Rear Admiral in '76. He became Flag Officer Sea Training Portland and then Flag Officer Gibraltar and NATO Commander Mediterranean. In 1981 after nearly forty years he was placed on the retired list and appointed Companion of the Order of the Bath. His crew thought that he handled 'Cavalier' like his old MTB! One of the names he was known by was 'Ard over Pritchard' because he invariably started violent manoeuvres about Tot time or lunch time. Many years later when asked why he did that he said; 'Just to show who was in charge'! He was a strict disciplinarian but fair with his men, if they were right he would stand up for them. It was a remarkable achievement to have risen from the lower deck to Rear Admiral.

This was the Author's commission. We, the next crew were flown out from Stansted airport which was then just a runway with a few wooden sheds. We went out in two flights in the Britannia a four engine turbo prop aircraft. Chartered by the Admiralty from Eagle Airlines, these aircraft were nicknamed the 'Whispering Giants'. In June the first of two flights were due to take off. The aircraft was a small dot at the end of the runway and we were taken there by bus. We asked the driver why we didn't board the plane at the terminal *'like we had seen film stars do in the pictures'*. The bus driver told us that they were afraid the undercarriage wouldn't take the weight taxiing out to the end of the runway! He was joking wasn't he? We were loaded aboard and were quite excited, only VIPs and film stars flew in those days. The pilot started the engines to warm them up and after a few minutes he got up from his seat, put his hat on picked up his briefcase and said as he left the aircraft 'I'm not taking that bloody thing up'. We waited but they couldn't find another pilot who would either! All our baggage was unloaded and the plane was taken to the sheds 'for some adjustments' (They hit it with a big hammer). Later we loaded again and finally got off the ground. About sixty miles downwind from the airport there was a bang and a shudder, one of the engines had blown up! We turned and headed back towards Stansted but had to fly around for the next three hours dropping fuel. You could see it streaming out of pipes in the wings... *'Please do not smoke'*, as if we needing telling! We finally came into land back at Stansted with fire engines and ambulances chasing us down the runway... if this was flying they could stuff it; it created a lot of extra dhobying!

A Britannia of British Eagle airlines used for trooping flights. As they passed through various foreign countries they wore civilian clothing and their passports stated they were 'Government officials'.

Some men were taken to Hendon to sleep for a couple of nights and some slept in huts at the airfield. Many of the crew went into London and made the most of an extra night on the town. We finally got away; we stopped at Istanbul to refuel and then flew on to Bombay. Over Bombay we hit the monsoon and were thrown all over the sky. As we landed the wheels hit several inches of water at the end of the runway and we thought the tail was going to overtake us, more dhobying! Six hours later and we were on our way again. On arrival at Singapore after a flight of twenty four hours we landed in the heat and humidity of the tropics, we thought it was the exhaust of the engines as we stepped off the plane. We went by navy bus to the Dockside accommodation, a shed in the dockyard, dumped all our kit on our beds and within an hour we were making the most of the bars in Bugis Street Singapore, such is youth!

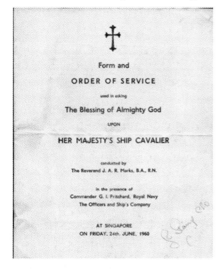

'Cavalier' had been left in Singapore Naval Base by the 59/60 crew when they flew home. They left her spick and span and shipshape.

Commissioning service sheet

On 24th June 1960 the new crew mustered on the dockside alongside the ship in their best No.6 white uniforms. CDR Pritchard, gave a speech and the Sin bosun said a prayer or two and for the first time we all walked across the gangway with our kit bags to find the mess deck that would be our cramped home for the next eighteen months. The coxswain CPO 'Sticky' Stamp took charge of the junior seamen; he said *'I shall never remember all your names so I will give you names that I will remember, you will be 'Katie', 'Blossom' 'Sally' and 'Petal'* and so on, and nearly sixty years later they are still known by those nicknames… over the years it has caused a bit of confusion! Blossom remembers 'Sticky' Stamp well, he was a big man and when he wore his shorts they were large and wide, when climbing up a ladder behind him it was like looking up the belfry of St Mary's church!

The junior seamen were then sent to one of the after messes to be supervised by a 'Sea Daddy', a senior A/B, for the first few months, the idea being that they would not be lead astray or corrupted by the older sailors in the other messdecks. It has to be remembered that some of these junior seamen were probably only just sixteen years old. The 'Sea Dad' system was a tradition dating back to the 18th century.

We sailed the following day for work up, those intense days when everyone is put through their paces. Night and day they train and prepare for any contingency that is likely to be thrown at them in a hostile world.

Three weeks later and having had very little sleep the powers that be consider you may need a bit of rest and relaxation, so it's off to Pulau Tioman. One of the crew of a submarine tried to swim back to his boat from the beach and was bitten by a huge sea snake; he was flown to Singapore hospital and luckily survived and with puncture scars to show for his experience. In HMS Terror sick bay they kept many stuffed snakes so that 'Jacque' could point to the one that may have bitten him!

Then we were off for our first visit to Hong Kong. On that first visit the Provost Marshall's team came aboard and gave a talk, they also showed some horrendous slides of what you might catch there if you were not careful; it put some of the men off for all of an hour! He said 'Give or take ten there were about three hundred and sixty bars and night clubs in the Wanchai district, not counting Kowloon. All of these were vying with each other to give 'Jack' a good time and relieve him of some of his shekels'. A good run ashore could be had for ten shillings (50p). We were vaguely aware of the poverty in China at that time but unaware of the total disaster that Mao Zedong's policies had caused. In 1960/1 whilst we were there it was later estimated that some thirty million people had starved to death. Many Chinese in Hong Kong had come across the border into the British Colony to escape the draconian regime and the poverty.

Pulau Tioman, the beautiful tropical island in the South China Sea where coconuts and bananas grew wild and where large iguana lizards roamed. Crew member AB Pitman is seen here walking along the beach.

Cinderella leave

In Hong Kong and other British colonies the Royal Navy crews were allowed ashore for a full 23 hours leave at a time. In practice this meant if you were over eighteen and not on duty you could go ashore all night but report to the ship for an hour in the morning and if not on duty you could go off again. However the Americans had to return onboard their ships by midnight. This was called 'Cinderella' leave by the British sailors and they worked it to their advantage. In the bars and nightclubs the Yanks would spend money on buying girls drinks all evening and when they had to leave before their carriage turned back into a pumpkin... the British matelots took over!

Officially the Yanks were not allowed tattoos. A group of 'Cavalier's met up with a couple of American sailors in a bar in old Wanchai, Hong Kong. They had a good friendly evening and after drinking

177

far too much than was good for them and having paid a visit to the Tattooist, the Americans returned to their ship at 'Midnight'. One of them awoke in the morning to find he had a lovely Union Jack tattooed on his back!

Rickshaws were the preferred way of travelling around Hong Kong; there were hundreds of them, bright red with a green painted hood. They were very comfortable and were cheap, about 30 or 40 cents (3p) to the bars or back to the ship. Very often 'Jack' on returning to the ship from the bars in the early hours would put the Chinese coolie in his rickshaw and then raced their mates through the town back to the harbour.

Dave Jobling A/B: 'Whilst in Hong Kong we normally lay to a buoy out in the harbour, but on one occasion we were entering the basin to go alongside, starboard side to the wall. There was a strong offshore wind blowing and it was blowing us away from the wall. The Skipper didn't panic he ordered full astern on one engine and full ahead on the other and spun the ship around almost on the spot. At the same time he ordered the seamen to pass the berthing wires over to the port side. He 'parked' that two and a half thousand ton ship as though it were a car! Our skipper was one of the best ship handlers I met in my time in the RN.'

The reason for us coming alongside in Hong Kong was that a crane was to hoist a large wooden packing crate onto the squid deck. We were then joined by some RAF personnel. Nobody knew what it was or where we were going. Several hours later we found that we were sailing up the Formosa Channel (Now Taiwan) with huge weighted Union Jack flags hanging over the side of the bridge and a large White Ensign flying from the yardarm. The Island of Quemoy, occupied by Chiang Kai-Shek's Republic of China, was under constant daily bombardment by the Peoples Republic of China and we were sailing between the two. The channel there is about sixty miles wide and through binoculars you could see quite clearly many gun emplacements on both sides. When the end of the packing crate was dropped there appeared to be a very large camera lens protruding from it. We assumed of course that the skipper had taken up photography!

Leaving at 0900hrs from Hong Kong in thick fog one morning for gunnery exercises, an SOS was received from the MS Mui Heng (CPT H Benneche); she had been entering Hong Kong by the Tathong Channel in fog and had collided with the MS Tong Poh (CPT M Norman). She was holed in the bow and the crew was standing by the lifeboats until they could assess the damage. 'Cavalier' found her

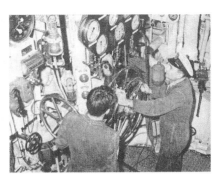

MS Mui Heng collided in fog and was holed (Photo H.K. newspapers)

MS Mui Heng collided in fog and was holed (Photo H.K. newspapers)

on radar and stood by her whilst she pumped water from frwd to bring the damage above the water line. Later the tug Taikoo was able to tow her into Hong Kong and 'Cavalier' resumed her voyage.

George English USN, writing many years later: I owe thanks to the men of 'Cavalier' for their interceding on my behalf in the fall of 1960 at the China Fleet club Hong Kong, B.C.C. (British Crown Colony). I was under physical assault by some American sailors in the heads. The 'Cavalier's' stepped in and halted that assault, thereby saving me from serious injury. Whomsoever they may have been… THANK YOU'.

Marshall 'Nobby' Clark A/B: 'On one occasion 'Cavalier' had been at sea on strenuous exercises for several weeks without any leave. When we did get back into Hong Kong, apart from the duty watch most of us went ashore. However, before visiting the bars many sailors went to the China Fleet Club on the corner of Nathan Road to play tombola, in the hope of winning some money. When the American fleet was in harbour their sailors were also allowed to use this club and generally the British and American sailors got on well together. On this particular night the Americans continually played a record on the Wurlitzer juke box, The Battle of New Orleans… sung by Johnny Horton, which was currently in the charts. After the Americans had played this record for the umpteenth time 'Lucy' Lutchford A/B RP, of "Cavalier's" crew told the Americans that we had heard enough of that one thank you. They put it on again to antagonize. 'Lucy' pulled the plug out of the socket, they put it back in! Someone ripped the plug off the wire; the Yanks stuck the wires back in the socket with matchsticks… The Chinese Mama San could see where this was all going to end and telephoned the Police and Naval patrol. About this time a group of 'Cavalier' Stokers pulled the Juke Box away from the wall trundled it across the room and pushed it down the flight of concrete stairs… just as the police arrived to be met by it crashing through the double doors. The American naval patrol, the 'Snowdrops' (They wore white helmets!) arrived and started beating ten bells out of their sailors with their huge 'night sticks' for bringing the USN uniforms into disrepute. Damn it we were winning before they arrived! The snowdrops didn't normally touch the British sailors unless they attacked them first. The following morning our 'Old Man', received an order to present himself before the Admiral at HMS Tamar, the Hong Kong shore base in his best uniform. When he returned to the ship he cleared lower deck of all the ship's company and told them that he had just been carpeted and we were to go to a buoy out in the harbour, all leave was cancelled. However he had pleaded our case and explained to the Admiral it was our first night ashore after several weeks at sea. The Admiral relented; but he still sent us to a buoy and stopped our leave for twenty four hours. As we were dismissed the Skipper said 'When you next go ashore I suggest you wear another ship's cap tally! The stokers also got involved in another incident which occurred in the Singapore Dockyard canteen. I was duty watch onboard when a patrol wagon was seen stopping by our gangway... what had the 'naughty boys' been up to this time I thought, were they returning a couple of drunks back to the ship? Stand by the duty watch! But no, from the driver's door emerged one of our drunken stokers and several more bailed out from the back, they came onboard, threw the keys to the Officer of the day, LT Dennison, saying 'You know where we are when they come looking' and went to their messdeck. It wasn't long before the dockside was crawling with Naval Patrolmen looking for their wagon. Of course there it stood alongside the dashing D73. They had no sense of humour and did not see the funny side of these stokers using their Black Maria as a taxi. They were charged and brought up as defaulters to the 1st Lieutenant's table who sent them on to the Captain's table. All the Naval Provost staff were there waiting for the 'hanging, drawing and quartering' of this rabble! The 'Old man' called forward one of the leading patrolmen witnesses and said to him 'When you went into the canteen to sort out the fracas that was taking place, where did you leave the ignition keys'? He replied 'In the van Sir'. The skipper consulted his minions and then turned to the Provost staff and said; 'That was rather a silly thing to do because my stokers are a very resourceful bunch and that was an open invitation for them to get a free ride back to the ship'. Instead of the expected 'hanging from the yard arm' he gave the offenders some minor punishment; the Provost staff couldn't believe their ears and the Master at Arms almost had a heart attack.

Terry 'Blossom' Bowser JS: This must have been the same day that Chats Harris' threw me in the grand piano! A fight started in the bar and, being just a 16 year old whipper snapper and Chats being quite a bit bigger and older, he lifted the lid on this big piano and threw me in the back of it saying 'Stay in there you'll be alright'.

Stevie Clare ME (sometimes LME!): 'The ship was in dry dock in Singapore and we were living in HMS Terror the shore base. This particular evening about eight of us stokers went for a 'quiet drink' in the Dockyard canteen and somehow got involved in bit of a fight with some Aussies, over a woman I think! The Naval Patrol was called and while they entered by one door we left by another, we just borrowed their van to get back to the ship. I don't remember who was driving, I was given thirty days stoppage of leave and whilst the rest of the crew lived in barracks we had to live onboard the ship which being refitted was dead and dirty (All the machinery was shut down). Although my leave was stopped I managed to get ashore in the evenings for a drink in the canteen by walking across the timber shores that held the ship up in the dry dock. This was great until one evening the chief caught me in the bar and I ended up in cells at the entrance gate to 'Terror' barracks. This was pretty grim, a potato and some gravy for meals and a cold tap in the yard for washing and drinking. I blocked the air holes up with toilet paper to stop the snakes coming in, the cells backed onto the marshes. It may have been 1961 but it was more like 1761, I had to pick so many pounds of oakum each day (old rope into fibre), they weighed it to make sure I had done enough. On New Year's Eve two of my oppo's, Oggy and Midge Beck, climbed on the roof of the cells and tried to get me out, I think they had had a drink or two! Velcro had not been invented then but it would have been handy to be able to put my Leading Hand's badge on and off instead of having to keep cutting it off and sewing it back on'.

December 1960 and the ship was in the King George VI dry dock for a self refit. The crew were living in 'Terror' the shore base and because of the heat of the day were on tropical routine, that is, start work at 0530hrs and finish the day at 1300hrs. Everything was overhauled and the ship's bottom painted. Chat's Harris a very good artist, painted a huge 'Cavalier' ship's crest on the wall of the dry dock for which he almost got into trouble for, but I think the skipper was actually secretly proud of it.

Christmas was spent in Singapore but unfortunately it was suspected that riots caused by Communist agitators were about to break out so all leave was cancelled. Those men not on watch celebrated in the dockyard canteen with a SODS opera.

Katie and Blossom JS, CAPTURED: 'Whilst the ship was in refit at Singapore Sub Lt. Cordrey, most of the junior seamen and a couple of senior AB's went on a trip on an MFV (Motor Fishing Vessel) It was part training and partly a break from the heat of Singapore for a few days, we would be visiting some small islands in the Malacca Straits. We were having a good time 'Mile Stoning' (Leaving beer cans every few hundred yards!) when some shots were fired across our bow and suddenly we were surrounded by three Indonesian gun boats. We were accused of being in their territorial waters and were taken in tow and escorted under armed guard to a harbour near Jakarta. We did not carry any weapons on this trip. Sub. Lt. Cordrey told us to expose any film we might have in our cameras which was just as well because our cameras were taken from us along with any other valuables, including all our money. We were held there for several days whilst a British civilian official from the Shell Oil Company tried to negotiate our release. After much political negotiation we were released and as we left the harbour we could see why... the cruiser 'Belfast' with her twelve six inch guns and three minesweepers were lying threateningly just outside and waiting for us! We never did get our property back though.

Shortly after this we were in Singapore when we were ordered ashore in platoons in riot gear. There was serious unrest between some Chinese communist's elements and the Malays and outbreaks of rioting. This was almost an annual event. Lt. Matthews the second gunnery officer and G.I. McCarthy were in charge. We laid a tape across the road and displayed signs in several languages for them not to cross this line on pain of death. We fixed bayonets. The marksman of the platoon had orders to shoot any ring leaders who crossed the line. It was a tense time but luckily they slowly dispersed'.

A much more relaxing time could be had at the Kota Tinggi falls about thirty miles north of Johor Bahru in Malaya; the water was always nice and cold there'.

Now it may seem that a great deal of our time was devoted to having fun, but it was only when we got ashore, which sometimes wasn't very often. At sea apart from being on watch, doing maintenance or washing and ironing or trying to grab a couple of hours sleep, it was training, training and more training. Rushing to your action station and going through drills until they became automatic, whatever the situation.

Kota Tinggi falls, Malaya

John 'Dinger' Bell AB: On closing up on 'A' gun:

'A' gun to TS, 'A' gun closed up and cleared away, bore clear, Tube inserted and mounting in Auto'.

The gun being in auto would immediately align itself with the Director's radar but with all the additional data added from the system. Wind speed and direction, Barometric pressure, Target speed and direction, own speed and direction, backlash within the system, wear on the barrel (each gun had a 'rounds fired' counter from which wear was calculated) and many more calculations. Add in the gyroscopic corrections to counter the constant rolling and pitching of the ship and a shell could be put on an aircraft that was travelling at perhaps up to eight hundred miles an hour or more. If in Anti Aircraft mode the shell would have a radar nose fuse which was activated with the inertia when it was fired through the rifling o the barrel, if it arrived within a few meters of the target it would go off. If the cartridge failed to fire perhaps because of a poor charge, you firstly left it for half an hour to make sure it wasn't just a slow burn and then tried firing it again, if it didn't go this time you had to remove it... vary carefully... and throw it over the side fairly smartish. If a shell jammed half way up the barrel it had to be rammed out with a pole with a bronze cup on the end so that it didn't strike the fuse! (Luckily this was a rare occurrence). January 1961 and we were off again to Hong Kong as guard ship.

Robert 'Paddy' Townsend OD; 17th March 1961 back in Hong Kong I was celebrating St Patrick's Day in the China Fleet Club. I had been holding a conversation with a French sailor, the Frenchman could not understand a word of English, especially with my Irish brogue and I could not understand French... we were getting on very well! At some stage we decided to swap uniforms, I thought it was just for a laugh for a few moments but when I looked around he had disappeared. Having consumed a few more San Migs I found myself wandering down Wanchai in the middle of the night and being challenged by some USN Snowdrops as to what I was doing out after midnight. (The French like the USN also only had Cinderella leave). I tried to explain but it was either my Irish accent or the beer talking! They threw me in the Jeep and I was taken all the time protesting, to the French ship. As they tried to hand me over to the French their Officer of the Watch was shouting 'Non, Non, Non', he had enough problems with his own inebriated shore goers. The Snowdrops finally got the message and took me back to 'Cavalier' where, to my surprise the OOW thanked the Yanks and just told me to turn in. I thought I had got away with it but in the morning I was in the rattle. I was made to parcel up the French uniform and was taken back to the French ship where a ceremony was held when I handed my parcel to the Frenchman and him my uniform to me. I then got weighed off and was very lucky to only get one day's stoppage of pay and leave. No sense of humour some people! I don't know what punishment the French matelot got'.

Paddy on joining the RN had been offered a commission but had turned it down preferring to experience serving on the lower deck.

Put me down: A group of our crew was returning off shore from Wanchai Hong Kong early in the morning singing their heads off. They were approached by a little Chinese policeman, very smart in his starched shorts and polished Sam Brown belt, he said 'You, stop makey noise'. One stoker, who was built like a brick chicken run, picked him up by the scruff of his neck lifted him up level with his face and said 'Who do you think you are talking to?' The little policeman pulled his revolver out and stuck it in the stoker's guts and said 'YOU'. He put him down smoothed his shirt and we all returned quietly to the ship. Well anything for a quiet life eh?

Cliff East J TO: 'Apart from a couple 'sparkers' and the Yeoman I was the only signalman left onboard one day in Hong Kong. We were at a buoy and the carrier 'Victorious' was on another nearby. We received a signal from the 'Vic' to say, 'Typhoon imminent, all men to be recalled and all ships will put to sea forthwith'. (It was the practice to ride storms out at sea, it was safer than getting battered against a jetty or beached). The Blue Peter and Two Black balls were hoisted to the yardarm informing everyone to return to the ship immediately as we were sailing. Most men hurried back but the communicators ashore on seeing the signal decided that they would take a ride up the Peak. Crafty lot knew that the first thing the authorities did when a typhoon was about to hit the city was to shut down the funicular railway to the Peak, it would leave them stranded at the top… where there happens to be a bar! As we left harbour it was decided by the powers that be that we would play war game whilst at sea to while away the time! This meant that with so few of the signals branch onboard I had to spend three days curled up on the deck underneath the 20" signals lamp. Just before leaving

Seamen of the quarter deck division in No 6's after Sunday church parade.
Back row L – R: 'Buster' Brown, Tex Williams, Ginge Cuckson, Paddy Salter-Townsend, Chris Barber, George McNally, Ian Kelman, 'Scouse' Jones, 'Ginge' Caudery, Dave Barker, Cleb Clarke, Soapy Watson, Jock Gilham, Bob Milne, 'Pat' Paterson.
Front row L – R: S LT 'Cowboy' Cordery, Eddie Vann, PO Taff Butler, 'Chats' Harris, 'Ginger' Norton, 'Buck' Ryan.

had been ashore to watch an English touring team play a game of football against Hong Kong. The Tom Finney X1 was good but the No6 didn't look up to much; however my Oppo 'Bob' Parry bet me HK$5 that in the future he, the No6 would play for England… I still owe him HK$5… the player was a man called 'Bobby' Moore! (One HK$ = 1s 3d or about £0.07 today!)

Fred Coates AB G: How to get on a diving course… 'Returning from the Singapore dockyard canteen one day and having enjoyed a few Tiger beers (Beer in Brain out!) I came across a diving team operating around the ship. Fun time said numb brain cell, got to take the P…. out of this lot and I did. A tap on the shoulder and there stood this dirty great hairy Chief Diver who had an uncanny resemblance to the 'Hulk'. Name, Number and Rate he asks, and, like the village numpty I gave him my details, I could have given him any of the other two hundred names but brain was not in gear. The following morning in response to a 'request' I went to the coxswain's office and Sticky Stamp, bless 'im handed me a temporary draft chit to HMS Terror barracks… for a diving course! Round things I said, I never volunteer for anything, I'll complain… on second thoughts it will be pointless! There I was standing looking like a tadpole (In black shiny diving suit) and doing alright as well, until, while dropping to the bottom by Red House Jetty some stupid PO Diver sneaked up on me in the murky water and tapped my mask to ask if I was OK. It frightened the brown stuff out of me. I let go of the rope and fell backwards into a deep mud hole. I was dragged out and spent some time in the decompression chamber and being treated for a burst ear drum. Shortly afterwards I was back in front of the Dirty great Chief Diver, 'Get your ear sorted and we'll have you back here' he says and handed me a draft chit back to 'Cavalier'. Like a streak of lightening I was off back to where I belonged, in the safety of the seamen gunner's mess!'

Extract from the 'Cavalier's' log now at the PRO Kew:

1900hrs Tuesday 15th September 1961 'Fleet diving team exercising under ship's stern'

Sick Bay

Overheard whilst in the queue outside the sick bay:

Doc; *'Well did you wear something?'*

Rating; *'Yes Doc, I kept my socks on'*

Jenny's Side Party: A Chinese lady, named Mrs Ng Muk Kah universally known as 'Jenny', and her gang of girls, were employed by most of the Royal Navy captains visiting Hong Kong between the 1940's and 70's to wash and paint their ship's sides. They were honest hard working and did not demand huge amounts of money for their work. Their payment was to take away all the food scraps and old rope, in fact anything they could recycle. She would place a sampan under the gash chute at the stern of the ship to collect all the scraps of food. They also had some of the left over paint and from time to time, dressed in their finery they acted as very attentive waitresses at cocktail parties. They could also be found onboard doing sailors washing or mending their clothes. When a new ship came in the harbour it was not unknown for her and her girls to stand in her sampan and hold a message up saying 'Your Ship Dirty'... it pays to advertise! Jenny was very proud to have been awarded the British Empire Medal in the 1980 Hong Kong honours list.

Jenny's side party on 'Cavalier's quarter deck, she is 2nd from left front row, to right of her is CPO Smale (Buffer) and the officer, right is the 'Jimmy', LT CDR James

Like many of the older Chiefs and Petty Officers Les Smale seen above with Jenny, were wartime served men. Les was a young seaman on HMS Hardy at the first battle of Narvik and when the coxswain was killed he steered her under fire onto the rocks to save her from sinking. He was one of the men who got Captain Warburton-Lee

(VC) ashore on a Carley float. Unfortunately as they landed him he died of his wounds and they buried him temporarily in the snow onshore. Luckily he and the others, who had been looked after overnight by the local villagers, were rescued from occupied Norway by another RN ship the following day. Les was a true patriot, a hero and gentleman.

One of the four torpedoes carried by the ship. This one is half withdrawn from its tube for servicing by PO Butler and his mate AB Howell both of the TAS department. Both were Welshmen.

Operation Pony Express, North Borneo: As we crossed the South China Sea we refuelled from the USS Kawishiwi. We approached them to take a line and could hear music being played; as we got nearer we saw that they had a very good Skiffle group on the quarter deck thumping out some of Lonnie Donegan's numbers just for us, different! On 28th April 1961 we joined the Operation Pony Express; it was to last fourteen days and involved some 20,000 naval personnel, 6,000 troops, two attack carrier groups, hundreds of aircraft and sixty ships. It was the biggest exercise since WWII and was the first to involve a nuclear submarine. Deployed in the landings were 42 Commando Royal Marines, Australian Infantry and US Marines and men from New Zealand, Philippines, and Thailand. Aircraft carriers of several nations were 'cross decking', that is landing on and taking off from each other's decks. Aircraft bombed and strafed shore targets, ships bombarded and troops landed. It was centred on the island of Balambangan, Borneo and was conducted by mainly British and American troops with an underwater demolition team from the Philippines. Two aircraft were lost during this exercise one being a Royal Navy top secret Scimitar which crashed into the sea. Luckily the pilots were able to bail out. These exercises were always watched by Russian 'spy trawlers' festooned with aerials so we had to locate the crashed plane by ASDIC then blow it to bits with squid bombs, this ensured that it could not be recovered by a foreign power. A Whirlwind helicopter from the commando carrier 'Bulwark' carrying six British soldiers crashed on landing in a clearing on the top of a hill in Borneo. As it touched down it caught a soft patch of soil and tumbled down the hill, no one was seriously hurt. The USS submarine 'Sargo' was detected before it was able to penetrate the screen. Live ammunition was used in the bombardment of an uninhabited island off White Rock Bay with Mount Kinabalu half covered in cloud in the background.

One ton of 'tin fish' on it's way over the side. They had a range of five miles at forty knots or seven miles at thirty five knots with a warhead weighing 750 lbs. Practice torpedoes had a reflective orange nose to facilitate finding them at the end of a run.

Recovering a practice torpedo at the end of its run, the smoke that can be seen is emitted by the torpedo automatically to aid in locating it. On 'Cavalier' there were no electric winches, everything was lifted by hand using block and tackle; this can be seen lying on the deck with a line of men ready to haul.

A dangerous workplace! Cavalier's 'A' gun bombarding over the starboard side at a shore target off Borneo. HMS Belfast is ahead firing her six inch guns; a large red flag can be seen on her port yardarm. Dave Jobling is standing by the net and 'Smudger' Smith next to him. On the deck behind them are live high explosive shells and cartridges and in the foreground are several empty cylinders. A section of guardrail (left) is folded down to allow the gun to depress as the ship rolls. Imagine trying to do this in darkness and in a rough sea with empties rolling around under your feet. On the right the OA is standing by in case of technical problems. Buckets of water stand nearby in case of fire. (Taken by the author)

HMS Belfast, our C in C's flag ship, fires a broadside in bombardment from her twelve 6" guns R. Hunt)

'Rog' Graham AB, 'A' gun Breach worker in his steel capped Jesus sandals!

Sponging out and loading Anti-submarine Squid bombs

'160 tons please'! Pumped at 150lbs psi, 'Cavalier' is refuelling astern, the hose can be seen trailing over the stern of the Royal Fleet Auxiliary tanker 'Wave Master'. She is also refuelling the Australian aircraft carrier Melbourne (left) and HMAS Voyager (right) at the same time. You need to know what you are doing on the wheel! The destroyer on the right now lies at the bottom of the ocean having been chopped in half by the carrier on the left. On 10.2.64 whilst on exercises in Jervis Bay she cut across 'Melbourne's' bow and was sliced in two, eighty two sailors were drowned.

'Cavalier' getting up close (perhaps a little too close) to an ammunition ship. Boxes of ammunition are being transferred up frwd by jackstay. Top right a red line around her funnel indicates explosives being carried. With both ships travelling at 15 knots it would not be prudent to collide with that little lot!

Photo taken from 'Cavalier' of destroyers deployed around two of the several aircraft carriers involved in Operation 'Pony Express'. The destroyer in the foreground is 'Cavalier's sister ship 'Cassandra'. They were operating off White Rock Bay North Borneo. One carrier is making smoke; to do this they deliberately sprayed thick oil into the boilers. Photo; Leigh Easton (Royal Artillery). (Naval terminology for soldiers: Pongo's – where the Army goes the Pong Goes!

After expending all that ammunition it was time to meet up with an RFA ship to replenish the magazines and refuel.

Leigh Easton, Gunner 23754275 Royal Artillery: I was attached to the No3 Amphibious Observation team. We were normally based at Whitfield barracks in Kowloon (Hong Kong), or on the Commando carrier 'Bulwark' but were seconded to 'Cavalier' for operation Pony Express. Our Royal Artillery team on 'Cavalier' as far as I can remember was, Sgt. Grogan, Gunners John French and Hood and me the Amphibious Observation Post Assistant. Normally a Royal Artillery Captain would stay onboard to liaise with the navy gunners but on this occasion it was Petty Officer Telegraphist McKay (he had a large scar down his cheek which was partially covered by a full set). A naval Radio Operator would go ashore with us (A ger kiddy on Morse at 25 words per minute). We would be landed on shore and spot and correct the fall of shot from the RN ships as they bombarded, I did not get off to a good start when I first arrived onboard the ship; At bedtime I took a hammock from the stowage and started to sling it when a matelot asked me what I thought I was doing with 'his' hammock! I thought you helped yourself to any one; I ended up sleeping on a camp bed on the deck. There were sixty ships taking part in the operation. We were landed on a beach alongside some Americans and became quite buddies with them. They had more equipment than us, including a bicycle that generated electricity to run their radios! We swapped our Compo rations of five types of tinned stew for their Chicken and Pineapple! I enjoyed the tinned egg and ham, which was just as well because no one else did. It rained constantly for three days and although it wasn't actually cold my fingers were blue and shrivelled. We strung our ponchos in pairs to make tents. I can still see it today, jungle to the right of us a stream to the left and the sea in the distance; it was as well we were on a slope because the water poured past us. It must have been a bit grim because the Commando RSM struggled up the muddy slope to deliver a tot of rum to everyone. I have to confess to a cardinal sin for spotters… I climbed the tallest tree and used it as a command post. However it worked and we had the shells from HMS Belfast and HMAS Queenborough smack on target... two hours before the 'Yanks' got through on their radio. It always pleased us to get one over on them, and they on us at times no doubt.

What the Navy did with their ships was quite spectacular. We carried out a refuelling at night from RFA Wave Master. This was an experience for me and as it happened for one of the matelots as well. He had tied a line around a hatch clip and it being quite rough the two ships moved apart, as they did so the line tightened, came off the clip and he was thrown into the 'oggin' (sea). The cry 'Man overboard' went up. There was an emergency break away, the fuel line was axed, a messy job, oil all over the place! Then the ship did a sharp turn. Searchlights came on and scoured the sea… and there he was; his lifejacket light flashing away and we pulled him back inboard.

I got a turn on the wheel! QM; *'Private Easton requests permission to take the wheel'*. Me; 'But I'm not a private' QM; *'If I say anything else the Old Man won't understand'*. OOW; *'Permission granted'*. And that was that I was driving a 'C' class destroyer in the South China Sea, a good day!'

It was about this time that we refuelled from the USS Caloosahatchee a huge 35,000 ton oil tanker and because of a mix up in communications she carried on pumping, even though our tanks were full. As a result the after messdecks were flooded with several tons of thick black fuel oil (FFO). It would take several days of cleaning to get them habitable again. The men who lost their kit were barely compensated for it and did not get paid for any personal items lost, including the presents they had bought for family back home. We had the last laugh… the 'Caloosahatchee' was towed to the UK in 2003 to be scrapped.

The communications man on 'Caloosahatchee' *'Sorry it's a bad line can you speak up… what was that…did you say stop pumping?!!'* (Photo, Jim Martino USN)

The huge tanker USS Caloosahatchee AO98. (Martino)   (Martino)

Japan. Beppu, Onomichi, Kobe

On 29th May 1961 our first port of call in Japan was at Beppu, a holiday resort with hot springs, here we had to lie off at anchor for three days and go ashore by 'Liberty boat'. The hospitality at the 'topless' bars and night clubs in these towns had to be seen to be believed. We sampled sushi for the first time and all the different sea foods that the Japanese are so well known for.

Our next port of call on the 3rd June 1961 was at Onomichi, this is a small town of mainly wooden buildings situated in the north of the inland sea. 'Cavalier' was the first British warship to ever enter the river. The old man confidently swung the ship round in the confined space; it was only a bit wider than the length of the ship and he put her alongside a commercial dock. The war with Japan had only been over just fourteen years ago and we were warned there may still be Samurai in certain areas who resented us; these areas were out of bounds (a magnet to Jack!). However the ordinary Japanese are lovely people and they gave us a wonderful reception. The ship was opened to visitors, a great deal of interest was shown and there were huge crowds waiting from dawn till dusk to come onboard, in two days over five thousand people came aboard. We entertained sixty under privileged children onboard for a day; we showed them around the ship, played games, fed them and at the end of the day gave them some goodies to take home.

The river and the wooden houses of Onomichi.

The town was criss crossed with
quaint narrow alleys and streets
but of course no traffic.

LS 'Hoppy' Hopkins in fancy dress at the top of the 'companion ladder',
he's waiting to greet some children from Onomichi. The ship's whaler,
which can just be seen, is dressed overall with flags and balloons.

200

On the 8th June the ships log shows two men under close arrest, these were two seamen who had 'jumped ship' at Beppu and were arrested at Nagasaki. They were later transported to HMS Hartland Point and placed in cells.

Clifford 'Windy' East JTO: We challenged the local Baseball team to a game and turned up in our Pusser's gym shoes, shorts and vests to find their team kitted out in the latest American gear. They loaned us the big gloves but when the ball came towards me I threw the glove off and caught it 'cricket' style, they thought this hugely funny! Whenever we played a foreign team, win or lose we always had a good party afterwards! With our job as 'ambassadors' having been done we left, leaving many new friends behind. As we slipped from our berth we played 'Auld Lang Syne' over the Tannoy and crowds waved us off'.

It wasn't all bars and night clubs, we took in some culture. There was a coach trip to Kyoto, the ancient capital of Japan. We went to a theatre in Takarazuka and saw the incredible Girls Choir there. Five hundred girls in the cast who took the parts of both men and women, a bit like our Panto. The Japanese are masters at drama and the scenery and sound effects were first class, it lasted three hours and we enjoyed every minute of it… even though we didn't understand a word!

The tickets cost 100yen. (Two shillings or 10p)

On the 9th June 1961 we arrived at Kobe, here we had to anchor off and go ashore by boat. Over the intervening years this town has been devastated by earthquakes and again rebuilt.

Whilst in Japan there was a cocktail party held on another ship and two of our messmates, Ginge and Ken decided they would like to go. Ratings would not normally be allowed anywhere near, except perhaps to serve drinks! However because they were unknown on this ship they dressed as officers and partook of a few drinks and casual conversation. Having had their fill they decided it was time they left before being discovered. As they were leaving their ruse was exposed when, not thinking one of them picked up the wrong cap (A very senior officers cap with scrambled egg round the front)… Muster for defaulters and stoppage of leave for three weeks. On the 14th Father Leonard joined the ship from the 'Belfast'; he left us on arrival in Manila on the 19th June.

Bob Styants POME: We were returning from Hong Kong to Singapore, the NAFFI canteen manager was in our mess. We called him the 'man with the frozen arm' because he kept all the beer in the fridge instead of the canteens chocolate… and his arm was always in there! One day he told me he was not feeling well. He said the Doc had told him he thought it was heat exhaustion and had given him Aspirin and salt tablets. The next morning he couldn't get off his camp bed, his lips were blue and he couldn't speak. We carried him up to the sick bay but just as we got him there he died, later it was discovered he had been suffering from pneumonia.

Australia.

We passed down the east coast of Sumatra and it was announced over the Tannoy that we were crossing the equator, it is said that Junior Seaman 'Sally' Rymer rushed up on deck with his camera… he had got to get a picture of the line! A temporary canvas pool is created on the deck amidships and filled with water from the salt water fire hoses and the time honoured ceremony is enacted

All the first timers are hunted down and initiated by being shaved by the surgeon barber and a ducking by the 'bears'. Everybody then gets a copy of a certificate certifying their membership of Neptune's club.

Passing through the Sunda Straits between Java and Sumatra we saw the evil looking volcano Anak Krakatau (Child of Krakatoa). The Straits here are fifteen miles wide at its narrowest point. As we passed the volcano it lay smoldering

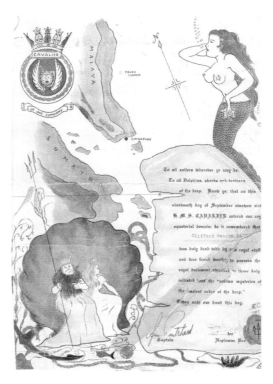

Everybody received a 'Crossing the Line' Certificate.

and looking very sinister. Thirty miles further on and well after dark we could still see it glowing in the distance. The Admiralty chart for this area in the 1920's, stated that: *'Owing to volcanic eruptions in this area it is considered unsafe for shipping'*. The last catastrophic eruption of this volcano in 1883 killed over 36,500 people and ships over thirty miles away were hit by huge flaming boulders of pumice. One boulder of coral which landed many miles away on Java was the size of a house. It was the largest known explosion to be witnessed by modern man, it caused a tsunami over 100 feet high and is said to have caused the global temperature to drop by two degrees for five years. *Six cubic miles* of the original island of Krakatoa literately disappeared, the shock wave was felt around the globe seven times and the noise was heard 3,000 miles away. The lava is constantly flowing and the present volcano, which appeared in 1927, is growing by five and a half inches *a week*. There had been several eruptions in the 1960's whilst 'Cavalier' was in the East.

Anak Krakatoa the smouldering menace which has grown out of the sea since the big explosion and continues to grow daily. (How Volcanoes Work, Vic Camp)

Bubbles from the gases, some estimated to be almost half a mile wide are still escaping and can cause negative buoyancy and drag a ship down… It was not a place you wanted to hang about for too long… and we had to come back this way! An interesting aside was that the first five Brazilian rubber trees destined to create the future Malayan rubber plantations, (And probably one of the reasons for us being there) were on a ship that survived the fall out, such is fate.

King Neptune comes aboard and is escorted by CDR Pritchard for an inspection of the guard. Brian Dunk AB slopes his broom. To the right GI McCarthy keeps out of the sun under a 'Wanchai' umbrella (Made by the Chinese from paper and glue and then varnished).

On the right is the 'Jimmy' in his white shorts talking to the captain… the 'Jimmy' was shortly to be caught by the bears, shaved by the barber then ducked.

After a very rough crossing of the Australian Bite the sea had stripped the paint down to the bare metal on the leading edges of the superstructure so we lay stopped at sea about eight miles out to repair, repaint and clean up the ship before entering harbour. We had had a telex from the hospital in Fremantle asking how many men would like to go on a picnic. Although it did not sound like our sort of scene some of us put our names down. On the appointed day we went by train from Perth and were met at the station by a huge crowd of nurses, now that was more like it! They really made us welcome and made a memorable day in the park. Because the pubs closed about 1830hrs we were invited to their houses for the evening. A little nurse borrowed daddy's Mercedes and drove us back to the ship just in time for the 0900 muster, now that's what you call a picnic!

On 6th September 1960 the ship sailed from Albany in Western Australia for Bunbury. All the junior seamen with the 'schoolie', S LT Cordrey in charge left the ship and hitchhiked to Bunbury, a distance of some 220 miles. They walked, got lifts in a 'road train' (A lorry towing four trailers full of sheep) and were then 'kidnapped' by a gang of nurses and held overnight in their hostel, such are the hazards for the sailor abroad!! They arrived at 0900hrs Friday the 9th September just in time to see their floating home enter Bunbury harbour.

The Bunbury Sun newspaper headlines reporting 'Cavalier's visit. Many local people would invite Jack 'up homers' to catch up with news from the old country.

A Cocktail party was held onboard for 150 local dignitaries and a dinner and reception was given at the Highway Hotel for the officers. A team from the ship played a football match against a team from the Bunbury Soccer Association, a shooting match against the Bunbury rifle club at their range and a game of golf at Clifton Park was organized. The four day visit was packed with activity including a boxing match… between two kangaroos!

Singapore Naval base, entering and leaving:

Our C in C occupied a house on the hill overlooking the Naval Base. Whenever a ship entered harbour, particularly during daylight hours, he would be on the veranda with a telescope to his eye and with his underlings hovering by his side. The crews of ships entering or leaving would all have to be in the rig of the day, usually No10's, that is white shorts and white fronts, and everything looking shipshape.

One particular day 'Cavalier' was entering harbour with everything just as it should be when… a stoker in his greasy stained boiler suit suddenly pops up out of the engine room hatch amidships, puts hand to eyes to shield them from the bright sunshine and looks to see how far up river the ship had got… where she had got to was right opposite the Admiral's house and this 'oily rag' had spoilt his vision of the perfect ship! Red hot messages shot across the ether; *'Cavalier' will proceed to sea immediately and come in again'*. She had to turn around, back down the Jahore Strait and come in again a journey of a good many miles and taking up a lot of shore time!

The classic lines of an immaculate 'Cavalier' leaving Singapore Naval Base, everyone on the upper deck would be in the rig of the day and fell in properly. In the background, opposite the base was virtually impenetrable jungle.

From time to time Captain 'D', the commander of the 8th DS would hold an inspection of each ship in his squadron. For the crew of the ship to be inspected it entailed a great deal of work. The ship had to be 'tiddly' (Neat and tidy) and everything working. If it wasn't all sorts of punishment could be inflicted, extra sea time or a re-inspection and a huge amount of extra work.

Alongside in Singapore, captain 'D' has just finished his inspection of the ship and is piped ashore by a full piping party. From Right: CDR Pritchard, LT CDR James, LT Scovell (Guns), CPO Stamp, the Quartermasters and Bosun's mates.

Jungle Warfare, Fraser's Hill:

During her short self refit in the King George VI dry dock in Singapore a few men at a time were sent up to a jungle camp in Pahang province in the Cameron Highlands, central Malaya. This was done for several reasons. Firstly it gave them rest and relaxation away from the ship and the dockyard and secondly it taught them how to fight and survive if they had to, in the harsh environment of the tropical jungle. The men travelled by sleeper train for two days via Kuala Lumpur and Rawang through central Malaya to a small railway station, Kuala Kubu Bahru. From there it was a lorry ride of six miles up a torturous narrow road cut through the jungle. So narrow was this road that vehicles were only allowed one way at a time, down in the mornings and up in the afternoons. During the recent terrorist attacks the Governor of Malaya, Sir Henry Gurney and several Malay police officers had been killed when ambushed on this road and it was believed there were still several terrorists hanging out there.

The camp was on the Titiwangsa Ridge and was originally created by the RAF; it was in a clearing in the jungle made for helicopters to land troops quickly to counter the attacks by terrorists. On the author's arrival at the camp there was a seven metre python that had just been shot by a Malayan with a twelve bore shot gun and he was cutting it open to retrieve a calf which the python had just swallowed. The first thing you were told was that you do not enter the jungle at all unless in a party with the right equipment, five meters into the dense jungle turn around and you could be lost!

Because of the unusual conditions that prevailed there, there was an abundance of exotic and rare wildlife. During the day it could be very hot and very humid but cool at night. There were strange insects and animals, ordinary insects grew to huge proportions, a fly could be big enough to cover the palm of a man's hand, moths with a six inch wing span, millipedes up to eight or ten inches long and an inch in diameter. There was a deer that barked like a dog, beautiful highly coloured birds and butterflies, many kinds of snakes, some poisonous others not. Rifles were carried when entering the jungle, not only against terrorists but the wild water buffalo (seladang) which could be very dangerous. The Gibbon monkeys screeching echoed for miles. On camp we slept in wooden huts, one of which had a nice bar in it. One evening a man shouted that there was a snake under a seat in the bar and everybody laughed... but he wasn't kidding, there was a green mamba lying there! We were fully kitted out with the proper clothing and equipment, a wide brimmed floppy hat to stop the leeches falling down your neck, rubber soled canvas lace up boots and a machete for hacking a path. We were shown how to make a temporary camp, a native basha, from large broad leaves. The favourite past time when not actually in the jungle was volleyball, we had a tournament going but it meant getting up at 0500 to play before going off into the jungle. There were two husky looking dogs on the camp, their names reflecting their condition… Fleas and Bugs.

Whilst in the jungle we were taught how to be safe, before hacking at a hanging vine you should check that there was not a hornet's nest on it… if you disturbed them they would attack you and, being almost the size of small fighter planes (so I exaggerate slightly) it would not take many to seriously injure or kill you. The easiest way to travel in the jungle is by following the water courses, however check any overhanging branches because that's where the black and green mamba snakes like to drape themselves and wait for their pray… Stop every hour or so and remove any leeches from your body by burning them off with a lighted cigarette, don't pull them off it will leave their pincers in there to fester (and we thought it could be dangerous at sea sometimes!).

Another couple of groups went off to a different part of the jungle and for different reasons.

Marshall 'Nobby' Clark AB: We went by overnight sleeper train to North of Kuala Lumpa, then on to Ipoh and from there by lorry to somewhere near the Thai border. In the below photograph we are going up river to the base camp. One of 'Cavalier's' signalmen, RO2T 'Jack' Frost who was in the group before us had been killed when he fell down a ravine whilst traversing some rocks. His body was being taken out of the camp when we arrived.

Going up river in the Malayan jungle, left, 'Nobby' Clark AB, right, 'Butch' Mercer AB, the ship's butcher (no doubt looking for big game to stock his freezer) behind him 'Pusser' Hill AB. The extreme heat and humidity can be seen by the steam rising from the river.

JS Terry 'Blossom' Bowser: We went by train to Ipoh and then to Baling, Perak state, near the Thai border. Here we were put into native boats with outboard engines with very long shafts. There was a long haired native covered in tattoos steering our boat. We travelled several miles 'up' river to a base run by the 1st Battalion the Royal Australian Regiment. It was literally 'uphill' where the rapids were. When we reached a certain point we were told to lay flat in the bottom of the boat with our rifles at the ready to watch the trees for terrorist snipers.

Our clothes were constantly wet and clammy from the heat and humidity.

We eventually reached a clearing in the jungle where there were a few native type huts. Strung across between two of the huts was a volley ball net. One night there was a hell of a commotion, an elephant had charged through the volley ball net and took the two huts with him! It was one of those moments when you discovered that adrenaline is brown, smells and causes a lot of extra dhobying! Another night the sentry heard a rustling in the trees so a flare was fired to illuminate the area, it wasn't terrorists it was another elephant. Our toilet was a plank over a pit dug in the ground. Our floppy hats had a white band round the inside of the rim, if we came under fire the idea was that you could turn your hat inside out and be able to identify friends from foe by the band. If I remember rightly the British troops had a red band and the Gurkhas a green one! On Christmas Eve 1960 a RAAF Dakota did a parachute drop with some Christmas fare. There were six chutes, one red and the others white. We went for the red one because we thought it contained the rum! It didn't, but it was still the best one to get because the red silk fetched money with the natives, they liked to make dresses from them.

Ron Rymer OD, RP: Whilst with the RAF regiment in the jungle I learnt from them how to literally sleep on a clothes line. It was unsafe to sleep on the ground (we had just seen a bootlace snake and were told not to 'disturb it'… and we took that advice!) A rope is strung across from tree to tree and you dangle your arms over it, put them in your pockets and sleep standing up. You couldn't get eight hours but sufficient to keep you going. We did four patrols in a month looking for a terrorist; I didn't enjoy it, because you couldn't wash till you got back to the huts (This could have been the leading terrorist Chin Peng who came and went over the Thai border for several years).

Cliff 'Windy' East JTO: Whilst refitting in dry dock in Singapore I was singing… not because I was happy, I was a tad nervous. There I was a 17 year old lad hanging upside down by my legs a hundred and thirty feet from the dry dock bottom painting the port yard arm, I had no safety harness. I was singing 'I'm such a fool' (Norman Wisdom) and all the lads below joined in singing with me!

Returning from Manila we went through a typhoon for three days. Typhoon 'Nancy' was one of the most powerful to be recorded in the region with winds of around 200 mph. HMS Victorious the aircraft carrier was in company and from time to time we could see her three propellers coming out of the water. I climbed into my hammock in the frwd messdeck to sleep in the evening and a short while later as we ducked under a huge wave I heard a terrific wrenching noise directly above me on the fo'c'sle, then a clattering noise as a heavy reel that carried two or three berthing wires had been ripped out of the deck, rattled across the deck and crashed through the guardrails into the sea. It left four large bolt holes in the deck above my hammock through which water poured every time we went under a wave. I took a blanket and staggered against the violent movement to the rear of the bridge and slept there until I was required for duty watch. We hit the eye of the storm and it went eerily quiet for a short while and then the noise and fury continued for another day or so. As dangerous as it was it was more so on land with all the flying debris and many people were killed. We later met up again with USS Cavalier in Hong Kong and found that they had passed through the same typhoon.

27th October '61 refuelling from the tanker RFA Olna, oil tanks overflowed and flooded the after messdecks with five tons of heavy black fuel oil... again.

28th October '61 we were in Oolongapo, Subic Bay in the Philippines for the centenary of Jose Rizal. We were hosted by the new destroyer USS Edson which was secured outboard of us, later we did firing exercises with her using live torpedoes and 4.5"s and firing at an uninhabited rock off the coast.

'Cavalier' alongside at Subic Bay, outboard of her is the USS Edson (DD946).
The Jack was flying at half mast for the funeral of UN Secretary General
Dag Hammarskjold who had been killed in an air crash in September. The
shadows on Cavalier's side highlight the wind scoops protruding from her
scuttles, the only form of air conditioning on the messdecks at that time.

We acquitted ourselves well and I think they were suffering teething
problems with their very new automatic equipment. We also met up
with our namesake, the USS Cavalier, PA37. She was launched in
'44 the same year as our 'Cavalier', as a Personnel Assault ship. She
took part in WWII, the Korean and the Vietnam War, which was still
ongoing. We took part in exercise 'Crosstie' with HMS Victorious
and the USS Ticonderoga, the big 'T', a USN aircraft carrier, we
did plane guard for her and were made honorary 'Tico Tigers' by
the Americans. Some congressmen were onboard whilst the ship
experimented with landing on some huge bombers, the wingspan
of which was so long they hit the deck with a shower of sparks as
they landed, this was quite spectacular at night. They put on a superb
air display with fighters breaking the sound barrier at wave top level.

'Ticonderoga' was also built the same year as 'Cavalier' and had also taken part in WWII, albeit in the Pacific. She just survived a hit by a Kamikaze. As I write the 'Tico' is being scrapped in the USA.

Looking very ship shape 'Cavalier's' namesake, USS Cavalier, a Personnel Assault ship. (USS Cavalier Association)

John 'Katie' Ironton A/B: We were warned on arrival in Oolongapo, in the Philippines about the dangers of the cheap white rum that could be found there, it could blind you. During the early hours of one morning I was Bosun's mate to Jamie Jamieson the QM when we saw three of our crew on the jetty returning to the ship. They had obviously had a good night... one had a ladies dress on over his uniform, another was carrying a grandmother clock over his shoulder and the third one had a duck on a lead, it was waddling along quite happily following them and quack quacking away...!'

Although hugely funny at the time there was unfortunately a darker side to this incident, one of the men had a revolver on him which he had taken from somewhere. Later back in Singapore he tried to get rid of it to a civilian ashore who turned out to be a plain clothes Singapore police officer. Having faced a Court Martial he would have been sent to a military prison in the UK.

Extract from "Cavalier's" log; '0310hrs telephone call from Regulating Petty Officer Singapore, 1 rating detained by Singapore Police' and ... 0640hrs 'Rating detained by Singapore Police returned to ship – placed under close arrest'. (Log now held at the Public Record Office).

On another occasion at Subic Bay the crew was invited to the American PX, the equivalent of our NAAFI. After several hours of their usual generous hospitality we left the American base late at night and had three miles to get back to the ship. Near the base was the fire station and on the forecourt some nice man had left this big red shiny fire engine with ladders on both sides and complete with keys in the ignition… Katie, Lou, Petal, Blossom, Sally and Stripey made it back to the ship OK. Blossom was duty bell ringer till he got fed up and Stripey took over.

Shortly after leaving the Philippines we refuelled from RFA Olna, this time without incident.

The 3rd of November and we were heading to Singapore for the last time, enroute we did a full power trial. We arrived there on the 4th and packed our kit ready for the long flight home. We probably didn't appreciate it then but we had experienced the Orient when it was still a distant place with strange customs and costumes, memories you could not buy.

The crew flew home in two groups just in time to be with their families for Christmas 1961. Some went off to London to attend the wedding of one of their shipmates, Ron 'Sally' Rymer to his girlfriend Phyllis.

Crew list 1960 – 61

Adams A.   CPO El.
Atkins 'Daisy' M. (E) 1
Atkins Dennis   NAAFI Mngr.
Badham 'Taff'   TO2
Bailey 'Scouse' M (E) 1
Baker Geoffrey   L/WRT
Barwis 'Stripey'   JS (G)
Beck   LME
Beirne Peter   POM (E)
Bell 'Dinger' J.   AB
Bell 'Dinger' John   AB (G)
Bowser 'Blossom'   JS (RP)
Brent 'Slim'   TO3 (W)
Broome 'Nobby'   ME (1)
Brown 'Buster'   AB (FC2) G
Brown 'Buster'   A/LS (TAS)
Bunting 'Bunts' W.   M (E) 1
Burge 'Taff' K.   C (EL)
Burke   LME
Butler 'Taff'   PO TAS
Button 'Bert' Paul   JS (RP)
Cameron 'Jock'   JS (G)
Cannon 'Tommy' PO (ME)
Carey   LCK (C)
Carpenter 'Chippy'   SWr 1
Carter   Sub. LT.
Carver David   LT.
Cassey 'Taff'   OD QA
Cawston 'Taff'   JME
Chalmers 'Jock'   A/LME
Charles M.   Lt CDR. 1st LT
Clarke Jan   JS TAS

Clare 'Stevie'   ME
Clarke 'Nobby' M   AB RP
Coates Fred   AB G
Coates Ian   AB
Cooper John   LT Elect O.
Cordery 'Ginge' AB TAS
Cordrey Sid   S LT. TASO
Corrin 'Paddy'   ME
Crowe Mike
Cuckson   JS TAS
Cull 'Ginge'   AB RP
Curd Dennis   LTO Comms
Dawber 'Scouse'   LME
Dennison   LT
Dent 'Doc'   SURG. LT
Derere Mike   RO2 G
Dingwall 'Jock' J.   TO C
Dowling Harry   Mech1
Dunk Brian   AB G
East 'Windy'   J TO
Easton Leigh   Royal Art.
Edmonds John   LT SO
Edwards 'Bungy'   ME1
Evans 'Tanky'   ME1
Faulkner Les   AB UW
Field 'Paddy'   ME1
Flaherty 'Scouse'   ME1
Floyd Mick   ME1
Fox 'Freddy'   AB G QA
Frost 'Jack'   RO2 T
Gary   LCK C
Gaskin   PO
Gavin Ron   POM E
George 'Doc'   LSBA

Goddard John	AB Nav.Yeo.	Loney F	PO TO
Graham Rog.	AB G	Lowther Les	CH Mech
Grieves Walt.	LMEM	Luchford 'Nellie'	RO1
Groves 'Granny'	LS G	Lynch 'Benny'	CPO OA
Hardy Jim	ME	Lyne 'Harry'	CEA1
Harris 'Chats' R.	AB	Macatany M	Mech2
Hatch 'Scratch'	LM E	Markey 'Scouse'	ME1
Haynes 'Duffy'	ERA1	Maskell Derek	L CK
Hayter 'Tubby'	JS	Matthews Dan	LT G
Head 'Jan' L	AB RP	May 'Yanto' P	PO RPI
Heap 'Buster'		McCabe 'Mac'	ME1
Hickman Ken	ALS G	McCarthy 'Mac'	PO Gi
Hopkins 'Hoppy'	LS G	McNally George	OD TAS
Houlihan Don	YS comms.	McNarry 'Albert'	AB RP2
Howell 'Taff'	AB TAS	McPetrie Jim	S LT
Humphries 'Taff'	ME	Mercier 'Butch'	AB Butcher
Hunter 'Tubby'	PO	Miller 'Dusty'	LSA S
Ironton 'Katie' J	JS G	Milne	JS TAS
Jackson 'Jock' D	ME1	Mirams A	CPO EA
James	EA	Morgan 'Rattler'	AB G
Jamieson 'Jamie'	AB	Murphy 'Spud' B	AB GL2
Jennings 'Jan'	RO2 G	Neave Peter	AB Postie
Jobling 'Jobs' D	OS G	Noble 'Jan'	OD
Johnstone	PO Tel	Norton M	JS TAS
Jones	AB UC2	Ogden 'Oggie'	ME1
Kelly 'Spider'	AB GA	Parry Robert	RO2 G
Kelman Ian	OD	Poynton Trevor	TO
Kidd 'Captain'	ME	Pritchard G. I.	CDR Capt★
Knell Barry	AB G	Prodger Joe	ME1
Kyprianou 'Kippers'	LME	Quinlan George	AB
Lamerton John		Randall 'Lofty'	AB G
Leatherbarrow 'Scouse'	SA	Rees Len	LME
Lee 'Tansy'	PO	Renilson 'Jock'	AB G
Littler 'Scouse'	TO2	Ridgeway Peter	AB G

Rimmington C   LT ME Off.
Rivett-Carnac Lou OD RP
Robinson 'Robbie' JS
Rochester 'Petal' JS RP
Rogerson 'Geordie' OD
Ryan 'Buck'   AB TAS
Rymer 'Sally'   OD RP
Salter-Townsend R OD RP
Saunders J   LSA V
Scovell 'Guns'   LT G
Shorrock 'Sham' AB RP2
Skinner 'Yorkie'   AB Putty
Slade 'Sam'   AB
Slater 'Gerry'   OA4
Smale 'Buffer'   CPO Smith
'Knuckles'   JS G
Smith R   RO S2
Smith 'Smudge'   POME
Smythe 'Sammy'   AB G
Souter 'Ginge'   UC1
Sprunt Ron
Stamp 'Sticky'   CPO Coxn
Stenhouse 'Doc'   SURG LT
Sturgess 'Sturge' ME1
Styants 'Bob'   POME
Sykes 'Bill'   ME1
Taylor 'Buck'   LRO
Timms 'Tiger'   CPO C
Tomlin F
Traill Colin   LT NAV. O
Vann 'Eddie'   LS   RP2
Wakinshaw G   LME
Watkins C   AB
Williams 'Scouse' LS

Williams 'Bungy'   CME
Young 'Brigham'   ME 2
*Later Rear Admiral.

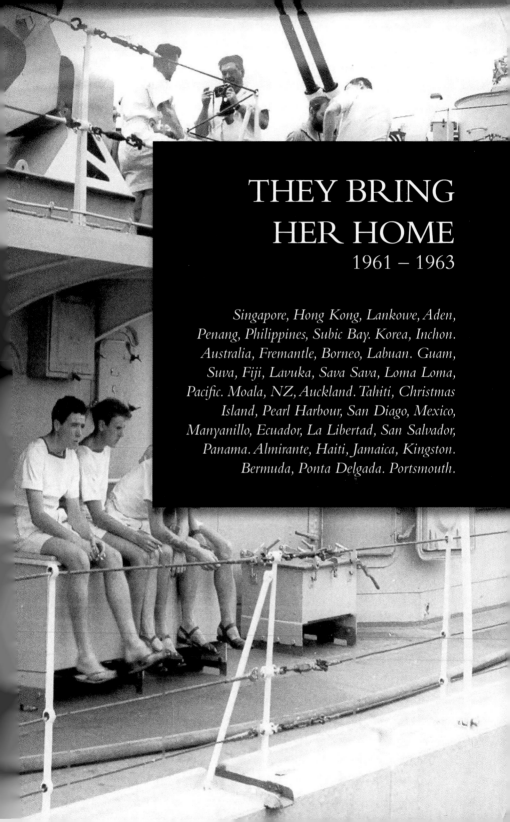

THEY BRING
HER HOME
1961 – 1963

*Singapore, Hong Kong, Lankowe, Aden,
Penang, Philippines, Subic Bay. Korea, Inchon.
Australia, Fremantle, Borneo, Labuan. Guam,
Suva, Fiji, Lavuka, Sava Sava, Loma Loma,
Pacific. Moala, NZ, Auckland. Tahiti, Christmas
Island, Pearl Harbour, San Diago, Mexico,
Manyanillo, Ecuador, La Libertad, San Salvador,
Panama. Almirante, Haiti, Jamaica, Kingston.
Bermuda, Ponta Delgada. Portsmouth.*

THEY BRING HER HOME
1961 – 1963

Cdr William G. B. Black
(Fifth commission)

It was the 18th October 1961 when the advance party flew into Singapore. They had left the UK on the 16th and had flown via Istanbul and Bombay. The remainder of the ship's company arrived on the 8th December; being so near to Christmas it was not a good time for the married men to be leaving their families. The commissioning ceremony was held the 11th on the dockside at Singapore and they wasted no time by sailing the same day and spent a month working up and on exercises in the Singapore area.

John 'Woosha' Mager RO: I was a 17 year old lad on HMS Tyne; a destroyer support ship based in Portsmouth Harbour and had just qualified as a junior Radio Operator. I was having what you might call an intimate relationship with a young lady from Gosport, I was in love… well that's what I called it! My mum God bless her, in her wisdom, decided that this girl was not good enough for me and wrote to my Divisional Officer saying she thought I was headed for a fate worse than death, and there I was enjoying myself. I was sent for by the D.O. who told me I was to be parted from my 'beloved' and was being drafted, I had two choices, the West Indies or the Far East, I chose the West Indies and the Admiralty of course in their usual perverse way drafted me to the Far East… and a destroyer named 'Cavalier'. I was flown to Singapore to join the ship and the next eighteen months was to be the most influential of my life. The ship was a lot smaller than I had expected. After a welcoming speech by Captain Black we marched over the gangway carrying our hammocks over our shoulders and found the mess deck that was to be our cramped home for the next eighteen months. I was to go from what you might have called a 'mummy's boy' to a man of the world in the Orient, a slight culture shock! The ship's company motto 'Of one company' seemed to take hold and remained so for the rest of the commission. Captain Black, unusually for a captain invited us all for a drink in HMS Terror, the shore base. He and I struck up an instant rapport, we agreed that he would call me Mager and I would be allowed to call him Sir! Our Skipper was the junior captain of the 8th Destroyer Squadron so we became what was affectionately known as the 'bum boat' or 'Canteen boat', it meant that we got all the crap jobs like acting as plane guard for all the carriers transiting the Indian Ocean. I was to become the drummer of a pop group that was formed onboard called the 'Caravels', we became quite well known in bars and clubs ashore and the youth club at RAAF Seletar. It was interesting when the C in C inspected the ship because to the amusement of the rest of the ship's company we were following him around the ship carrying the drums and equipment to keep him from seeing them onboard'.

Sheila Bailey, wife of Bill, CPOME: Bill went off to join the 'Cavalier' as advance party for the December 1961 commission in October 1961. He left me at home with our son Kevin who was fourteen months old at the time and came home twenty months later to a three year old 'who didn't know his dad'. I can remember Christmas 1962 Kevin and I went to stay with my mother in Eltham for a couple of days... and ended up there for six weeks because we were snowed in. 'Cavalier' had just arrived in Hong Kong from Singapore and Bill wrote to complain that it was so cold there... it had gone from the 90's Fahrenheit down to the 70's! I sent a letter back telling him in no uncertain terms to stop moaning.'

On the 12 January '62 after that normal stressful work up period they rested on the sailor's favourite Banyan Island, Pulau Tioman. It wasn't all roses though; they had evaporator problems and were on water rationing. There were more exercises for a month and if that wasn't enough they departed Singapore 26th February '62 to take part in a joint SEATO exercise, 'Jet 62'. Before arriving they diverted to Penang to drop off OA Ken Wozencroft who had to fly home.

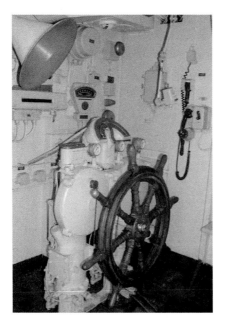

12th March and they were off to Aden, in the Indian Ocean they refuelled from RFA Tidesurge... and yes they had another flood of oil in the after mess decks, albeit not quite so much this time (just a couple of tons!). Off Aden they rendezvoused with the carrier 'Ark Royal' to escort her to the East.

The wheelhouse from where the quartermaster steered the ship, he was assisted by his Bosun's mate. They also ran the ship's daily routine from here using the ship's broadcast system. They could also call the ship to action stations with an alarm bell.

It has to be remembered that the quartermaster steering the ship could not see where he was going, he steered by a strip gyro compass in front of him and followed the course given him by the officer of the watch on the bridge. The main reason for this was so that the officer of the watch had complete control and the quartermaster did not anticipate where the officer wanted him to go. Another reason was that in the past huge seas had sometimes smashed the windows of the exposed wheelhouse when it faced forward rendering it unusable. Communication was by means of a microphone but in emergency by voice pipe, the large red 'trumpet to the upper left in the photograph above. As well as steering the ship he controlled the speed by applying the revolutions on the engine room telegraphs as required by the officer on the bridge.

Jeremy Blackham a young Midshipman: I joined 'Cavalier' in Singapore dockyard on Monday 19th October having spent a short time on 'Ark Royal'. The last time I had seen 'Cavalier' she was refitting and looked a mess, now she looked every bit the classic warship and lay glistening in a new coat of paint. Shortly after joining her I was invited to a party in one of the Hindu homes in the Naval Base to celebrate the festival of Deepavalli (or Diwali). It is the festival of the lights, the day when the darkness of evil was overcome by the lord of light and good. They had bathed in oils and dressed in all their finery. I was a bit nervous not knowing what to expect, however the Indians still have a great deal of old world charm and welcomed us with great formality and with a bow to each of us. What would we be asked to drink on this festival day and would we find it pleasant? 'But it is just like beer' said our host filling our glasses with... whiskey! Contrary to their normal custom the women and children joined us for a short while showing off their beautiful clothes, the host's wife wore a shimmering blue sari. Custom then prevailed and they retired to another room to prepare the meal. We were fed a very tasty curry along with numerous other smaller dishes; curry puffs, noodles, sweat meets, nuts and fruit. The whole meal was conducted with a punctilious courtesy and formality, accompanied by the whole story of Deepavalli in the traditional Indian manner, but with due allowance for our ignorance. Meanwhile the whiskey bottle, or more likely the third one by now, was still circulating... and tasting less like beer as time went on! The small room was decorated with lights and, with coloured candles burning had a beautiful effect. After the meal came the long formality of taking leave with bowing, hand shaking and wishes of prosperity for each other. Then it was back to reality and my world onboard'.

Another life saved: On 10th November '62 whilst en-route to Fremantle, Australia for the Commonwealth Games, 'Cavalier' was fifty miles West of Geography Bay when she received an urgent message from the American research vessel 'Horizon', she was way out in the Pacific, over a thousand miles away and had a seriously ill man onboard. Seaman David O'Connor was suffering from internal bleeding and pneumonia. 'Cavalier' was sent because not only did she have the speed but she also happened to be carrying the squadron surgeon, SURG LT Alistair Scott-Brown. Everybody onboard felt the urgency as the ship vibrated and shuddered hour after hour at high speed. For two days the signals staff had very little sleep whilst they kept in touch with 'Horizon'.

US Research ship Horizon (David Carver)

Medical information was being passed over the radio to the ship before they met up and at one stage SUB LT COMMS 'Dave' Davies was in touch with an amateur radio ham ashore to assist in keeping in touch with 'Horizon'. 1,200 miles later when they met up in fairly heavy seas they were unable to attempt to transfer him by jackstay transfer. The sea boat was lowered and managed to get alongside the 'Horizon'. O'Connor was dropped into the boat whilst they manoeuvred in five metre seas. It took them one and a half hours to get him onboard 'Cavalier' but thankfully without further injury and without getting him wet! A heaving line transfer then had to be carried out to get some of his equipment over from 'Horizon'. During the 1,600 miles return journey, again at high speed the surgeon assisted by the SBA gave the sick man six blood transfusions, half his total blood. Having travelled so far at high speed they knew they would be running short of fuel so they had arranged to meet up with the RFA tanker 'Wave Ruler', ordered to steam out and meet up with 'Cavalier' as she returned towards Australia. 'Cavalier' was down to 30 per cent of her fuel; this was rarely allowed to happen as 75 tons was normally kept for better stability. Having refuelled she worked up to full speed again for Fremantle where an ambulance was waiting on the jetty.

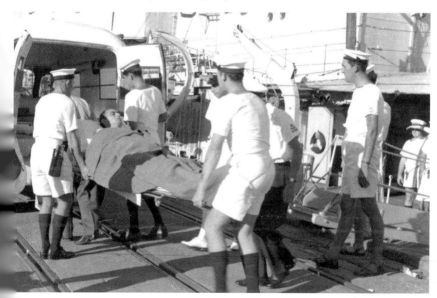

American Seaman David O'Connor is carried by 'Cavalier' crew to a waiting ambulance at Fremantle. 'Cavalier' can be seen in the background. All seamen carried 'pusser's' dirk (knife) around their waist so these are seamen here who worked the upper deck. Notice the ship's whaler is not on its davits, if they were going to the port side to the jetty it was lowered beforehand so that it could be used.

O'Connor was rushed to Fremantle General Hospital where the newspapers reported that he was considered to be 'fairly satisfactory'. During these long high speed runs the guy wires to the funnel have to be slackened as the heat expands them and buckles the plating on the funnel and the captain takes exception at seeing the funnel looking like a crushed beer can! However being sprung steel it does resume its shape when it cools down.

Fremantle Harbour.

David Carver Lt: When the 60/61 commission flew home I stayed on for the changeover. After about two months the navigating Officer, Lt. Garth Ridgers suffered from serious heat exhaustion and had to be flown home and, although not qualified I was given his job of Navigator. We sailed towards Aden escorting the carrier 'Centaur' to the Suez Canal; she was on her way home. We would then escort the carrier 'Ark Royal' back to the East. One carrier had to transit the canal into the Indian Ocean before the other returned; this was so that if for any reason the Canal was blocked we would always have a carrier east of Suez for emergencies. As this was to be my first effort as navigator we carried the squadron navigator, CDR Tim Beaver with us.

The whaler would be turned out ready for immediate launching. (D. Carver)

'Cavalier' chasing 'Ark Royal' at thirty knots and acting as Plane guard to pick up any ditched pilots. An aircraft can just be seen about to land on. "Cavalier's' whaler would be fully manned and turned out ready for lowering in the event of an accident. (D. Carver)

28th March 1962 in the Bay of Bengal, 'Cavalier' refuels aft from the aircraft carrier 'Ark Royal'. At the same time she is carrying out a ackstay transfer, Lt David Carver being transferred. (D. Carver)

Victoria harbour Hong Kong 1962 taken from The Peak. Five of the C class destroyers of the 8th DS along with aircraft carrier 'Ark Royal' are laying to buoys in the harbour Centre: 'Cavalier' is alongside the wall in the harbour. Wanchai district is to the right, Kowloon and the Whampoa docks to the top left; in the background are the hills of the New Territories and China.

Learning Chinese: Some men found it quite easy to learn a few Chinese phrases. Try this: *'He stayed out of sight'* – He Lei Lo. *'I got this for free'* – Ai No Pei. *'Are you hiding a fugitive'?* – Hu Yu Hai Ding? *'Your body odour is offensive'* – Yu Stin Ki Pu.

22nd May 1962 crossed the Yellow Sea to Inchon, on the North West coast of Korea. 27th May to 26th June visited Yokohama and Okinawa in Japan, back to Hong Kong by 19th July. Returned to Singapore for self refit July to September.

Borneo 'Confrontation': A war by any other name? (Confrontation and Emergency are names used instead of 'war' because insurance is still paid out, but not if war is declared) On the 8th December 1962 a rebellion broke out in North Borneo. Returning on the 9th December from her Australian trip covering the 7th British Empire and Commonwealth games, 'Cavalier' received a coded order from C in C Far East Station to 'Proceed to Singapore at highest speed'. An armed rebellion had broken out in Brunei, Sarawak and North Borneo and Britain had a treaty obligation to them, they were to sail to their aid. A Mr. Ahazari backed by the Indonesians had formed a group who styled themselves as the North Borneo National Army; they were against the formation of a federation of the trading states of Malaysia. He was directing the rebellion from Manila in the Philippines and they had already taken three major towns and the Shell oil fields at Seria.

Brian Beniston, Royal Marine: 'My first connection to 'Cavalier' was whilst serving on the commando carrier 'Bulwark'; we were ashore in Hong Kong and became pals with some of her crew. Needless to say after a few drinks they got me into 'Pinkies' tattoo parlour even though I hated needles!

The next occasion was whilst I was based on shore in Singapore and my job was driver to Lt Col Bridges RM. One Saturday night in December '62 I had been on a 'run ashore' to Nee Soon village. I was awoken early on the Sunday morning to be told I was required by the Lt Col urgently. I had to drive him and other officers to GHQ Singapore. On arrival I noticed a large contingent of officers from other services already there. On return to unit all shore leave was cancelled and all 'outliers' (Men living away from barracks) were recalled to the unit. Lower deck was cleared and they were informed of the situation in Brunei. 42 Commando (L Company) would spearhead a rescue mission for hostages being held at Limbang. L Company flew in and the rest of them would catch up with them travelling on the Commando carrier 'Bulwark'. My party and I, a group numbering thirty, drove to Singapore dockyard to embark on the destroyer HMS Cavalier. My Land Rover and trailer was lowered onto the deck where they had already removed the torpedo tubes.

Brian with Land Rover and trailer, one of seven transported on 'Cavalier', it was stripped down for active service with the windscreen down in order to mount a gun, and the doors could also be removed.

42 Commando Royal Marines deploying in Brunei.

The voyage was not particularly that memorable except I remember we watched a film called South Pacific and whenever I see that it brings back memories of this campaign. We Marines slept on the mess deck and the Gurkhas slept on the after superstructure. On arrival at Labuan we received a pep talk and as we were leaving the skipper lent over from the bridge and shouted: 'My sailors have done a good job getting you here in record time now I'm sure the Royals will do well ashore'. We drove to the airport and were flown by RAF Beverly to Brunei airport. We deployed to the Brunei Hotel which was in bit of a state, I was ordered to take down the rebel flag and as I was doing so I was shot at by the rebels. I made my way to Limbang with the CO's orderly via some jungle tracks and then landed at Limbang by landing craft at dawn. I and another driver (they are all combat marines first and foremost) took charge of the prisoners there and got them to dig pits to bury the dead that had been killed by L Company. The local police chief asked me to lead a raid on a house where a terrorist was known to be holding out and we took him prisoner. After this we had little use for the vehicles that 'Cavalier' had brought up for us, we left them behind and did jungle patrols on foot. The prisoners we captured were held at the Commissioner's House stables under guard until they were transferred to Limbang prison where some of them were later hung by the local authorities'.

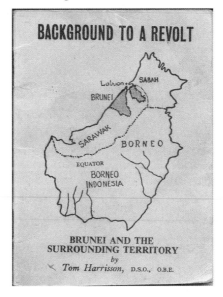

Troops entering Brunei were given a booklet about the customs of the country and what to and what not to do.

'Bill' Cracher, Queen's Own Highlanders
played them out of Singapore harbour

Bill Arbin AB TAS: We arrived alongside in Singapore where there was bit of a rush on. In four hours we had refuelled, removed some of our ammunition (for stability) and to make room for further ammunition and stores for the troops. We also embarked a Royal Army Service Corp officer. The torpedo tubes were removed by the dockyard and seven Land Rovers were tied down in their place. We embarked one hundred Gurkhas (OIC Bruce Jackman), one hundred Scots of the Queens Own Highlanders and some Royal Marines. We sailed from Singapore for an evening voyage to Labuan; with bagpipes playing it was quite a stirring moment. We arrived at midnight. As soon as we arrived the Gurkhas were off and disappeared into the jungle.

Because there were no cranes on the jetty we had to roll the Land Rovers and trailers onto the jetty using planks and some old doors. With everyone working together the unloading of troops, stores and ammunition was completed in one hour. Shortly after that we went to anchor off shore. I was detailed to go off with the party to the nearby airfield. We were given .303 rifles with ten rounds of ammunition each to protect the airfield so that the RAF could fly in. Four hundred rebels were captured within a short while and "Cavalier's" crew acted as guards and awaited the arrival of the cruiser HMS Tiger with a further detachment of Royal Marines. (The torpedo tubes which were removed were never replaced)

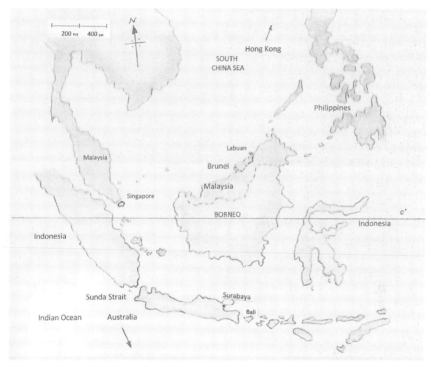

The area of conflict in Brunei and Borneo, Singapore to Labuan is nearly 900 nautical miles. (Author)

Lt David Carver: 'We approached Labuan harbour during the night of the 11th, although the pilot book had a note which stated; *'Warning not to enter Labuan during the hours of darkness'*. We just had to get in with the troops and as a result we nearly came a cropper. We saw ahead of us a nice well lit jetty, as we approached it someone suddenly realized it was not a jetty but street lights and a road; we were just a few yards from running aground on a nice sandy beach! The actual jetty was another quarter of a mile further on. Although our trip up was in a flat calm sea all the Gurkhas were seasick, this left us with lots of extra food after we had landed them!

Having landed I was sent to the harbour master's office where with others we acted as controllers of shipping. Our Engineering Officer Lt CDR Gerry Burnan was sent up to the airfield with a landing party to take charge of the captured rebels. We then received a report that a 'battleship' had been sighted entering the harbour and as we had no battleships we got a bit concerned and went to action stations. (The Indonesians had two very large Russian Slerdov class cruisers) As it was it turned out to be our cruiser HMS Tiger. She had brought a larger contingent of Royal Marines and being a bigger ship was able to take over Control and comms from us'.

For their participation in the confrontation all British troops were awarded the 'Malay Peninsula' General Service medal. Those involved in the fighting ashore received the Borneo Medal. In 2005 the grateful Malaysian government issued a medal (the Pingat Jasa Malaysia or PJM) themselves to all British and Commonwealth troops who fought to secure their freedom. The Queen gave her approval for veterans to wear this medal alongside their British issue.

Dave Davies SUB LT COMMS: 'I had the morning watch, 0400 – 0800, we had rounded the North West corner of Borneo then passed Kuching and I remember giving my bunk to one of the Marines before going on watch as he was trying to sleep on the iron deck. As we passed Seria we could see flames on shore, but that turned out to be gas burn off from an oil well! On arrival at Labuan we discharged our passengers and changed from being troopship to a forward communications ship. Amongst other things we set up a POW camp on Pappan Island. All our radios were in use and one of the messages I saw come in was reporting the death of five of our Royal Marines, one of them I believe may have been the one I had given the use of my bunk. It brings it home to you that you are in a war. We saw Hunter fighter aircraft going up the Limbang River to support the Marines in the interior. RAF Beverly transport aircraft flew in to Brunei airfield. It was amusing to see the criteria that the RAF had for keeping the Beverly in the air, five bullet holes and it could still take off, six and it was grounded'! After being relieved 'Cavalier' returned to Singapore.

In late 1962 before leaving Singapore to return home to pay off, the Captain cleared lower deck and explained to the crew what the itinerary would be for the trip home. He explained they would be going via the scenic route, across the Pacific to South America and the Panama Canal. They would also be visiting Christmas Island which was undergoing a huge 'clean up' at the closure of the recent Atomic bomb tests. What the nice travel agent at the Admiralty had not told them was that the radiation still lingered there. (Some elements of radiation have a half-life of 50K years) Of course it was Secret then and anyway even had they known they were hardly in a position to say 'No thanks we'll give it a miss'! The last test, the fortieth, had taken place in July 1962, just seven months before their latest visit'.

1st January they sailed for Hong Kong arriving on the 5th. The temperature dropped that much that they shifted into blues. After five good days there they left for Subic Bay where it is said there are a thousand bars and night clubs, every third house is a bar, club or more probably a brothel, at that time VD was rife and much of the area was out of bounds (A magnet to some people!) they spent six days there.

In January they were exercising and acting as plane guard for the carrier HMS Hermes. The normal position during this evolution is for the rescue ship to lie about 1000 yards astern and to the carrier's port side. They suddenly got a message that a helicopter that was doing flying-on exercises had ditched. The spot was marked and 'Cavalier' steamed at high speed to the area, another helicopter hovering above warned 'Cavalier' that she was 'on top' (the spot). The sea boat, always turned out ready on these occasions was launched and after a quick search the entire helicopter crew where found and pulled safely inboard. They were transferred back to 'Hermes' within 33 minutes of their ditching, a testimony to the efficiency of "Cavalier's" crew and their training. They re-ammunitioned from RFA Resurgent in a difficult sea, it took two and a half hours to get 25 loads onboard. With waves up to ten feet high they then went on to transfer stores from RFA Fort Dunvegan, it took three attempts to get a line across, during this Transfer a guard rail stanchion was ripped out the deck. Notwithstanding the difficulties they went on to do a personnel transfer with the destroyer HMS Barossa, a Battle Class destroyer.

In company with her sister ship 'Cassandra' and the frigate HMS Llandaff they arrived in Guam in the Marianas Islands on the 21st January. There is a large USA naval base here. A cricket team made up from the three ship's wardrooms was put together when challenged by the 'Yanks'! Apparently their rules were slightly different to ours and included the fact that you had to have a waist over 32 inches round and be able to drink at least ten cans of beer during the match. What we didn't know was that they had been practicing under the tuition of a couple of Brit ex pats… and they won! The fact that the ref had had twelve cans of beer, may have affected the scoring. And so on to Pearl Harbour, the well-known American naval base surprised by the Japanese attack in WWII. Just before entering there they did a 'sleeve' shoot (that is a drogue towed by an American aircraft). They surprised everyone by scoring four hits on the first run and then actually shooting down three, (by cutting it away from its towing wire) very good shooting for a relatively old system.

They left Guam to act as Search and Rescue ship for Queen's flight. This was a standard operation whenever Royalty was travelling over the sea. As she was on a tour of Australia, various ships would be strung out across the course of the Royal aircraft to cover any emergency.

Their next port of call was at Suva in the Fijian Islands 1,200 miles north of New Zealand. To keep the crew occupied during these long voyages across the oceans various games were organized. One was a Tug 'O war between the seaman and stokers, it is not easy to find the room on deck for this.

Several hundred miles from the nearest land and it's not easy finding space for things like Tug 'O' War on the decks of a destroyer.

'Radio Cavalier' broadcast every evening and would have done credit to a commercial radio station. Shooting and fishing matches were held. After two hours of fishing the biggest imaginary one won, as they caught nothing.

Jeremy Blackham, Midshipman: 'The ship anchored off Suva and we lowered the whaler. I and six others plus a Rotuman boy interpreter were going to sail it to Beqa Island twenty five miles away whilst the ship went on to Sevuka. It took us five hours to reach the Beqa lagoon where we had to negotiate various coral reefs. Then a sudden squall and downpour cut visibility to ten yards, luckily this went as quick as it came and when it cleared we found before us the village of Dahuimbeqa, a collection of grass huts housing a population of seventy natives. We anchored near the shoreline and went to meet the Buli, governor and hereditary chief, whose word is law in the village. He arranged for some help to unload the whaler and beach it and then took us to the biggest grass hut in the village and told us that that was where we would stay whilst on the island. His wife unasked gave us a cooked meal of yams and breadfruit. Each morning and evening a line of children would queue to give us bananas and mangoes and the Buli's wife cooked our meals. After our first meal we met the old men of the village, we saw no women for the first twenty four hours after our arrival (They must have had sailors there before!). We presented them with a gift of yaqomo, this led to a ceremony of Kava drinking, something which we were to become familiar with. We were unsure of the part we were to play in the proceedings; however we soon learned a few words and the formalities of the ceremony. We heard for the first time the men singing, it was one of the most impressive things we saw on the island, they are a very musical people who are deeply conscious of rhythm and spontaneous harmony. We walked and explored the island for a couple of days then sailed to explore another island called Natheva. There we were greeted by the head man and offered the traditional greeting of… kava. They were virtually self-sufficient surviving on fish they caught and vegetables they grew. Their houses and fishing nets were all made from grass or coconut fibre. There was dense vegetation on the lower lying land and long sandy beaches. It was the beautiful idyllic South Sea Island that many people dream of but few actually experience. We went on fishing trips with the natives, they didn't use lines they used spears, some were twenty feet long with a barbed point. They swam on the surface and jabbed them downwards, they caught octopus and a sort of flat fish. They had no fear of sharks and laughed at us because we scrambled out of the water at the first sight of one. Back on Beqa we held a football match against the villagers and as usual… we lost: Fiji 5 England 1, we put it down to their enormous size, their stamina and ignorance of the rules! After the game we were shepherded into the Village meeting house and sat crossed legged on the floor. We were served tea and buttered scones (how England has influenced the Commonwealth) by the women, only one of which had a limited amount of English.

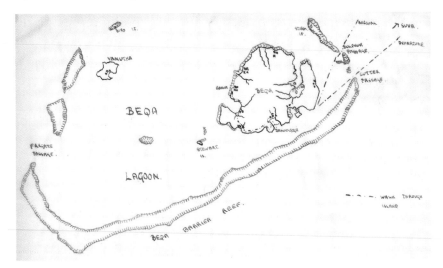

Jeremy's contemporary map of Beqa Lagoon and Island, Fiji.

After dinner we were treated to a display of mahe, or hand dancing outside. A line of women in colourful costumes did their beautifully executed hand movements with harmony and rhythm. When they had finished they stood up and placed their garlands around our necks, in the darkness, lit only by the fire it was magical moment and a spectacle none of us would ever forget. After taking a shower we entered the village meeting hut for a dinner, the hall had been decorated with palms leaves and fruit and on a mat on the floor (the table) there lay a mass of rich foods: chicken, all kinds of fish, prawns and the octopus we had caught that day. The Buli made a wonderful speech of welcome and I replied with one in Fijian (which had cost me hours of practice under the tuition of the village school master). The meal was cleared away when finished and an enormous bowl was produced, the first of several mixes of kava. During this a group of women appeared and a band of solid wooden drums, bamboo poles and a guitar struck up. We were introduced to the Fijian form of dancing, the Ta-ra-la-la, where ones walks alongside ones partner rather sedately but in strict military fashion, left, right, left, right. Eventually with many regrets the evening came to an end and we returned to our hut. Having spent a week on the island we prepared to leave the following morning. Having launched the boat and loaded our gear we were invited back onshore for a leaving ceremony of another dance and farewell bowl of kava. We shook hands with the whole village and made our way to the shore where a punt took us out to our whaler, as we left the shore they broke into the traditional Fijian song of farewell, 'Isa Lei' and as they sang they waded into the sea waving us off. The Buli needed to go to Suva on business so we took him with us. As we approached Suva harbour again a squall of rain blotted it out and we had to navigate with the boats compass. We cleaned up the whaler and returned to the ship which was now berthed on the jetty. We thought we had seen the last of the Buli but on the day we sailed he appeared on the jetty waving us off with tears streaming down his cheeks, it seemed to symbolize the warmth and generosity of the welcome we had been given on Beqa'.

The Islanders of Fiji prepare a welcome. (Roger Hunt).

They visited Levuka, Savu Savu, Loma Loma and Moala, spending two days at each before going back to Suva, finally departing for New Zealand. On leaving Fiji they refuelled from RFA Wave Sovereign, the man firing the Costain gun line from the tanker fired too soon, quite a common error which had resulted in fatalities in the past. On this occasion one man saw it coming and just managed to duck in time but it was a close shave as the bronze rod carrying the line ricocheted off the ship's structure.

They arrived in Auckland in New Zealand on the 20nd February and some members of the crew took leave and travelled the country visiting places like the Maori village and hot pools at Rotorua. The ship underwent a self-maintenance period in the Devonport dockyard, HMNZS Penguin. They sailed from Auckland for Tahiti on the 6th March and into the teeth of a gale. On the 7th they had two Thursdays… they crossed the International Date Line.

They reached Papeete, Tahiti in French Polynesia by the 12th March. Tahiti is one of 130 islands that go to make up the Windward, Leeward and Society islands. It is the beautiful tropical island of everyone's dreams with blue coral lagoons, coconuts and bananas, white sandy beaches and numerous brightly coloured flowers like bougainvillea and beautiful rare birds. The men dress in bright coloured clothing and the women are said to be some of the most beautiful in the world.

On the 16th March they were on course for Christmas Island (Native Kiribati in the Pacific, not the Christmas Island in the Indian Ocean). They were steering by the morning and evening star sightings and enjoying a leisurely trip when it was reported to the bridge that they now had an acute appendicitis case onboard. They speeded up to 22 knots which gave them an ETA of 0230hrs on the 19th. The condition of the patient was such that they prepared if necessary to carry out the operation onboard, this can be done in an emergency but is not done lightly! It was an anxious time but luckily they didn't have to and luckily their navigation was spot on, Christmas Island is very low in the water and can only be seen from eight miles away, although they had it on radar before that. There is not a great deal on the island, apart from the military camps, there are villages called London and Paris! On arrival a bus was laid on and many of the crew, ignorant of the possible consequences did the grand tour of the bomb sites!

For all the mixed services there were lots of activities such as, Drama, football, cricket, tennis, sailing and other water sports. The fishing was good with catches of Wahoo up to 65lbs. The night before sailing the village meeting house was the scene of singing and dancing and the drinking of Kava. The natives had gone to a great deal of trouble to put on a show in honour of the ship's visit. The girls had made their grass skirts and garlands and danced their traditional 'Batere'. The dancing went on for two hours, such lovely friendly people.

By April 9th they were in San Diego, again they had another successful shoot before arriving. Their host ship there was the very modern USS Kings. They left there on the 14th.

From San Diego to Marzonillo on the Mexican Pacific coast, they entered the harbour there on the 22nd March. This is the Mexican Navy's base. As a precaution here they were using hurricane hawsers to secure the ship to the jetty... just in case! After two enjoyable days with busy social engagements they sailed to refuel astern from RFA Plumleaf and then escorted her for part of her homeward journey.

The next stop was La Libertad on the 26th April. Another busy round of cocktail parties ensued, with official engagements and invitations by the British residents to their club in San Salvador. The governor of Bocos Del Toro entertained the ship's officers and the two countries flags were flown side by side. The football match played against them became an international event with the National guard for security and the Army producing a band... they lost... again. It would be nice to think that for international relations it was deliberate but it probably wasn't! However the visit was a success and a letter from the British Embassy there to the Foreign Office, dated May 8 1963 (Public Record Office) states that it was so successful that it should occur more often than the previous visit, which had been eight years ago. The letter also stated that it was appreciated locally that all officers onboard had grown beards in keeping with local custom, however it was added that: 'A suggestion that this should be regarded as evidence of Castroist tendencies in the Royal Navy has, you will be glad to hear, been firmly rejected'.

All of 'Cavalier's' officers had grown beards for the occasion in San Salvador. (Public Record Office)

April 30th and they were making for Rodman in the Panama Canal Zone. On arrival they took on a pilot to transit Gallun Lake and enter the locks. They really felt as though they had left behind the Far East fleet and were on their way home as they entered the Caribbean. Their last port of call for flag waving was at Almirante, they then expected to refuel in the Bahamas and make straight for home. They had had enough of flag waving and needed to get home to their families. However they still had more duty ahead of them as they received a message to make for Haiti at highest speed. The Dominican Republic seemed intent on invading Haiti, and the Haitian people had problems with their despotic leader President Duvalier (Papa Doc). They arrived off Navasa Island at 0700hrs on the 4th May and patrolled up and down that area to prevent any landings. After a couple of days they we ordered to proceed nearer to Port 'O Prince at high speed and again they patrolled off Roches Pirogues. The Canadians and Americans were arranging to fly their nationals out and 'Cavalier' would take onboard any British should it be necessary. On the 8th they were relieved by the frigate HMS Londonderry in order that they could enter Kingston to refuel and store ship. They loaded three tons of potatoes in twelve minutes and the whole operation was over within three hours. She returned to take over from 'Londonderry'. On the 11th May they were relieved by their sister ship 'Caprice' and they made their way towards Bermuda. It seemed strange to be meeting up with 'Caprice' so far from our old stomping grounds in the east. On May 22nd they were at Ponta Delgada, Sao Miguel in the Azores and then left for the last leg home.

In April 1963 whilst the ship was en-route to the UK, wedding Banns were called at a church service on the quarter deck for several men who were intending to marry on arrival home. The service was conducted by the captain CDR Black. Amongst those called were Roger Hunt and John Natham. She arrived in Portsmouth on the 26th May 1963 and anchored at Spithead. She spent one day in Portsmouth and then sailed for Chatham to pay off. Her crew disbanded and she was placed in reserve again.

Marriage banns called for, on the left Roger Hunt and John Natham

That could have been the end of her but the cold war was still on and could at any time go 'hot', the Russian's were building more and more submarines, we might need every ship with an anti-submarine capability. Send her to Gibraltar for a major refit!

Pig's ear: To the rear of the bridge was a urinal for the use of the officer of the watch so that he did not have to leave the bridge. This was known as the 'pig's ear', (Hence the saying 'In a pig's ear'?).

The pig's ear!

Known Crew List 1961 – 63

Allen M	LME
Anderson	OA
Anning S	AB G
Annison E	AB G
Arbin W 'Bill'	AB TAS
Arnold W	PO G
Bagg J	LT G
Bailey D	AB G
Bailey D	CPO ME
Barnes	AB
Barter N	S LT
Bentley	AB
Bevir T	SQD NAV OFF
Biggs H	
Black W	CDR CO
Blackham J	MID★
Blenkinsopp	AB RP
Bright R	ELM
Broughton 'Les'	REA3
Burnan G	LT CDR EO
Carrie G	ME
Carrol P	AB
Carver D	LT NAV O
Chadwick R	SA V
Chapman D	LS
Chinery A	RO
Church	ME
Coleman C	CPO
Cornish B	JME
Coughlin D	ME
Cringle D	RO3 S
Cross J	LT CDR
Cubitt L	ERA
Curtis	
Davey	L WRT
Davey B	ME
Davies P	
Davies D	EO
Davies D	S LT COMMS
Denholm V	LT CDR
Dennehy T	RO
Doyle A	RO G
Dimmock J	L CK
Dominey J	LSBA
Dormer H	AB RP
Dowson G	
Dowie C 'Jock'	RO
Elliot G	JSG
Ellis R	EM
Elson G	PO
Embleton H	EM
Evans T	SQDN Padre
Evans	PO TEL
Fletcher A	AB
Fisher E	JS
Foskitt R	AB RP
Gibbs V	LT SO
Glenn	AB G
Good	ME
Goodall J	ME
Griffiths M	AB G
Haffenden T	AB TAS
Hale M	TO
Hall	POME
Hallett C.	LT CDR W&RO
Hart	CK

Harte G 'Spike'	AB RP2	McCormick R	ME1
Hay W	PO	McCrossan D	LT G
Hayball R 'Screwball'	AB G	McFarlane M	MID
Hayward T	CK	McGee	ME
Hendry A	ME	McGirr R	AB
Hodges	ME	McGrath B	LTO
Holmes P	SA S	McGrath A	AB
Hopkins	LT S	McInroy	ME1
Howard J	ME	McMahone P	ME1
Howe J	EM	McRoberts A	ME1
Hunking M	LS	Meldrum 'Jock'	RS
Hughes A	AB FC2	Middleditch D	RO2
Hunt R	LME	Millington	
Hunter	LT CONS	Mitchell R	LS PTI
Hunter M	AB	Mitchell R	OS
Ingram R	L WRT	Mitchem	ME
Johnson D	AB	Moir J	ME
Jones P	ME	Money J	CK
Keefe R		Moore	ME
Kemp D	AB	Moore M	LME
Knight	ERA	Moorhouse J	ME
Knox P	ME	Morgan A	JS
Lamb	MID	Morris J	LS G
Lansburgh T	ME	Moss	PO TASI
Leonard E	ERA	Natham J	ME
Lincoln E	ERA	Ninnim J	S LT TASO
Lindsay R	ME	Nixon R	RO2 S
Lysons P	ME	Nolan L	POME
MacCartney	ME	Ostler B	
Mackay S	ME	Paterson	ME
Mager 'Jan'	RO2	Patrick N	AB TAS
Manning W	RO	Petchey B	AB TAS
Margetts M	EA	Pinckard K	
Martindale D	ERA2	Portlock M	PO G

Priestley J	POME	Unwin J	POME
Primrose	EM	Upton K	EA
Proctor	POME	Vidler	AB
Pye D	LME	Wadey P	RO
Pyne	AB	Walker C	MID
Radford J	AB	Watson P	AB G
Reek	EM	Weare P	AB
Ridgers D	LT NAVO	Welby-Everard R	MID
Robson J	PO	Wickers S	LME
Rodwell A	AB	Wilkinson	PO GI
Ross T	ME	Williams G	AB
Roy R	AB RP	Williams N	
Savage W	ELM	Williamson J	AB G
Sayer J	ME	Winter S 'Fred'	PO RP
Scott-Brown A	SURG LT	Wood D	
Scrivens B	CY	Wooding P	LS
Searle B	AB G	Wozencroft K	OA
Shanks F	NAAFI	Wright J	ERA
Shields K	AB G	Yates A	
Sibley	LEM	Young B	CPO EL
Simmons D	AB G	Young 'Brigham'	AB TAS
Smith	AB		
Stabler	POME		
Staines J			
Stamp J	ME1		
Stanley D	AB		
Stockley P	AB		
Sykes A	PO CK		
Sykes F			
Tee Thanabalisingham R	COAWE		
Toop F	MID		
Toy T	RO2S		
Trevellion	POME		
Truby D	EM		

*Later Admiral Sir Jeremy Blackham KCB

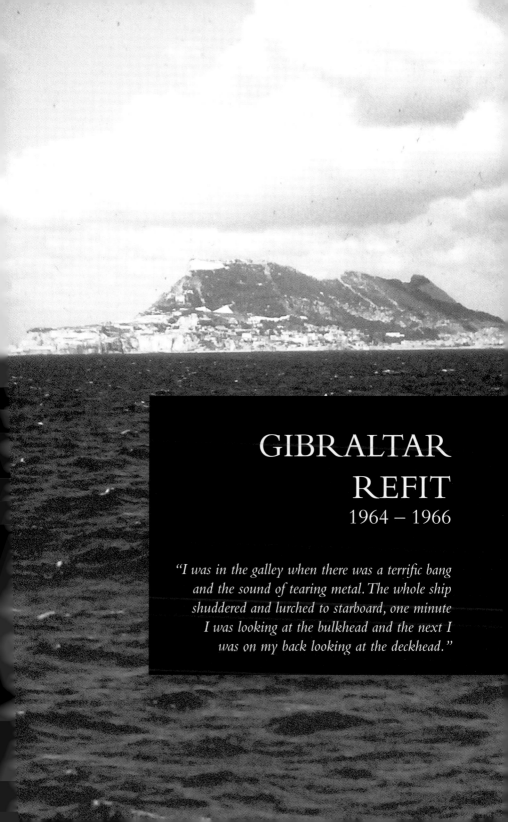

GIBRALTAR REFIT
1964 – 1966

"I was in the galley when there was a terrific bang and the sound of tearing metal. The whole ship shuddered and lurched to starboard, one minute I was looking at the bulkhead and the next I was on my back looking at the deckhead."

GIBRALTAR REFIT
1964 – 1966

After paying off at Portsmouth in 1963 'Cavalier' was moved from Portsmouth to Chatham dockyard. Here they made preparations for a tow to Gibraltar for a long major refit and upgrade. A skeleton crew, some of whom had stayed on from the 1961-3 commission, would man her and stay with her there. It had the dual purpose of giving work to the Gibraltar dockyard and would also work out cheaper with the sailors doing some of the work. In May she left Chatham under the tow of one of the navy's own ocean going tugs HMS Reward. On the 21st May '64 whilst negotiating the English Channel in thick fog off the Sussex coast, the 17,905 ton Liberian registered tanker *MS Burean* cut across the tow and with a huge rending of steel collided with 'Cavalier'. Luckily there were no injuries to the crew, although they probably needed to do some extra dhobying! One man on the tanker was quite badly injured and a surgeon and SBA from the frigate HMS Aurora, which was exercising nearby, went aboard to attend to him. He was then airlifted by helicopter to the hospital in Chichester.

Sid Anning, AB: 'I was in the galley with Les Johnson when there was a terrific bang and the sound of tearing metal; this seemed to go on for ages. The whole ship shuddered and lurched to starboard, one minute I was looking at the bulkhead and the next I was on my back looking at the deckhead. I was sure the ship was going to 'turn turtle'. Les, using the navy vernacular, suggested we get out of there fast, but for a while I couldn't move with the ship rolling'.

In case the ship was going to sink I started to turn the sea boat out, but realized I had not released the gripes... all that training gone to waste! I can laugh now (gripes = straps that hold the boat into the davits). When we tried to see what had hit us, all we could see was this huge tanker going down our side with lots of Italian sailors waving to us as they disappeared into the fog. We went forward and could not believe the damage that had been done; twenty feet of the bow had been crushed in. 'Dinger' Bell, our Jack Dusty (Storeman) and 'Nobby' Goodall had been down in the store below the frwd messdeck and had been the thickness of the bulkhead (4mm) away from being crushed.

Wallowing in the Channel, the stern of the whaler can just be been seen partly turned out due to Sid's efforts. (Newspaper cutting)

Able Seaman Ben Searle had been on the bridge sounding the hand operated mechanical fog horn, he saw the Tanker coming through the fog and called the Officer of the watch on the armament broadcast system and pumped the fog horn even faster but to no avail. The tug 'Reward' attached a tow aft and towed us stern first into Portsmouth, where a new bow was constructed.

She finally arrived in Gibraltar for her major refit which would last over two years. For many of the temporary refit crew it was a 'married accompanied draft', that is, some were able to have their wives and children living ashore in Gibraltar for the duration.

More than just a panel beating job! 'Cavalier' enters Portsmouth for repairs. Her gun ports had already been welded over at Chatham for the tow to Gibraltar. The paint store was situated in the crushed part of the bow hence the paint running down the ship's side, it was just as well that no one had been in that compartment at the time. Dinger and Nobby would have been next to where the paint is running down the ship's side over the black boot topping. (Times Newspapers Ltd)

There were huge changes made to the ship's accommodation; whereas up till now it had been all hammocks it was now to be mostly bunks. The twin Bofors mounting aft was removed and replaced by the new Sea Cat missile close range system and its magazine. This is the tall structure aft which is said by many to spoil her WWII 'classic' sleek destroyer look. The Seacat was the RNs first close range missile system, it had been developed from the late 1950's and early sixties. It was optically guided along two radio beams and was so successful (For that time) that it was purchased by over thirty foreign countries.

It had its limitations and about the time of the Falkland's war in 1982 it was in the process of being superseded by the much more versatile Seawolf missile. The refit was completed in September 1966 and the new crew, under CDR John Hervey flew to Gibraltar to join her for her sixth and penultimate commission.

Mark Ruddle, LT CDR, H.M.S. Caprice: My abiding memory of

'Cavalier' was whilst she was in refit in Gibraltar. She was undergoing full power trials and going astern at 19.5 knots with her rudder jammed hard over, out of control and with her decks awash from the stern through to the iron deck! (Half way along the length of the ship).

The subsonic Seacat missile, the upper fins, made of fibreglass were moved by radio control, the fixed lower fins had flares in small tubes so that it was visible to the aimer in poor visibility or darkness. It had a maximum effective range of about five miles and was initially Anti Aircraft, later it was developed for use against surface targets. In the nose was a small explosive charge which when set off scattered steel rods at the aircraft and cut it to pieces. (Author)

Skeleton Crew list for 1964 – 66 refit

Anning S	AB G
Baker D	LME
Bell T 'Dinger'	SA V
Brighton J	CK
Brown 'Buster'	ME
Campbell J	ME
Fidoe	ERA
Gates 'Tony'	AB G
Goodall 'Nobby'	
Godfrey	AB G
Haughton 'Scouse'	AB
Jenkins 'Taff'	AB QA
Johnson Les	AB
Johnston 'Johnno'	ME1
Kelly R	LEM
Kelly 'Spider'	REM
Marley R	LEM
Mason 'Perry'	LME
Moore 'Pony'	LEM WRTR
Nutley	C ME
Pugh	LT G CO EO
Roberts C	OS
Roamer	LT EL
Ross	LS
Roxborough 'Black Alf'	AB
Ryder B	LEM
Searle B	AB
Smith B	
Spinner C	LS
Steel	LT E
Walsh 'Scouse'	EL M

TWO CAPTAINS
1966 – 1967

*UK, Portsmouth Devonport, South Africa,
Cape Town, Mombasa. Beira, Singapore,
Hong Kong, Australia. Gibraltar,
Naples, Lisbon. Marseilles, Toulon.*

TWO CAPTAINS
1966 – 1967

CDR John B. HERVEY RN
(Sixth commission)

John joined the Royal Navy in 1946; he had a very impressive and varied career, by 1950 he had specialized in submarines, progressing to a nuclear boat in 1968. Between 1956 and 1976 he had commanded seven ships, an inshore minelayer, three diesel submarines, two destroyers and a nuclear submarine. He had vast experience in subs, commanding the 6th submarine division in Canada and the 7th squadron in the UK. Other commands were Flotilla Ops Officer (30 Subs), Senior Naval Officer Defence Op requirement Staff, responsible for getting Harriers onto carriers and arming nuclear subs with Sub Harpoon missiles. From 1976 to 1980 he had the posts of Deputy Chief of staff allied staffs to C in C Channel and C in C Eastern Atlantic at Northwood HQ. Director Task Force seven NATO. TF7 examined every aspect of electronic warfare throughout the Alliance and produced recommendation that were still being implemented many years later. From 1980 to 82, the period of the Falkland's war, he held the important post of Commander of the British Naval Staff Washington USA and negotiated the assistance given to the RN by the USN. He wrote a book on submarine warfare a large number of which went to the USN. One US officer commented that 'This book should be the bible of all aspiring submariners'. He was considered by all who met him as a professional and a true gentleman.

After her refit she commissioned and left Gibraltar on 22nd September 1966 for Portsmouth. She would now become a part of the 4th Destroyer flotilla and be sporting a large No.4 on her funnel. Having worked up she joined the Home Fleet on the 4th November 1966.

Keith 'Taff' Hewett JME: 'I was only 16years old when I joined 'Cavalier', we were flown out to Gib to pick the ship up in September 1966 and I was onboard when she paid off there in March 1969. I was later flown home but in between that time we travelled the world. I had a bunk in the after mess and slept directly under 'Y' gun, every time it fired my bunk filled with cork insulation and flakes of paint dislodged from the deckhead'.

John Hervey CDR: 'My crew had been 'rubbed down with an oily rag' in the UK before being flown out to Gibraltar to join 'Cavalier'. I commissioned her there and found she was in bit of a sorry state, the starboard side looked good, but the port side was still in red lead paint. Many of my officers were not suited to the ship, some did not want to be there or were due out of the service shortly and later on one had a nervous breakdown. To top it all when we started practicing with the main armament we found we could not have hit a Russian barn door from one hundred yards. The whole system needed overhauling. I and my new Weapons Electrical Officer, Bryan Mosdell who was really on top of his job gave me the confidence to approach the FOS (Fleet Officer Staff) technical staff at Portsmouth to outline the problems with the gunnery system. The Third Sea Lord – Controller of the Navy via his Executive Assistant suggested we sail for the Far East as planned and 'your staff can work on it enroute!

I told them that; *'If this ship sails for the Far East it will be with a new (deleted expletive) captain, I refuse to take this ship to sea without the main armament working and possibly to war and possibly the ignominious and undeserved end to the lives of the crew'.* The weapon systems had not been overhauled properly in the past because everyone thought that she would be going into reserve and probably never coming out again. The excuses were made that Admiral Reserve Fleet thought Admiral Fleet would be sorting the problem and Fleet thought Reserve would sort it! After much argument it was accepted that she would need another sixteen weeks in dockyard hands to rewire the fly plane 5 system. The director had the wrong magnetron fitted and because some of the wiring was frayed current was passing from one direction to another when the ship rolled and 'B' gun would suddenly acquire an extra 5 degrees of elevation… with the potential to shoot down the aircraft towing the target!

The guns crews were sent to gunnery school at HMS Cambridge in Devon so that when the guns and the electronics had been overhauled we could not have wished for a better system. We went to sea and did a test shoot with a Pilotless Target Aircraft (PTA).

'B' gun fired seven rounds and got seven Target Triggered Bursts (TTB's). 'A' gun fired seven rounds with six bursts and 'Y' gun six rounds with five bursts (A burst occurred when the shell got close enough to trigger the proximity fuse and bring a plane down, which makes the above pretty good shooting). My making a stand had been vindicated. Both Bryan and I had put ourselves in the firing line, so to speak, in the promotion stakes. Admiral Wise of Fleet Tech suppor wrote demanding to know why 'Cavalier' was delayed for so long i sailing for the East. So enroute for Gibraltar I wrote a long letter c reply pointing out the neglect of previous years and using Bryan technical knowledge of the system as back up. I did not post the reply until we sailed from South Africa knowing that by the time he received it, I and the ship would be under the command of the Far East Fleet and any flack that came back would only expose the short comings of the Home Fleet. I was thankful that I received support from two Admirals for my stance. The first was Rear Admiral Sharp CB DSC, Flag Officer Sea Training and the other was C in C Far East Admiral 'Bill' O'Brien, who of course did not want to be lumbered with an addition to his fleet of a lame duck'.

The fact that she was now a very efficient addition to the fleet once again probably contributed to her eventual salvation instead of her going to the reserve fleet and ultimately the scrap yard.

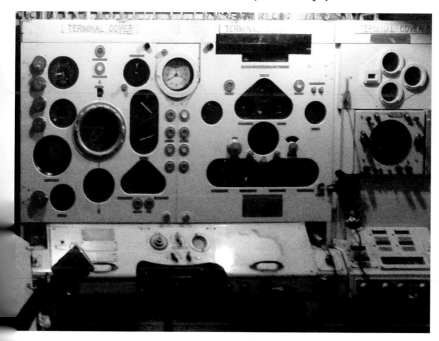

The console of the electro – mechanical predictor (computer) for surface gunnery. This part was operated by three men.

Peter Stone LT CDR, engineering Officer: 'I joined Cavalier in Guzz (Devonport) in February 1967 after the ship had failed her workup at Portland. Apparently she had defective guns and damage control systems. The Fleet Tech staff wanted us to sail anyway but our CO, CDR John Hervey was having none of it. After several weeks in dockyard hands and with on the 5th June 1967 the Arab – Israeli war breaking out and the canal subsequently closing on the 7th June, we loaded with extra live 4.5" ammunition and with a full compliment set off for Gib. We waited there for three days to hear from the politicians whether we may get involved or whether we would just

wait for the canal to open again. On the evening of the third day, during a cocktail party JH warned me we would be sailing at midnight, only he knew when we sailed from Gib whether we would turn right or left. Lo and behold we turned right; we were off to Simonstown Naval Base, South Africa we would be going via the Cape.

The inside showing a part of the computer. State of the art technology in the 1950s but by 1966 it needed overhauling.

I could not guarantee that we could make it on one bunker of fuel. However as luck would have it there happened to be an RFA tanker off Biafra (There was another conflict going on there) so we topped up from them. The Beira patrols were boring except when intercepting suspect tankers. Our mail and other essentials were dropped from RAF transport aircraft. After the Beira patrols we sailed across the Indian Ocean as escort for the carrier Eagle, it became our job because of our high speed, the modern anti

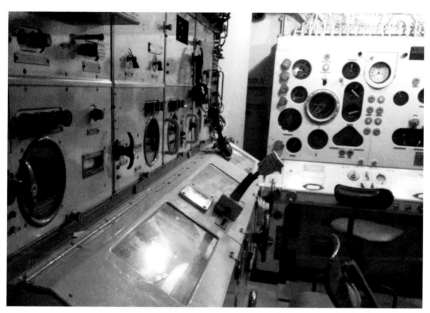

The anti-aircraft side of the gunnery computer. Three men operated this part. When the guns were in auto they would be following the pointers of these predictors. The orange disc, top left is the repeater screen for the overall anti-aircraft radar picture from the big cheese radar aerial near the top of the mast.

Left; The GRU, Gyro rate unit which stabilized the guns. Right; The computer bank for the gunnery system (All overhauled), defective units ould be removed and replaced for repair later, a fairly new concept then.

submarine frigates could not keep up with a carrier doing in excess of 30 knots for flying off her aircraft. We spent Christmas and the New Year in Hong Kong and whilst there JH left the ship for another advanced posting and he was replaced by CDR Tony Wavish. Tony was a specialist navigator and he showed his skills in ship handling on his first trip when we did the measured mile runs in the busy Singapore Roads. We did a five port visit around Australia; the hospitality was terrific wherever we went and as I was wine caterer for the wardroom I took advantage of some 'smoke damaged' crates of beer that came our way in Tasmania. The official reception there was held at Government house, it was expected to be rather boring… it was anything but! After some nibbles and a few drinks the ADC explained that we were going to play a game of special 'house cricket'. Now before that happened it was explained that the ladies would be queuing up for the loos so, led by the Governor himself it was suggested it would easier for all the men to go out the front door and piddle over the parapet! The game of cricket was played in the ballroom with besom brooms and a soft ball. Fours were scored against the ballroom walls, no sixes allowed, if your ball hit the wall without touching the ground you were out. The ladies were easily able to stop the ball because they were wearing long evening dresses… a night to remember!

On our way home we did yet another three weeks of Beira patrol and then headed for Gus, refuelling at Dakar.

I could not speak more highly of all my staff from ERA's down to the ME's they were a great team and many went on to further promotion.'

Cavalier's first visit to Mombasa and the monotonous Beira patrols was during July and August of 1967. Whilst lying alongside in Mombasa they put patrols ashore to police the behaviour of the crew. This consisted of one leading hand and two ratings to the Silversand area and another group to patrol the town. These patrols were made up from the duty watch of the day and the following day those ashore would become the duty patrol for that day. All night leave was granted here, from 0930hrs to 0730hrs, although junior seamen had to be back onboard by 2300hrs.

From the 14th August until the 31st they were patrolling, they went to and fro between the Macuti light and the Ingomaimo light, backwards and forwards stopping and checking merchant ships, boats and yachts and logging aircraft movements.

John Hervey CDR: 'In Mombasa I recall 'Chats' Harris, one of my seamen was presented at my table as a defaulter, I had to weigh him off. Yomo (Jomo) Kenyatta, the then president with a British Admiral and other VIPs had been due to travel round the harbour in his yacht. Ships in the harbour would be expected to salute him as he passed. Harris was ready to go ashore for leave with his oppo's but, as he was a trained bugler he was detailed by the officer of the watch to stay behind and play the alert as the yacht passed. Come the important moment he duly played the 'alert' as the yacht passed, then threw the bugle into the sea and jumped in after it – in full uniform! I asked him why he had done this and he gave some cock and bull story about the heat getting to him and he had had a vision of his girlfriend across the sea and dived in to be with her! I knew that was a load of bull, he had done it because he hadn't got ashore. I had to punish him somehow, but did not want to cause too much of a fuss over it. I ordered that he be detained under close arrest onboard for four days. This did not go down too well with certain members of the ship's company because they would have to act as his jailers and stand watches. A sequel to this was that later, in Hong Kong I was waiting on the gangway in full regalia to greet the Admiral when I noticed Harris was standing by to play the alert on his bugle! In trepidation I went over to him and said 'I don't want to see any of your aquatic skills demonstrated today thank you Harris'.

Alan Yates AB G: 'The memory of this incident can still reduce me to pulp if I don't take a grip! After a substantial time at sea we moored to ahead and stern buoys in the harbour at Mombasa. Our rugby team was due to play a big match ashore and many of the ship's company would be attending. As the final liberty boat was due to leave for shore Chats Harris (God bless him wherever he is) who was already in the boat in civvies and anticipating a few beers and fun ashore, was suddenly turfed out of the boat and ordered to report to the Officer of the watch's cabin. He was informed that he was to change into his best whites and as he was the only bugler onboard, be ready to sound the alert on the bugle. His protests at this injustice fell on deaf ears and he went to the mess deck to press his No6 uniform and whiten his canvas shoes. He had time to stew on the situation whilst he imagined his oppo's ashore enjoying their beer, I think he may have also had girlfriend problems at home at the time which didn't help…! At the appointed time he joined the OOD, Duty PO, Quartermaster and Bosun's mate (Yours truly) all looking spick and span under the awning on the iron deck. The yacht was ninety minutes late which didn't help matters, more stewing time! The Officer Of the Day (I believe LT CDR Pisani, the gunnery officer) then chose to dismiss Chats as 'not required' because the yacht did not come close enough! This was the straw that broke the camel's back and Chats defiantly blew a few desultory raspberries on the bugle… and then threw it into the sea… followed by him fully clothed doing a magnificent swallow dive over the guardrails after it. The OOD was mortified and his face turned a peculiar colour. Young Harris was moving seaward at a fair lick with his cap bobbing about behind him. The ship's whaler was lying at the boom and was quickly manned by a scratch crew in an assortment of rigs, some of them stokers in their boiler suits. They went after him in what can only be loosely termed as a 'seaman like manner', to retrieve him Other members of the ship's company on hearing the commotion stuck their heads out of the scuttles to watch and started shouting encouragement to Chats in his endeavours! The Admiral in the yacht, engine now idling, was probably mesmerized by what was going on and no doubt dictating notes to his aide. Our man Chats was dragged from the oggin and brought back to the ship, however half way up the ladder he did another backward dive and was soon thrashing his way down the harbour. He was eventually brought onboard and taken below and restrained. The re-percussions from this event rattled around for some time and quite a few people caught a dollop of poo from the fan. The Admiral's inevitable signal was 'lengthy' and contained references to 'Fred Kano's' and something about a 'cattle boat'.

On arrival in Singapore a few weeks later Chats was sent to see a 'trick cyclist' who pronounced that the incident was a one off aberration! Our 'old man', the illustrious John Hervey was I think absolutely tickled pink over the whole affair and I don't think the notoriety did him any harm in the promotion stakes!

About the same time as the Chats incident I was under punishment, No9's (Stoppage of leave and tot plus extra work). As part of our punishment, when everyone else had a Make and Mend Taffy Evans and myself were detailed to wash down and paint the tall superstructure over the iron deck. To do this we had to work from a cradle lowered over from the top. We washed one part, dried it and painted it and then had to lower ourselves down for the next stretch. Now although we were under stoppage of our tot, Taffy had had a fair amount of rum from his oppo's and when we lowered ourselves down he grabbed the wrong two pieces of rope and his end of the staging crashed down leaving me hanging in mid air. He fell, but luckily the canvas awning was rigged below us and he landed on it, along with a pot of ship's side grey paint and a bucket of soapy water… all mixed in together! The duty supervising Petty Officer hearing the commotion stood on the guardrail to look over the top of the awning to see what was going on and as he did so he was met by one body and a mixture of paint and soapy water. It was like a farce from a 'Carry on' film!

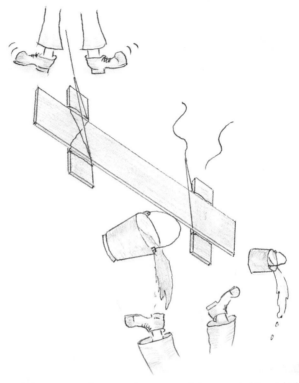

With two men sitting on a staging several metres up it is suggested it might be a good idea to untie the correct rope when lowering yourself down!

From Mombasa she went on to Port Louis on the island of Mauritius.

Keith 'Taff' Hewett, JME: 'We arrived in Port Louis on a Sunday and anchored in the main harbour. There was an American destroyer also there. We all got into our best tropical uniforms and went ashore in the motor boat, unfortunately being a Sunday none of the bars were open. However a word with some taxi drivers revealed there was one bar open in a village called Rose Hill, so off we all trotted the Yanks had also found it. We got on well with them and after a few beers it developed into a sea shanty singing contest, the more beers the louder it got. A big crowd of locals were peering through the windows laughing at the drunken proceedings. By the time we got back to the ship we were the worse for wear and our whiter than white uniforms were grubby, the skipper was not amused... I ended up with four days No9's'.

After Port Louis they went east and met up with the carrier 'Eagle' and acted as her plane guard. On arrival they moored in the naval base at Singapore for Christmas.

A Singapore bar advertising card.

In January 1967 she was again in the Indian Ocean exercising with 'Eagle' off the island of Gan when they received an urgent message. The Greek merchant ship *Thebean* was requesting urgent medical help, her chief engineer was seriously ill. Once again 'Cavalier's' speed dictated that she should be the one to proceed to their assistance, a helicopter from 'Eagle' brought the Doc over to us because we were only carrying an SBA. After a high speed dash she transferred the engineer onboard and rushed him to the island of Gan. Within no time she was back alongside 'Eagle' to continue the exercises. Another job well done, another life saved another person on the world's oceans had been 'touched' by 'Cavalier'.

Howard Bissell, Midshipman; 'On the 4th February I was flown by Gannet aircraft from the carrier 'Eagle' to the island of Gan in the Indian Ocean. There I was to join the 'Cavalier' for six months; she was lying in the Gan lagoon, beautiful blue water and fishing to make any fisherman's day. Arriving onboard I was assigned a camp bed in the wardroom, not a good idea, the wardroom was in

The Doc being lowered onto the quarter deck from a
Wessex helicopter, a view from the squid deck.

use seventeen hours a day and I could get very little sleep. I moved
from there into the Electronic Warfare Office (EWO) which wasn't
used too much during the night. We left the lagoon for Australia
and spent what seemed like a whole week of Replenishments, fuel
from RFA Olna and stores and more fuel from RFA Stromness. It
was the first time I had been put in charge of lowering the whaler.
On 'Cavalier' the whole lower deck was cleared to lower or hoist
the boats because there were no powered winches (The whaler was
usually lowered into the sea whilst the ship was still under way and

you needed to have some idea of what you were doing!). I was a bit nervous but seemed to be doing alright shouting out all the correct orders, however having ordered the pins to be pulled out of the releasing gear, I gave the order to 'slip' when the boat was still too high and she dropped into the trough of a wave with a huge splash, luckily no one was injured or damage done – especially as the captain was in the boat at the time'!

Terry Willis, Leading seaman UW2, Christmas 1967: 'Whilst in Singapore a group of us decided that it would be a good idea if we were to spend Christmas in the Malayan jungle! This wasn't the normal jungle warfare training it was our own venture. We put in a request for leave and it was duly granted. Having got it in writing we went to the HMS Terror shore base and arranged a supply of jungle clothing, machetes, tents, maps and 'K' rations. Five of us were given a lift in one of the base Lorries, we travelled over the Causeway, through Johor Bahru and on up through central Malaya. After about two hours we were dropped off on the roadside with jungle either side of us. We cut our way into this jungle and after some time found a suitable site to camp. We erected our tents and got a brew on the go and then proceeded to dam a small stream so that we would have a place to have a good scrub down and do our dhobying. We had some mosquito repellent but not nets, we could have done with some nets because later two of the lads ended up in Sick Bay with suspected Malaria, I was lucky I had no problems, I suppose they didn't like me. We made it our aim to find the source of the stream we were camped by. We consulted our map which indicated the direction we were going to have to go and set off; it showed we would have to climb a waterfall. It was quite an experience to see all the exotic plants and wildlife. Having struggled to cut our way through thick jungle and climb this water fall we discovered yet another… and then another, it was time to turn back. Unfortunately we never did find the source! One morning on waking we found some huge paw prints by the tents and going down to the stream, it looked like a tiger had come down for a drink… we were just glad he wasn't hungry as well, for we only had our machetes and a 'Very' pistol for protection'.

OD M. Dilks, Jan Early, AB Peter Rowe and LS Terry Willis, kneeling. The machetes they have for cutting a path through the jungle were navy issue.

Keith 'Taff' Hewett JME: 'You can imagine the first time I went through the airlock from the boiler room and saw Hong Kong I was so excited… and relieved! Because on arrival I was in the boiler room with POME 'Scouse' Flaherty and we started to shut the boilers down, one of the steam driven fans that keep the pressure up in the boiler room was shut down, however the stoker by mistake shut down one but opened the other one's exhaust steam valve. Very quickly the room filled with extremely hot steam at high pressure and the noise of escaping steam was horrendous. In a short time it became very difficult to breath, we all started to make for the vertical ladder to the air lock but the POME was standing at the bottom to stop us, luckily it was realised what had happened and it was very quickly brought under control before we were 'cooked'. Dangerous places these boiler rooms. I also remember about that time young JME Phil Curley he was jumping up and down on a bunk when he hit his head on a hammock hook in the deckhead, the split in his head was several inches long and needed ten stitches'.

In December 1967 CDR Hervey left the ship to take up another command and eventually became the captain of one of the new nuclear submarines. The crew stayed the same but under the command of the new captain, CDR Tony Wavish.

CDR A. R. Wavish RN,
December 1967 to February 1969

Alan Yates, AB G: On arrival in Sydney, Australia we went alongside with the 'Troubridge'. Australia was very enjoyable after our Beira patrol and exercises with the Far East Fleet. I was on duty as Bosun's mate on the gangway minding my own business when I was approached by the Physical Training Instructor who told me in such a charming manner... that I was a 'long streak of p...' and I was just what he was looking for. He said, 'Have you any experience in walking races?' 'No' I said, 'Great you'll do, get into your sports gear and fall in on the jetty'. And so began an interesting experience of which I still have fond memories. It seems there was an annual walking race held in Sydney in which teams and individuals from all over Australia train to compete in. It was a six mile course through the streets of the city, over the harbour bridge and finishing on the steps of the town hall. The race was sponsored by the Guinness brewing company; there was a first prize of $500 and a two week holiday for two up at Surfers Paradise. Of course I knew nothing of this on the coach travelling to the venue... in typical naval fashion I had just been detailed off. I only knew there were five of us and another five from 'Troubridge' who had been invited to take part in some sports event. So there we were with three hundred other people and suddenly a whistle went, a flag went up and we were off. I did my best to copy the others with that toe heel gait that they use and before long we were well strung out. Along the way you pass collection points where you are given little gizmos to prove you have passed. At one point I thought I'd gone off track and had to ask for directions... the next thing I know I'm going across the finishing line about twenty yards in the lead to huge cheers from a large crowd. After presenting my gizmos I am declared the winner, to say that I was totally gob smacked would be an understatement. I am carried shoulder high up the town hall steps where I am interviewed by a cluster of reporters and local radio and television people. It was all camera flashes, microphones and handshaking followed by meeting the mayor and an Australian actor whose face I knew but whose name eludes me and the actress Susanna York.

The rest of the day passed in a blur, I was much celebrated, went ashore and was soon plastered. I recall sitting in a Returned Serviceman's Club where everyone was shouting for me to watch the TV where I was being featured… but I didn't seem to be able to focus!

The following day I was on the mess deck when I received a call to report to the gangway. There was a flat back lorry and the driver needed a signature on an invoice from me. The load, under a tarpaulin was *two thousand pint bottles of Guinness!* 'Well shiver me timbers' I said… or words to that effect. What the hell was I going to do with that lot; I hardly had room in my locker for my kit let alone two thousand pints of Guinness, and anyway would it affect my rum ration? I sought my D.O's advice and it was decided that we would divide it up, half of it going to 'Troubridge', crates to every senior rates mess and the wardroom and of course one crate to each captain. The remainder was stowed in the spirit room along with the rum and I had a pint of Guinness every day in the dog watches for the rest of the commission and it didn't affect my rum issue! After some discussion the captain and the MD of Guinness decided to reduce the $500 to $200 and because the ship's programme would not allow two weeks away I was given a week's leave. The MD telephoned and said I could go anywhere I wanted by first class. Actually thinking on it that was day light robbery, I think I might sue, I wonder what the statute of limitations is? We had recently visited Newcastle further up the coast and I had met a lovely girl there, so I phoned her and went to stay with her. We had a great time, eating out every night, dancing, barbecues and all at the best venues and all paid for by my sponsors. I took her family out as well and we talked long into the night. Her father was an interesting chap, ex RAN and Japanese POW.

One final highlight was that the ship had sailed to Hobart, Tasmania and I had to fly down to catch her up. There were several officers and senior rates on the flight; the difference between us was that they were flying tourist class and I was in club class... I couldn't resist swanning down the aisle a couple of times with an umbrella cocktail. I don't think it would have done my career much good though!'

Alan receives the Guinness Trophy... and two thousand pints of Guinness!

During his initial training and before joining 'Cavalier' Alan received the following assessment: 'Junior Seaman Yates is quite a pleasant boy, but is a bit dim in many respects. Cheerful, but tends to be scruffy and casual. He is quite unreliable and is considered a liability to have around during evolutions. It was a mistake to have him in the platoon where he can come into contact with loaded weapons!'

And the following is an extract from his final assessment after twenty four years of service, a career that he ended as a Chief Petty Officer at HMS Eaglet in Liverpool: Chief Petty officer Yates has proved himself to be a most adept manager and administrator. Rarely if ever, in a long career have I met a more tactful, loyal and totally reliable senior rate, it has been a pleasure to serve with him'.

CDR Wavish and his officers

E Skillin, D Swetman, D Cunningham, W Benbow, P White, P Windley C Pool
P Stone, D Barrow, CDR Wavish – CO. M Gude, G Pincott

David Hall ERA1: 'We left Australia on 27th March 1968 to escort the frigate HMS Troubridge across the Indian Ocean, she had major problems with her boilers, and in the event of her breaking down a thousand miles from land we would be on hand to take her in tow.

Peter Stone, LT CDR EO: Having left Australia we were due to refuel from a tanker in the Indian Ocean, we were running low on fuel, when we received a message that the tanker had engine trouble and we would not be able to meet up with her. The crew got quite excited because it looked as though our best option was to return to Australia. Fortunately, or otherwise, before we reached the point where we would have to turn back the tanker radioed to say she had repaired the fault and would be able to refuel us after all'.

It suited the powers that be that whilst they were 'that way' they could do another Beira Patrol. This they did steaming up and down between the 12th and 30th April 1968. It became a bit monotonous and various things were arranged to keep the crew occupied, amongst these was a SOD's opera....'

Beira patrol, SOD's opera: PO GI Machin, Tommo, Perry, Ginge and Tom Kean AB. In the bottom right hand corner can just be seen the corner of the canvas swimming pool rigged for the occasion. (A. Yates)

In Mombasa the ship berthed at Kilindini and it was here that two sailors fell afoul of the law. When visiting a foreign country it was a very easy thing to do, something that would be tolerated or ignored at home would not be accepted. They had been drinking at the Castle Hotel in Mombasa and had made several offensive remarks about President Kenyatta being a 'dictator'. This was taken as a serious breach of the peace and they were arrested. They appeared before the magistrate Mr. R Bhandari at the local court and were sentenced to two months in prison, missing the ship when she sailed. Kilindini had been a Royal Navy Japanese code breaking station during WWII.

Beira SOD's opera: Bonny & Clyde, Miss Australia (Smudger Smith AB) & escort (Jan Roe AB) and Armand and Michaela Dennis (1950's wild life film makers). (A.Yates)

Supply and Secretariat branch (Store men, Cooks, Chefs and writers)
Back row L. to R: OSTWD Penn. LSA Spratt. STWD Thompson. CK(S) Denman. CK(S)Smith. CK(S) Jones. SA Mace. SA Talbot. STWD Salisbury. W Horsfall CK(S) Stroud. Middle row: POSA Armitage, LCK(S) Edwards. LSTWD Lewis. LCK Clewes. LSA Keith. NT3 Saunders. Front row: POCK Evans. POWRT Thurston. CDR Wavish. LT CDR Gude POSA Anson. POSTWD.

Derek Pevier RFA, Merchant seaman Deckhand: I was a deckhand on the Royal Fleet Auxiliary oil tanker 'Tidereach' (A69). I flew out to Singapore in a British Eagle's Bristol Britannia, with the crew of HMS Plymouth and joined the ship with them. A week later, somewhere in the middle of the Indian Ocean I was transferred to 'Tidereach' by jackstay transfer, an experience not to be missed! One of my jobs during refuelling the warships was on the communications telephone to them. Normally at the end of fuelling we would blow air through the hundred foot of pipe to clean the rest of the oil out before disconnecting it. However we sometimes practiced an emergency break away in the middle of refuelling, either for a broken hose or, on this particular occasion at the signal that an enemy submarine had been spotted. Our tanker sounded three long blasts on the siren, hearing this; the sailor on the other end of the pipe line smashed the connection off with a large hammer. The end of the disconnected pipe started to thrash around spewing oil with a great whoosh all over the decks... including the officer standing nearby in his beautiful white shirt, shorts and cap. Everybody thought it so funny and we gave him a big chuck up as the two ships broke away at high speed'.

The iron deck, torpedo tubes and one officer covered in thick black oil.
(HMS Caprice Association)

On arrival in most ports the 'Red Devil' was brought out by 'postie', this was a bicycle painted red and kept stored amidships. The postman usually a leading hand would ride to the nearest post office to collect the ship's mail which would have been sent on ahead to her next known destination.

Postie's Red Devil.

This was OK if she hadn't been diverted somewhere else, in which case her mail could be chasing her from port to port sometimes for several weeks. When you eventually got your mail there would be a backlog and you had several bags at one time. The advent of the helicopter delivery changed this arrangement somewhat.

Postie arrives in the form of a Wessex helicopter with two bags of mail. Splash targets are placed to guide the pilot. 'Y' gun is trained forward out of the way and a firefighter stands by in a Fearnought (Asbestos!) suit.

On the 30th May 1968 she returned to Devonport in the UK and joined the Western Fleet. She spent time in home waters and the Mediterranean. There in December 1968 they took part in the large NATO exercise in the North Sea 'Silver town'. She sailed for Gibraltar, and whilst in the Med, she paid visits to Marseilles and Toulon and took part in another exercise, 'Eden Apple'. Between the 16th and 20th She paid a visit to Naples and between 23rd and 27th visited Lisbon. She then made her way back to Devonport only to return in January to take up Guard Ship duties back at Gibraltar.

On 21st February '69 they sailed out from Gibraltar for radar calibration and exercises, she carried various guests including newspaper reporters. One reporter wrote that he got quite alarmed when a Hunter fighter aircraft appeared coming up fast astern and he thought he was to be amongst the first to see a jet aircraft land on the quarter deck of a destroyer! It was piloted by Flying Officer Chris Humphrey RAF and it ruffled their hair as it barely missed the top of the bridge.

Nancy Vaughan columnist 'Gibraltar Chronicle' February 1969: 'Never will I complain about the size of my kitchen again – I've seen the galley where food is prepared for 200 odd men! It is minute, everything in miniature – cookers, hot plate, the lot. No conglomeration of muck and dirty utensils, discipline I suppose. In the scullery section which couldn't have been more than two yards, potatoes were being eyed. The potato peelers have to be started at 4 a.m. each day, don't know how long it took to eye them, they weren't Cyclops! Hungry encouraging smells were coming from the meat and peas of large pies which were waiting for their lid of pastry which was being processed in the mixer by cook Evans. Fish piled in dishes waited to be fried; it all looked wholesome and appetizing. Could teach a lot of women their job I'm sure. Perhaps we should start a tour of her Majesty's ships like the 'Cavalier'. In order to get hot food ready in the correct sequence careful planning went into preparing meals in such a small space'.

The ship finally entered Gibraltar on the 23rd February 1969 to pay off and undergo another refit.

Officer of the watch of warship to Base; *'Am now tied up to buoy No5.'*

Base to OOW; *'Shoe laces are tied up, ships are secured'.*

Comment of a Divisional Officer on an officer's annual report: *'It is difficult to believe that this man is the end result of a million years of evolution'!*

Crew list 1966 – 69

Baker P	ME2
Balaam J	Stwd
Ballentine D	OS
Barker J	JS
Barlow B	ERA
Barnett Fred	POME
Barrett R	RO3
Barrow D	LT CDR
Bartlett J	CPO OA1
Bass 'Alfie'	AB RPY
Bassett K	LREM
Beckham 'Max'	JRO
Bell 'Dinger'	CY
Bellchamber J	JS
Benbow W	LT
Bent P	ERA3
Bexon B	PO GI
Biggs H	ME2
Bissell P. H	MSHMN
Blake B	AB
Booth W	JS
Bowell C	POME
Bower J	REM
Bowling 'Jim'	JME2
Boyle P	JS
Breckon K	AB
Bristow D	ERA1
Brooks D	LRO G
Bryan E	OS
Budd D	JS G
Bunton A	OS
Burgess A	OS
Burman G	LS
Burn R	ERA1
Butler T	
Caple L	OS
Carpenter M	A/CPO
Charge R	LS
Charlton	ME2
Cillard D	CLRA
Clews M	CK S
Colledge G	AB
Cooke E	SHPT 1
Cooper L	OS
Cornier M	PO EL
Cotton 'Bill'	RS W
Couroux D	JS
Cox 'Tony'	JME 1
Cross C	ME 2
Crowhurst C	
Cunngham D	LT NAV
Curley D	JS
Curtis R	L CK O
Davies A	JS
Davies 'Dewi'	PO
Dedman 'Bob'	RO
Denham P	ACK S
Devans 'Taff'	RO 3
Dilks M	OS
Dobson R	AB
Dormer H	
Driver J	CCAW
Duckworth C	CRS
Earle C	MIDSMN
Eastwood J	ERA 1
Edwards G	CAW

Edwards P	OA 1	Hills 'Pusser'	AB
Edwards W	L CK S	Hinglis 'Bill'	LWEM O
Elliot P	AB	Hughes D	ME1
Ellis M	AB	Iche J	JRO
Fackrell P	AB	Irons R	LME
Farr N	AB	Jackman 'Tony'	JME2
Flukes R	ME 1	Jacob W	PO
Forbes T	JS	Jakeway M	LS
Foster E	JS	Jarvis A	JS
Francis T	AB	Johnson S	LS
Froud J	LS	Jones J	OS
Gates 'Tony'	OS G	Jones J	CK O
Gibby 'Taff'	RO 2	Jones M	PO TEL
Gillard D	CERA	Kean 'Tom'	AB G
Goddard M	JRO	Keightle E	EM
Gommo R	AB G	Keith A	SA S
Gordon-Lennox M	LT NAV	Kelly B	RO3
Green J	AB G	King C	CH ME
Griffiths B	LS	Lally D	AB FC
Gude M	LT SUP	Lavender F	REA1
Gustard H	JS	Lawn 'Bill'	RS
Gyseman K	LME	Lawton J	LME
Hague 'Chas'	RO 3	Lee G	AB
Hall D	ERA 1	Lewis D	L STWD
Halligan J	LMA	Lingguard R	AB G
Harbour D	CAW APP	Lloyd P	AB
Harris D	AB	Lordon J	AB
Harrison L	LEM	Mace P	SA
Haynorth J	POME	Makin J	ME2
Hervey J	CDR CO★★	Maple K	PO
Heslop G	LEM	Marshall M	EM
Hewett K	JME 2	Martin B	AB
Hidden J	OA 1	Martin 'Pincher'	ME
Hill D	OS	Mathews 'Pedro'	AB

McCAulay P			Polin J	OS
McIntosh D	SUB LT. Diver		Pool C	S LT
MacMahon T	AB		Port V	RA
Meads N	ME2		Prestwich J	AB
Mellor R	LME		Priestley D	AB
Mellers G	RO2 T		Puddifoot G	PO SA S
Miller K	CH EL		Ralph I	PO CK S
Millward W	LME		Read J	LEM
Mohammed I	Officer N.N.		Richards P	OS
Moore G	POME		Richardson D	AB
Mosdell Brian	LT 2ndWEO		Riley P	OS
Mumford I	ELM1		Ringham	LME
Murray R	EA1		Roberts F	RO G
Musson J. CB	LT SUPP ★		Robins R	EM
Nesbitt J	LME		Robinson G	CK S
New A	PO		Robson G	POME
Newnes K	LRO T		Rolfe 'Rolfey'	ME1
Norton R	JME1		Rosenkranz 'Rosie'	AB RP2
O'Donoghue J	EA3		Rosser D	OS
O'regan T	CK S		Rowe P	AB
Palmer A	AB		Rule K	AB
Parkes G	ME2		Russell I	ME1
Parrot 'Polly'	RO3		Rustin R	JME2
Parrish G	POME		Salisbury A	JA STWD
Paton A			Sanderson J	CPO GI
Payne 'Bob'	RO3		Scriven M	OS
Peake W	OS		Shardlow 'Sharky'	ME1
Penn A	PO STWD		Shield R	ERA3
Penney J	A/L CK S		Skillin E	SUB LT G
Pierce Jones R	ERA3		Smith K	JA STWD
Pike I	CPO		Smith N	MIDSMN
Pincott G	LT CDR		Smith T	AB
Pisani P			Smith B	AB
Pitcairn T	ELM		Sosso D	STWD

Spencer M	WRTR	Weaver M	JS
Spratt D	SA V	Webb R	REL
Steel R	LT EO	Webster V	LT 1st. WEO
Stephen V	CK	Wesson P	ME1
Stevens R	JRO	Wharton R	RO2
Stevens T	EM	Whetler S	W APP
Stewart T	AB	White J	AB
Stone P	LT CDR	White P	LT
Streetling A	ME1	Widley C	LT?
Sutcliffe B	EM	Wilkie K	OS
Swales A	WM3	Wilkinson B	ME1
Swetman D	LT?	Wilkinson M	PO SA V
Swick L	ME2	Williams J	ME2
Talbot T	SA	Willis G	EM
Taylor T	OS	Willis T	LS UW2
Tennant A	AB	Wilson E	JME1
Thomas R	AB	Wilson R	ME1
Thomas 'Billy'	OEM	Woods F	AB
Thompson B	COMMS	Wright I	ME1
Thurston C	PO WRTR	Yates A	AB G
Tiley W	ERA2		
Toland 'Jock'	RO2		
Trapnell M	AB		
Tremlett K	PO		
Trigg M	LSA S		
Vale J	ME1		
Van Der Steen A			
Warne W	CHME		
Warner A	REA2		
Waterhouse R	LME		
Watkinson M	LT CDR		
Watson 'Soapy'	AB G		
Wattam B	EM		
Wavish A (1969)	CDR CO		

★ Later Rear Admiral Robin
Musson.

★★ Later Rear Admiral John
Hervey CB OBE FIMGT

No surgeon was normally carried

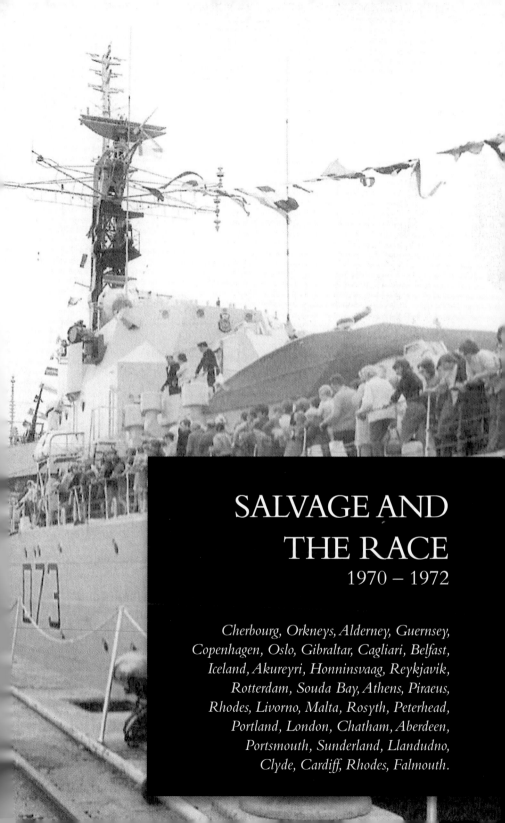

SALVAGE AND
THE RACE
1970 – 1972

*Cherbourg, Orkneys, Alderney, Guernsey,
Copenhagen, Oslo, Gibraltar, Cagliari, Belfast,
Iceland, Akureyri, Honninsvaag, Reykjavik,
Rotterdam, Souda Bay, Athens, Piraeus,
Rhodes, Livorno, Malta, Rosyth, Peterhead,
Portland, London, Chatham, Aberdeen,
Portsmouth, Sunderland, Llandudno,
Clyde, Cardiff, Rhodes, Falmouth.*

SALVAGE AND THE RACE
1970 – 1972

CDR Clifford A. Snell RN
(Seventh commission)

CDR Snell joined the RN in 1945 as a 17 year old cadet and served in many ships among them 'Launceston Castle' and 'Diligence' the shore base and as the 1st LT of HMS Cassandra, 'Cavalier's' sister ship. He was Commander of the Blackwood frigate 'Russell' and training commander at HMS Ganges the boys training establishment. A short spell as executive officer of the County class destroyer 'Devonshire and then command of 'Cavalier' from 6th March 70 till the 7th July 1970. He left her to take up a post at the NATO Staff College in Rome. On retirement with the rank of captain he went on to serve for several years with the Royal Bahamas' defence force.

The commissioning ceremony took place on the 6th March 1971 at South Railway jetty Portsmouth, during the ceremony a snow storm developed. The Fleet Chaplain, the Venerable Archdeacon A. Weekes conducted the service. A Free Churches and a Catholic padre along with three of her former captains were also present.

LS REM Colin Powell; I joined 'Cavalier' as a member of the refit crew in Gibraltar in '69 and was onboard her when she sailed for Portsmouth and the commissioning service. The weather deteriorated as soon as we left harbour, by the time we got to the Bay of Biscay, of all places, it was at storm force 10 and the worst weather I ever experienced in my twelve years at sea. It happened at that time that the masthead steaming light failed. In view of the situation a volunteer was called for and I broke the golden rule of all sailors… 'You never volunteer for anything'. With the help of my immediate boss LREM Cliff 'Sharpie' Sharpe I was rigged out with tools and two replacement lamps which were attached to me by a line. A harness was fitted so that I would have both hands free. Before starting the climb I reported to CDR Snell on the bridge that I was going aloft (Normally the fuses were pulled and a board stating 'Man aloft' placed for safety). I managed to climb the mast up to the steaming light and just had time to secure the harness when I looked ahead and saw the biggest wave I had ever seen racing towards us and about to engulf the ship. I looked down and saw the bridge personnel scatter and dive under the shelter. The next two minutes was like being on a fun fair ride as the whole bow, including 'A' and 'B' guns disappeared under water. As the ship shook and shuddered and resurfaced the wave rolled along amidships and I was able to get a replacement lamp fitted before she dived under the next wave. Everyone on the bridge looked up frantically wondering whether I would still be there when the spray cleared. 'Cavalier' was the last ship in the Royal Navy with an open bridge. As I got down to the bridge the skipper came over and said 'Well done Powell an extra tot of rum for you tomorrow', and true to his word I had two tots that day'.

'They could not get forward for a couple of days to the galley for food'.
(Peter Fowler 'Caprice')

For a couple of days we were unable to get forward to the galley for food, some people didn't want it anyway. In the 'greenies' (electricians) mess most men were in their bunks but I was hungry so I heated a tin of tomato soup by hanging it over the toaster by a piece of string. The smell I think upset some people! By the second day my hunger was overcoming my fear so choosing my moment I went forward over the flying catwalk. In the port passage by the galley was sprawled a group of soldiers who were on passage with us to the UK, they were not well! I collected some fish chips and peas and started to make my way aft the way I had come. Half way there the peas and chips blew away, the fish which I was holding down with my thumb went next, leaving the little tail bit under my thumb! I went back for more, which luckily they gave me and I ate it there. I must say although the food was not exactly gourmet the cooks we had were brilliant.

Ron Cooper AB: 'I joined 'Cavalier' in February 1970, I had just returned from the Far East on the frigate 'Jaguar'. I was in the first leave party from her and just before my leave expired I found myself in the Army Hospital at Woolwich with a big abscess on my shoulder. I was operated on and then spent two weeks convalescing with the Army. Then I found that due to a lack of communication I had been posted by the Navy as a deserter, AWOL from leave. That was eventually sorted out before I got jailed, but on returning to 'Jaguar' at Chatham I discovered that my kit bag and kit had gone missing, it wasn't on the ship or in the 'Pembroke' baggage store. The Rating Control centre staff had an idea; it may have been sent on to Portsmouth or direct to 'Cavalier', so they issued me a travel warrant and sent me off to Portsmouth, thereby washing their hands of me! 'No Son your kit's not here' said the Coxswain as I joined 'Cavalier' and stood there in my No.8 working dress, with no cap and a pair of brown suede shoes! I did my joining routine, watch and station bill and then met the GI, who looked me up and down; 'I'm glad you're tall, he said 'cos you are in the guard for the commissioning ceremony'. 'But I haven't got a blue suit GI' I said. 'Or shoes' he said looking down! 'You'd better get one, we commission next week and you'll stick out like a sore thumb in a guard dressed like that'. The Coxswain found a hat and steaming boots for me so that I didn't attract too much comment and was sent ashore to 'Victory' barracks store and scran bag (lost/found uniform). There a suit was cobbled together for me, the top was a different tone from the bottom but it was passable. I eventually replaced all I'd lost... but it took four years to get a kit bag. On commissioning day I stepped onto the upper deck fully booted and gaitered and carrying my rifle ready to join the guard. I heard the gunnery officer say to the GI 'If they all look like that GI we are laughing', I breathed a big sigh of relief.

During the commission I once had the misfortune of making my way up the port side break ladder and as my head popped over the top I saw a wall of green water sweeping along the deck towards me. There was nothing for it but head down, hug the ladder as tight as I could and pray that I and the ladder were still there when my bath had finished. Whilst operating with the 'Ark Royal' one day we were making towards Oslo for a visit, as we had been at sea for some time we looked like a bunch of pirates with long hair, so, the captain had the civilian NAAFI barber from the 'Ark' brought over by helicopter to sheer us all like a lot of sheep… however his plan backfired because with the ship going up and down about thirty feet at a time (Approx. 10 metres) the barber, being used to big ships was soon turning from grey to green and then became very seasick before he could sheer anyone'.

In May 1970 she was taking part in operation 'Oceanex' after which she sailed from Plymouth to Cherbourg. From there on the 30th May she took ex WWII Alderney Deportees, who had been concentration camp victims, to take part in the memorial service on Alderney.

Because of her speed she was in demand for escorting the carriers, firstly 'Albion' and then 'Ark Royal' off the Orkneys and between 1st July and the 9th down in the Bristol Channel. This was followed by a further visit back to Alderney on the 18th August and then on to Copenhagen.

On the 31st July 1970 over three hundred years of the navy's traditional rum issue come to an end, black armbands were worn and the last tot was drunk with great ceremony throughout the fleet. The actual last official tot was believed to have been drunk onboard HMS Fife as she was in Pearl Harbour and being over the date line on the 1st August put her calendar back to the 31st July

Afterwards they buried the rum barrel at sea from under a Union Jack and rifles were carried reversed during the ceremony. A passing Japanese Admiral thinking it was a pucker burial stopped his barge and saluted... then watched bemused as the barrel was retrieved on the end of a line and the crew danced the hula hula in grass skirts!

Major J. Rodwell, A brown job (army): 17th August 1970. I was a young officer in the Grenadier Guards when I had the great pleasure of being seconded to 'Cavalier' as temporary ADC to an Admiral who was to be delivered to the Channel Islands and the Lt. Colonel's visit to Guernsey. Following this duty I was asked to stay aboard when on the 21st August we would pay a visit to Copenhagen. I managed to obtain a small military band from the Guards Depot and they provided musical entertainment on the trip. As we entered harbour we passed the USS Guadalcanal which had lined her decks to pipe us in.

The stokers mess deck, the last tot is drunk, black arm bands are worn. This picture also illustrates just how over crowded the messes were when most of them were present at the same time.

I caused embarrassment to the Captain by having the Band play *'Any Old Iron'* as we sailed past her! Signals were exchanged but luckily most of the ship's company thought it highly amusing. I somehow managed to stay onboard when we later took part in an exercise called 'Northern Wedding' and was allowed to fire one of the guns. I still have as prized possessions two brass cartridges either side of my fireplace. I so enjoyed my experience on 'Cavalier' that I went on to become Army Directing Staff at the RN College at Greenwich and served more time on other ships.

Ship's Company fell in for divisions on the jetty in Copenhagen 21st – 26th August 1970. This gives a good illustration of how many men were crammed into this small ship.

MS *Saint Brandon* salvage: This ship was a small coaster which caught fire in storm force ten winds in the Bristol Channel. Fire at sea is a frightening experience at the best of times but in rough weather it can be absolutely terrifying. After several explosions the crew was unable to contain the fire and sent off an SOS. They abandoned the coaster and took to their life rafts; they were picked up by the French Trawler *'Henri Callogh'*. At 2300hrs on Tuesday the 8th September

1970 whilst exercising in the Bristol Channel with 'Ark Royal', 'Cavalier' picked up a message from the St Anne's Coastguard about the fire on the *Saint Brandon* and raced towards the area. She arrived at 0300hrs on Wednesday to find the ship burning furiously and with occasional explosions still taking place at the stern end. It was too rough to board and take her in tow so she stood by her to act as a navigation warning to other shipping. At dawn the next day they considered taking her in tow, but before they could do that the wind increased to storm force eleven and then to force twelve and, as putting a boarding party aboard her was out of the question they retired to the leeward of Lundy Island, which lies eleven miles north of Hartland Point in Devon to ride out the worst of the weather. They had worked out that, with the current, wind and tides the *Saint Brandon* would pass about seven miles north of Lundy at about 2100hrs. Lo and behold there she was as expected on radar; however the radar contact was eventually lost at 0515hrs when it drifted out of range. At 0600hrs on the Thursday 'Cavalier' left the lee of Lundy and closed the expected position of the derelict. They found her at 0730hrs still afloat and with the fires died down to a smoulder. There was still a storm force ten wind but the seas had moderated, it was now time to consider attempting to board her and take her in tow.

They found her gutted by fire and her hatches blown off in an explosion.

A volunteer boarding party was mustered and the Rigid Inflatable Boat was launched. The boarding party managed to get into the RIB and despite the rough seas made their way to the derelict which was being thrown about violently. After an extremely hazardous operation they managed to get the party onto her deck and by 1030hrs they had got a tow line passed to 'Cavalier's' quarterdeck, the men working there were continuously being swamped by waves breaking over them.

The small RIB was launched to get a towing party onto the wreck.

The boarding party has got onto the derelict and 'Cavalier' edges closer to fire a Costain gun line across; this will be used to pull a much heavier tow line over. The gun line had a bronze rod attached to it which went into the barrel of a .303 rifle. The towing crew had to keep under cover until the line was fired! (D. Thompson)

Very slowly both ships started to move forward at about three knots; just about walking pace, but at 1615hrs the tow parted and hopes that had been slowly rising were dashed. The storm by this time had moderated to force eight and 'Cavalier' was able to manoeuvre back into position and the tow was again secured in record time. After much agonizing and fine adjustments to the ship's speed at 0400hrs on the Friday the *Saint Brandon* was finally brought into Milford Haven and handed over to the Port Authorities.

Towing the MS *Saint Brandon* in a storm involved quite a feat of seamanship, to get aboard and rig a towing cable would have been extremely dangerous. Cables when breaking under stress have been known to whip back with fatal consequences. In this picture some of "Cavalier's" life rafts down aft have been washed away. (RAF St Mawgan)

Members of the boarding party were: LT CDR 'Mike' Jones, LS 'Mike' Dann, AB Peter Reynolds, AB Keith Hart, AB Mario Sanderson, PO 'Bill' Blake, LS Eric Sanderson, AB 'Tony' Grayson and AB John Gerrard. Tradition and the law of the sea dictated that the salvage reward would be divided amongst the crew onboard at the time in the following manner; CPT = 60 shares, CPO's = 10, PO's = 8, LS = 6, AB's = 5, and each OD = 3 shares. The ship was valued at £7,000 and the cargo, a huge copper boiler was £160,000; however the net salvage was expected to be a total of £70, 000. A comment was jokingly made by one of the crew that he would see everyone in the Bahamas… and coincidentally that is where, several years later, CDR Snell went to work and then retire to!

OD Danny Spinks; 'I was just sixteen years old and a junior seaman, when I joined 'Cavalier' I was very green around the ears; I was shy and did not drink! The ship was in Pompey and I can remember going aboard struggling with my kit bag and thinking 'This ship is a bit old'. When I made it down to the mess I was approached by the butcher, John Danforth, who took me to the frwd showers and lectured me on hygiene, I was to shower every day and wash my hammock once a week. He told me he was to be my 'Sea Dad'. He took me on my first run ashore in Pompey and introduced me to Scrumpy (Very rough, cheap, strong cider), I had two pints and felt ill, he then bought me a rum telling me it would make me feel better…I believed him… it didn't and I was Tom and Dick! I was not allowed in the mess when the rum was being dished out, I used to stand in the doorway looking on in amazement; however my 'Sea Dad' was also the rum bosun so on occasions he would let me have sippers. My action station was on 'B' gun and if we had a bad shoot the G.I. would make us stand with a shell above our heads (approx. 24 kilo).

When we were towing the *Saint Brandon* I was on the rope when it parted and it flung me into the back of 'Y' gun. I had no feeling in my arms and was transferred by helicopter to the sick bay of the aircraft carrier 'Ark Royal' for x-rays. Luckily no bones were broken; I was brought back to 'Cavalier' and put into the sick cot in the sick bay for a short while.

I didn't know what a cockroach was until I joined 'Cavalier'! Whilst we were alongside in Malta the G.I. said he was organizing a Maltese dog shoot, he said the Maltese government wanted the wild dogs culled, anybody interested in taking part was to fall in on the jetty dressed in No8's, trousers tucked in socks, sleeves rolled down with full anti flash gear and helmets. About ten men fell in kitted out and waiting… luckily I had already been told it was a 'wind up'! (Maltese Dog is a navy euphemism for the runs or diarrhoea after a drinking session) I soon learned not to backchat my elders though, having done so one day I was cut out of my hammock and deposited on the deck'!

Harry Dormer, LT CDR, Royal Naval Reserve: 'I was a merchant navy officer and had been on the Royal Naval Reserve list since the 1950's. From time to time the navy would draft me to a ship for refresher training. Amongst others I had spent time on the 'Acute' and the 'Galatea' at that time I was the First Officer (training) on the QE2. In 1971 whilst serving on the liner 'Lanconia' I received orders to join HMS Cavalier in Malta. I flew to Malta and arrived onboard at 0100hrs, I could do very little at that time of night so I kipped on the wardroom sofa! After breakfast we sailed for Cagliari, Italy to show the flag. I went onto the bridge and met the captain CDR Snell, a charming man. It was a bit of a shock to the system to find she had an open bridge… I was used to a well heated glass-enclosed bridge on liners! My draft had been at short notice and I had no foul weather gear, but someone kindly kitted me out with some. We had not long left Grand Harbour when the Captain asked for a meeting of his officers about the forthcoming visit to Italy… he asked me if I was happy to take over the con. *I had only just arrived and this man was handing over his ship to me…* I was hooked! It was then brought home to me one of the principal differences between being on the bridge of a Royal navy warship and a passenger ship, rapid, quick fire messages were coming and going over the radio and Aldis lamp which required answering. I had to quickly introduce myself as a Reserve Officer and ask for them to slow down their delivery slightly… this they did with heavy exaggeration! Back alongside in Malta the 1st LT, Mike Jones buckled his sword round my waist and told me I was to meet and greet CPT 'D' who was coming aboard shortly, this came as a bit of a shock, although I also felt it to be an honour. There was something about that ship. I look back with great fondness on the times I spent with her and her crew. When I was finally due to return to the real world the Petty Officers saw to it that I felt no pain!'

Harry Dormer LT CDR RNR greets CPT 'D' on the iron deck amidships.

Harry's wife Hermione had had connections with 'Cavalier's old stomping grounds, Malaya, and it was one of the reasons that 'Cavalier' whilst there did 'guard ship' (Standing by to evacuate civilians in the event of trouble). During WWII Hermione was just a young girl and her father was a rubber plantation manager. He just managed to get her and her mother to Singapore and away on one of the ships that managed to escape before the Japanese invasion overwhelmed them. Her father was a volunteer in the local defence force and was later captured and spent several years in the infamous Changi jail.

CDR P.M. Goddard RN, a 'Hairy Fairy' (Fleet Air Arm pilot)

At Chatham on the 6th July 1971 CDR Snell left to take up another post and CDR Goddard took command on the 12th. To start with the crew was slightly bemused to see a 'Hairy Fairy' driving a destroyer. In the past it was usually because they'd crashed several planes that they were grounded. However this was not so in this case, these commanders had to do a period in command of a smaller ship to qualify for further advancement.

He joined the Royal Navy in 1955, trained as an observer in the Fleet Air Arm and served with 849 Squadron (Airborne Early Warning). He flew in aircraft from carriers such as 'Ocean', 'Eagle' and 'Ark Royal'. In 1960 he trained on Sea Vixens and Venoms, all weather jet fighter aircraft from 'Victorious' and 'Hermes'. He planned the RN team challenge in the Trans-Atlantic Air Race and was in the winning Phantom. He was later appointed as Senior Observer of 892 Squadron (Phantoms) in the carrier 'Ark Royal'. He took command of 'Cavalier' on the 12th July 1971.

CDR Peter Goddard in his day cabin

In October 1971 whilst in the Med, an inspection by the ship's divers showed there was a crack in one of the propellers, as a result they ordered a spare prop to be on hand when she was dry docked in Gibraltar on 22nd October, she was there until 2nd November. The spare prop (about four tons of it) was flown out from England but after the ship was docked down they discovered that the crack was actually an old repair! This particular propeller, removed from the ship is now mounted on a plinth and is on display on the sea front at Cowes on the Isle of Wight, it is a memorial to her builders: the repair is still evident.

Ice cream man's convention… no, some of the Chiefs in their tropical uniforms. They had just paraded for Sunday Divisions in Gibraltar. From L to R: Nick Carter MEA (H)1, John Lesley REMN1, Harry Wood COEA, Gerry Gooding CHMEM, Tom McGhee CPO (Buffer), Barry Russell OEA(O)1, Charlie Partridge CEMN1, David Thompson OEA(O)1 and Charlie Thompson CCEMN(L). In the background is the harbour mole.

David Thompson OEA: 'One morning in October whilst we were in the dry dock in Gibraltar, I and my party were about to carry out some routine maintenance on 'A' gun, someone noticed what they thought was a bundle of rags on the bottom of the dry dock. On closer inspection it was realised that it was a body. It is believed he had been drinking in a night club near the 'English Steps' during the night and on his return had fallen into the dock some fifty feet down'.

John Skelton LT CDR (Engineering Officer) – Prelude to The Race: 'On 18th September 1970 we were taking part in the NATO exercise 'Northern Wedding'. It was that time of the year when the shore based staff officers can play 'cops and robbers' with real ships! We had been in commission about six months and had shaken down pretty well… considering all my engine room staff were Diesel trained… (*'Cavalier' was FFO, oil*) I thought this was the warped sense of humour of the Commodore Naval Drafting but it turned out they were destined to join HMS Jaguar but because 'Lincoln' had lost a propeller in the West Indies, rather careless I thought, 'Jaguar went into refit at Chatham to eventually take her place, Chatham dockyard on seeing the state of her fell about laughing and suggested three years would be nearer to a completion date than three months… hence we ended up with their engine room staff.

LT CDR John Skelton, Engineering officer, with his team of stokers ready for divisions on the jetty in Copenhagen, 14th May 1971. The propeller on their sleeves indicates engineering.

'Cavalier' was good news to 'Ark Royal' as she was fast enough to act as plane guard and keep up with her when flying off her aircraft. This went on night and day. In between times we went out to the edge of the screen to watch for any 'enemy' that may be attacking. We chased the 'Ark' at 0600hrs to launch her first flight of the day and then resumed our position in the screen. Shortly after arriving we picked up a surface contact on radar which we assumed was 'enemy' (Orange Force) and made our way towards her at 30 knots. A stern chase developed and as we started to gain on her the gunnery teams were carrying out tracking runs.

At 'stand easy' in the stoker's mess. Behind can be seen one rating in his bunk, probably on 'make and mend' having had the middle watch. Behind him can just be seen the hammocks in their stowage. From the right 'Lonely' Harris LMEM, P.Yarman MEM1, P. Swanston LMEM, A. Hirst JMEM, D. Dugmore MEM1, F.Ware JMEM and one of the 'Tiffies' (Artificers) in the foreground.

As we got within visual range we discovered it was HMS Rapid, another wartime destroyer converted to a frigate and commanded by LT CDR W. Kelly. She was not taking part in the exercise; she was based at Rosyth and had a training team onboard from HMS Caledonia, (Engineering training school). We returned to the fleet exercise and forgot about the diversion until about two weeks later a signal was received… *'Rapid to Cavalier; my full speed power trial – 31.5 knots. The gauntlet is down'*. We saw this as impertinence coming from a destroyer de-rated to a frigate! Back went the reply; *'Not bad for a frigate. Hope to take you up on it sometime'*. It was to be nine months later.'

Before returning to Chatham she paid a visit to Belfast (2 – 7th June) and then Aberdeen on the 8th June. It was in Aberdeen that Miss World; Jennifer Hosten came onboard along with the Aberdeen Festival Queen Heather Green and Miss Grant's Whiskey Linda Paterson.

A visit by the beauty queens to Cavalier's wardroom.

David Thompson OA: 'On the 29th April 1971 my son Roy was born in Portsmouth whilst 'Cavalier' was in Liverpool for the Captain Walker Old boys reunion. On the 1st August 1971 on our return to Chatham he was christened in the ship's Wardroom by the padre, the Reverend D. Prosser (Chaplain from HMS Pembroke). As is the custom his name was etched on the inside rim of the ship's best bell'.

It was then back to work and a spell off Iceland on Fishery protection, patrolling up and down keeping the Icelandic gunboats from attacking our trawlers. From time to time they were supplied with some lovely fresh cod from the trawlers, it didn't come any fresher. They also paid visits to Reykjavik and Akureyri. Very often during these patrols, which could last up to several weeks, some captain's would order the crew to stop shaving, then have a competition at the end to see who had grown the biggest beard.

Roger 'Iggy' Bliss, AB: 'Whilst we were in the Med. We were sent to Malta in bit of a rush. Dom Mintoff who was the anti-British Prime Minister at the time of an independent Malta was ejecting all British troops from the island and allying himself with Colonel Gaddafi. It was a tense time and I was part of an armed party that was sent to cover the withdrawal. Along with the GI Alf Batley we guarded the old Admiralty buildings in Valetta whilst they were vacated. Everything was left there even down to the furniture, cutlery and crockery'.

The other extreme, the Arctic. Roger 'Iggy' Bliss AB (Navigators Yeoman)
sporting a full set during fishery protection patrol off Iceland.

Back in the UK, on the 5th July 1971 they called in at Peterhead
and were due to conduct a full power trial the following day. These
were carried out about once or twice a year or in emergency
situations. After a night at Rosyth they would RAS (refuel) and head
to Chatham for leave. However whilst at Peterhead there was an
incident which occurred ashore that would have fitted well in a
scene from the comedy film the 'Navy Lark'! Cavalier's motor boat
was alongside in the harbour when a dispute arose between some

of 'Cavalier's crew and the crew of the Leith fishing boat *'Elysian'*. One of the fishermen tried to untie the rope holding the boat and as it pulled away he was dragged into the water and towed some way into the harbour. He was eventually dragged out of the water and returned to the dock where, on seeing one of 'Cavalier's crew bending over... booted him up the backside and pitched him into the harbour! He was arrested and ended up paying a fine of £15 at court for a breach of the peace!

Saviour 'Tony' Falzon, LMEM: 'Whilst escorting the 'Ark Royal' one day we were diverted to investigate a Russian cruiser that had entered British waters and was shadowing a NATO exercise. We went off at near full speed after them. When we caught up with them we went quite close to them and some of the men stood on the iron deck throwing spuds at them (I bet that got them worried, no wonder they never attacked the West!). Having 'seen them off the premises' we had run lower on fuel than was normally permissible and as we were now a long way off from our RFA tanker, it was arranged that we would call in at Honninsvaag in Norway to refuel. I can't remember now why but we had to gravity feed the fuel into the tanks, either there was something wrong with their pumping gear or it wasn't compatible and it took nearly all day. My abiding memory of that place was the smell: I presume it was a fishing port, I do remember it was extremely cold'.

John Skelton EO, The Race: 'Careful liaison between the two CO's over several weeks had ensured that the two ships would meet off Peterhead on the 6th and race down the North Sea. It was one of the Navy's worse kept secrets, not only had it been arranged that press representatives would have a place onboard but odds were being quoted by Ladbrokes bookies! The Daily Telegraph newspaper was offering a silver salver to the winner and it was arranged that the losing ship would host a party for the winners in their wardroom. This nearly all went for a ball of chalk when 'Cavalier' was diverted from her fishery patrol to go chasing some Russians who were close to entering our waters off North Cape. We shadowed them and were uncertain as to whether we would get back in time for the race. We were also conscious that 'Rapid' had all the time to prepare and with the added specialist engineering team from 'Caledonia'. These types of ship run better when deep loaded but we had already used quite a bit of our fuel. The 6th July arrived and with it an air of expectancy by everyone onboard, after all we had coped with everything that Western Fleet had thrown our way'.

Taking on fuel, 'Cavalier' alongside in Honninsvaag Norway. Seen here is 'Tony' Falzon, being an LMEM he would have been involved in the refuelling. Snow can be seen on the mountains ahead of the ship.

'Rapid' appeared on time at 0830hrs and we got under way making for the start line. (The race was to take place off Kinnaird Head, Aberdeen). BY the time we reached the start line the boilers were nicely warmed up, a few adjustments to position, a flare was fired and they were off with both ships already doing in excess of 30 knots. It was truly a magnificent sight – huge bow waves; propellers throwing up great jets of water astern which seemed to hover over the vibrating quarterdeck. The press was fascinated by this and crowded the quarterdeck to feel the power and look at the wake above them. The roar of the engine room fans pumping air directly into the boilers could be heard throughout the ship. Everything was controlled by hand, fan speed, fuel pressure and temperature, check the burners were atomizing correctly, check the mirror to keep a clear funnel. It was too noisy to even shout so the POME passed his orders by hand signal and his team responded instantly – they had to – each of those

boilers had 20,000 horses at full pelt and you don't control them with a slack rein'.

LT CDR William Kelly on Rapid's bridge checks the bearing of 'Cavalier' as the two ships line up for the start. (Scottish Daily Express)

A flare goes up over 'Rapid' and they were off with her building up a huge bow wave. (Phil Cowling SA)

'Cavalier' in a floating dock and showing her two huge propellers.

As in the past light hearted messages were sent from ship to ship using biblical phrases:

'Cavalier' to 'Rapid': *'Job 15-21'*. (If you did not know what it meant then you looked it up…) *'A dreadful sound is in his ears, in prosperity the destroyer shall come upon him.'*

'Rapid' to 'Cavalier': *'And he saith unto me, seal not the saying of the prophecy of this (signal) for the time is at hand.'*

'Cavalier' to 'Rapid': *'Jeremiah 22-7… And I will prepare destroyers against thee, everyone with his weapons, and they shall cut down my choice cedars and cast them into the fire.'*

In the engine room the great throttles had been wound wide open. The engines were turning at maximum revolutions and the whine of the generators and feed pumps added to the sense of speed. The Chief of the watch and his team were checking the hundred and one parameters that kept everything running – levels in the main feed tank and condensers, check the feed water with silver nitrate, keep the condenser vacuum up. With the speed of the ship the main circulators would not need steam – more for the main engines. All was controlled activity; teamwork with everyone involved. After the start of the run 'Rapid' drew very slightly ahead and the press was under the impression that this was to be the pattern of the race. Our Officer of the watch on the bridge and other observers passed information down to the engine room staff. Constant checking down below bore fruit, a group valve, almost redundant and never used was found to be partially closed. It was opened fully and the revolutions crept up and yard by yard we started to overhaul 'Rapid'. 'Rapid' ordered some of her men aft to allow the props to bite deeper then 'Cavalier' did the same.

'Cavalier' right and 'Rapid' both at full power. It was exhilarating to stand on the vibrating quarter deck and feel the power under your feet. The jet of water being expelled behind the ship was higher than a man standing on the deck. Both of the ten foot diameter bronze propellers weighing nearly four tons each, at this stage would be turning some 317 revolutions per minute.

An hour and a half after the start and we were abeam of her and still slowly gaining, then 'Rapid' lifted a safety valve and we knew we had it in the bag. Two hours after the starting gun and sixty four miles later the green Very light was fired to signal the end of the race…. 'Cavalier' was ahead by all of thirty yards. We were checked doing over 32 knots, not bad for a twenty seven year old destroyer. I do remember our wardroom team did an excellent job in drinking 'Rapid's' wardroom dry in Rosyth that evening'.

Migrating swallows stopped off to watch the race. Very often birds being wet and tired from long ocean journeys would rest on the ship before flying on to their destination.

Josh Cosnett, LT CDR: 'Some time prior to the race I was approached by members of the wardroom who wanted to know what the prize would be. I told them that there was no prize; it would be for the prestige. Whilst in London one day I decided to call on the transport manager of Courage's brewery at their Anchor Brewery on the south side of Tower Bridge. I suggested that as a cockerel was the traditional symbol of the winner of fleet exercises a cockerel from the roof of one of their Lorries, which was their company's symbol, would make an ideal prize. He told me that they had requests almost daily for these cockerels, particularly from the supporters of the Tottenham Hotspur football club. It was near lunchtime so I suggested that we go for lunch at a nearby pub and, having almost completed the second bottle of wine he said that we should repair to his office, get me a cockerel and let him get on with his work! The skipper arranged for the cockerel, which was all gold, to be painted by the dockyard, it came back with plumes looking like a magnificent Leghorn'.

For the next few months they were kept busy in the Med, and in home waters on exercises 'Deep Furrow', 'Highwood' and 'Easy Life'. On Operation 'Deep Furrow' she showed all the other ships, which included Greek, Italian and the USN how to shoot. They had all missed the target and when it came to 'Cavalier's' turn she blew it to pieces with one salvo.

They paid visits to Cagliari and in Livorno Italy, and Athens, Piraeus, Rhodes and a further visit to the Channel Islands.

John 'Yorkie' Emerson AB on the loss of one of his digits: We had just entered Chatham dockyard having been at sea and completed a shoot on the 4.5's. We had to drop the breaches on all three guns (They weighed about 300 kilos each) but had to wait until we had entered the basin before doing so. The armourers for all three guns. John 'Nobby' Hall, Mick Davies and I, got together and having done 'A' and 'B' guns went to 'Y' gun down aft. Without going into too many technicalities I had to get under the gun, release two cams and then put the spring cover back on. I heard Mick shout 'I'm going to release the tray', both I and Nobby shouted 'NO Mike, not covered yet', but it was too late the spring shot forward and took one of my fingers clean off at the knuckle. Thinking about it reminded me of the old school guillotine! I was taken by car to the Pembroke Hospital where they operated on me. I was discharged shortly after that because they needed the beds for a railway accident. The coxswain on seeing me gave me a railway warrant and told me to 'B.....r off on weekend till Tuesday'.

Mick Davies: I had removed the Breach Mechanism lever and unknown to me Yorkie had his hand in the spring when I closed it. It took his finger off. The SBA 'Doc' Murdoch cleaned it and covered it before getting him off to the hospital. They asked for the detached digit but it had fallen into a tin of graphite grease and was in bit of a mess. We later put it in cotton wool, put it in a matchbox and made a presentation of it to him. We wanted it as a mess trophy but he threw it away. He had a job scratching his nose from that day on'!

David Griggs PO: I was duty Petty Officer just before I left the ship when one of the gunnery ratings put his finger in a hole where he shouldn't have and it was chopped off. It was me who was given the job of driving him to the hospital with his greasy finger in an oily rag. I had a reliant three wheeler car, like the Trotters van in the TV series but mine was red not yellow!

Phil Bailey AB: 'This wasn't the only incident involving 'Y' gun. At Portland after doing some maintenance someone forgot to put the training stop back in. The next time we did a shoot the gun traversed a lot further round past the safety stops than it should have done and when it fired it came close to taking off the Squid handling room bulkhead! I was in there at the time and my hearing has never been the same since: I always blame 'Cavalier' when my boss asks me a question which I cannot answer… I revert to my 'war wound' deafness'!

David Thompson OA; 'We were touring the UK visiting various ports on a recruitment drive. Schools and cadet forces were invited to visit the ship. Before entering one port I asked the lads who looked after the 40-60 Bofors guns (either side of the bridge) to smarten them up and give them a coat of paint.

It may have been because I asked them to do it in the evening that I later got piped to the bridge! There I was faced by an irate Captain and the Weapons Electrical Officer waiting for me. 'Did you order someone to paint the Bofors?', 'Yes I did sir, I asked them to smarten them up for our visit tomorrow'. He said; 'Why are they being painted PINK?' 'PINK' I said as I dashed round the side of the bridge to look. Sure enough the starboard gun was a lovely bright pink. At the time there was a Pink Panther theme thing going on and the culprit said he thought the children would like it! I forget now what I said to the lad but I know I reported him and he appeared at the Jimmy's defaulters table the next day. It is not easy to wipe off a coat of wet paint and apply another but he was to paint it grey ASAP and in the morning … It was grey! In December we called in to Greenock, following exercises that had been going on since November. For one member of the Chief Petty Officers mess it was about as close to home as he was likely to get and he had his own 'up channel' (Stored rum) celebration and afterwards he crashed out on his bunk. Shortly afterwards a large chauffeur driven Rolls Royce appeared on the jetty with a Lady (for that's what she was) in the back. The quartermaster piped for her son, the chief and when I turned up I explained that he was 'unavailable' at the moment. She said 'Is he pissed then?' Although taken aback by such a question from such a lady I had to admit that he was… she replied 'That's my boy, can you bring him up for me so we can take him home please?'. So several men carried him up to the Rolls and off they went for the weekend. He returned to the ship on the Monday refreshed and ready to go'.

During the latter part of this commission schools from the ports they visited were invited to tour the ship: 1st and 2nd Feb, Cardiff, five schools. The 4th to the 8th Feb, Birkenhead, 2 sea cadet units, 30 blind children, 11 schools, 1 Sea Scout unit and 1 Scout unit, the Mayor and nearly two thousand other visitors came aboard. She returned to Chatham the 11th Feb.

Open to visitors

On the 18th February she left two men in the cells at 'Pembroke' barracks and then sailed for London, arriving on the 19th and berthing on the port side of 'Belfast'. 'Belfast' of course had been her old C in C flagship from the days in the Far East. On the outside of 'Cavalier' was berthed the frigate 'Hermione', one of the ships that the Prince of Wales had served on. Whilst in London a party of volunteers went off to the kitchens in the Savoy Hotel, four schools, a Sea Cadet unit, Brentwood Football club and Rear Admiral Pope visited the ship.

CH yeoman 'Tony' Batten poses for the press. Sometime after the 'great race' with 'Rapid', they moored in the river Thames alongside 'Belfast' in the centre of London; here they were presented with the magnificent 'Cock 'o the fleet' by Courage Brewery and a silver salver by the Daily Telegraph. (Courage Brewery)

Sport figured highly throughout the commission and they excelled in most:

The football team twice reached the semifinals of the Fleet Knock-out with professional coaching from Frank Blunstone and tuition from Gerry Gooding. Main strength was in midfield with John Richards, 'Scouse' Abley, Freddy Fredson, and Mick Miln. 'Scouse scored all five goals when we beat the cruiser 'Blake'. At the back George Temple, 'Burbs' McIntosh and Jonah did well against 'Penelope' in the KO cup in Gib. Others who did well were Pete Yarman and Jock Buchanan. On the wings was Steve Littlefair and Emms and up front

Shiner Wright and Phil Cowling. Memories of the drunks around the edge of the No1 pitch in Gib. will remain with us!

Alf Batley, PO GI: Whilst in Gibraltar we took the opportunity of doing our annual rifle shoot. Everything was going fine until Barry Crook the RPI, who had a .303 rifle in his hands with a full magazine, suddenly had a fit! Someone shouted to 'Put something between his teeth so that he doesn't bite his tongue'. I shouted, 'Never mind his bloody tongue, get the bloody rifle away from him'!

John Plumber, ASWO: 'For some unknown reason it became customary for the officers on the bridge to wear Deer Stalker hats during refuelling, in fact during a wardroom run ashore in Gibraltar the same deer stalkers were worn. We were thrown out of the officers club because we spilt beer on the dance floor whilst filling one of the deer stalkers'!

Hands across the sea, Livorno Italy 1972. A ship's crest is presented to the home team.

Before leaving Gibraltar they took some of the Gibraltar garrison out for a day at sea. They took the opportunity to get some Bren gun and live 81mm Mortar firing practice in, something they had difficulty doing in the limited space on the Rock. April 1972.

Another sport they excelled at was rifle shooting. A proud PO Gunnery
Instructor Alf Batley showing off the cup his lads won for their .22 shooting.
Judging by the smile on his face it was probably filled with rum!

She left the Med, for what was to be the last time on the 5th May
and made for home. There was a visit to Sunderland and Portsmouth
and an exercise with 'Ark Royal'. Then between the 22nd and 29th
June she paid her last foreign visit to Rotterdam before returning
to Portsmouth to de-store and de-ammunition ship. They knew it
was time for her to go. They had recently had trouble with some of
the pumps and when they had contacted 'Wiers', the manufacturers
they were told that the man who knew all about them had died a
couple of years ago and that they couldn't help! They had to resort
to rabbiting trips for spares from the ships waiting to go for scrap.

On the 5th July 'Cavalier' entered the Medway and tugs met her off
Sheppey carrying press and radiomen who boarded her for the trip
up the river. She moored in the river at Chatham for an official visit
and entertained the local dignitaries at Rochester.

5th July 1972, moored in the river Medway to fore and after buoys.
(Photo Section HMS Pembroke)

The Licensee and all the Staff of the
Ship Inn, Rochester
Extend a very hearty welcome to all
the company of

H.M.S. Cavalier
Bring along this card and receive a
pint of " TAVERN " Keg with our
Compliments
CHEERS

The crew was welcomed by the
city. I wonder if this is still valid!

On the 7th July 1972 she entered the Bull's Nose entrance to
Chatham docks (For what was thought to be the last time!). She was
flying a very long paying off pennant, supported at the end by two
inflated devices from the sickbay (Durex) to keep it out of the water!
A Royal Marine band was there to play her in and she sounded off
three long blasts on her ship's siren in reply. As she entered the basin
at Chatham, tugs nudged her alongside, the lines were secured to the
dockside and the captain spoke down the voice pipe for the last time

'Finished with main engines' and after twenty eight years of travelling the world and the millions of revolutions the props had turned... they would turn no more. She had travelled almost three quarters of a million miles during her twenty eight year career. For many of the some fifteen hundred men who had served in her over that time, it had been their formative years, she had been their home, and they had seen the world and fought the elements. Their memories and many of the friendships they had made would last a lifetime.

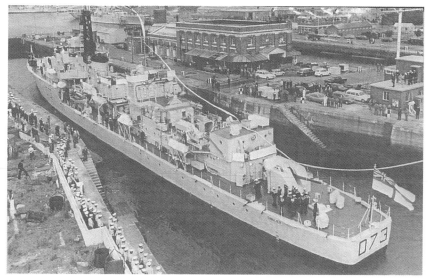

'Cavalier' enters the Bull's Nose lock to No3 Basin at Chatham looking as though she could go on for another 28 years.

Two weeks later the ensign was hauled down for the last time and she was put on the disposal list; **'For Sale, one well used destroyer'.** She appeared to be destined for the scrap heap again.

Little did they know that she was to survive for many years to come.

Being pre computer age someone must have trawled through a great deal of paper work to find this lot:

Since the 1970 commission started the ship has steamed 169,242 miles and visited 32 ports in nine countries.

730 gallons of grey paint had been used… (most of which went on the ship's side!).

420 gallons of deck paint.

1,032 paint brushes (many of which were lost over the side!).

428 torches and 3,510 batteries.

They ate:

16,000 yards of sausages (eight nautical miles).

130 tons of potatoes.

30,000,000 square inches of bread (three football pitches).

180,000 eggs (it would take one chicken 722 years to lay them.).

Tons of paper had been 'pushed' by the offices onboard but the clear winner was the GO who averaged 34 words per round fired from the guns.

The Naval Stores department was responsible for some 8,000 different items from ordinary nuts and bolts to complicated electronic components to strange items like 'Hand Portable Fog Horn … for the sounding of'!

Sports played and excelled at were basketball, volleyball, squash, tennis, badminton, cricket, rifle shooting, golf and water polo.

Since 1944 she had steamed a total of 564,140 nautical miles, nearly three quarters of a million land miles.

Mirror, mirror, on the wall

Who's the brightest of them all?

You are POTs without a doubt,

Thank you mirror, Roger, out.

(POT = Petty Officer Telegraphist)

Crew list 1970 – 72

There may be more men shown in this list than were required for one crew. The reason for this was that a new system of 'trickle drafting' had been introduced and men joined and left throughout the two year period instead of all joining on one date. This also accounts for why there are listed two 1st LT's, two canteen managers and so on.

Abley W	RO2 T
Acred T	L REM
Adams D	L REM
Addison A	MEA P1
Adlem V	AB
Allbut A	AB
Allen M	AB
Allen N	PO MEM
Ambler R	AB
Ashton H	LT CDR 1st LT
Back P	LS QA1
Backus A	LT
Bailey E	LMEM
Bailey P	AB
Bailey R	LSA
Baldechino V	NAAFI
Baldwin G	RO2 G
Barber K	OEMN3
Barclay M	L MEM
Barnes A	AB
Bate	C AB
Bateman R	L MEM
Batley N	PO GI
Batten A	PO CY
Battesworth G	RO3 G
Beard P	OEM1
Bee M	RS
Bennett R	J STWD
Beresford G	AB
Bevan D	AB
Birch C	S LT
Bird P	RO2 T
Blackhall W	PO OEL
Blake W	PO QA1
Bliss R	LS RP2
Bliss R	AB RP
Bond J	MEA P1
Bowden M	RO3 G
Brittain B	OD
Broad R	L MEM
Brooker D	SHRT 1
Brookes E	PO MEM
Brown I	L OEM
Brown S	L RO T
Byrne S	PO MEM
Buchanan D	AB
Burton T	L MEM
Bushnall E	AB
Calverley F	CPO COXN
Carrington L	CEA2
Carter C	MEA H1
Carter N	JA CK
Cartwright K	PO MEM
Chandler H	SURG LT
Chapman B	PO MEM

Chappell D	A STWD	Doherty A	JS
Chee Yee C	Laundry	Dormer H	LT Cdr
Chun Man Y	Laundry No1	Douglas M	OD
Clark J	AB	Downs G	AB
Clayton S	J MEM	Dray L	A CK
Cohen A	MEM1	Duffy M	JMEM
Colclough P	MEA P2	Dugmore G	MEM1
Conner F	L REM	Dunthorne J	AB
Cook I	MEM1	Dyball B	MEM2
Cooke R	CEM1	Dyson R	LSA
Cooper R	AB G	Easterbrook J	MID
Corrington T	PO OEL	Edwards G	MEM1
Cosnett J	LT CDR	Elliot P	AB
Counihan C	MEM1	Ellis D	AB
Cowling P	SA	Embery I	MECH1
Cox P	LSA	Emerson 'Yorkie' J	AB
Crawsham R	MEM1	Emms T	MID
Crocutt K	CH REL	Ethel W	L RO G
Crook B	PO RP	Evans D	JS
Crowley M	LT	Fagg G	OD
Cullen P	JA CK	Falzon S 'Tony'	L MEM
Curley P	AB	Farrow D	CEA1
Daly E	MECH1	Fish R	L CK
Dann M	LS GA	Fisher P	LS GL1
Davies D	CPO	Fleming F	PO RP
Davies M	AB	Fleming R	RO2 W
Davies M	MEA P2	Fowler J	CPO
Davison J	MEM1	Fox T	MEM
Deadman M	PO STWD	Franklin P	LS
Deeming D	MEM2	Fredson G	MEM1
Degorgio R	L MEM	Freeman C	LT
De Villiers see Miln		Frogley I	MEM1
Dicker M	CEM1	Gat J	NAAFI
Dixon R	AB	Gerrard J	LS

Giles W	LS	Horton P	RO2 G
Goddard P	CDR 2nd CO	Houghton K	PO CK
Gooding G	C MEM	Huddestone F	NAAFI
Grayson A	AB	Hull I	MECH3
Green N	AB	Hurrell L	AB RP
Griffiths P	LS FC	Husband P	MEA P2
Griggs D	PO	Hutchings M	AB
Grimsey R	RS	Irvine A	PO OEL
Gymer D	CK	Irvine G	PO STWD
Hall JH	AB	Ivens C	CK
Hall JI	AB	Jack R	MID
Hallet C	PO Ck	Jackson L	RO2 G
Hamersley R	LT	Johnson D	REM1
Harrington T	MEM1	Johnson J	PO
Harris B	RO2 T	Jones A	LT GO
Harris D	RO1 G	Jones C	L STWD
Harris L	JS	Jones M 2nd.	LT CDR 1st LT
Hart K	AB	Kay C	PO WTR
Harty D	REMN2	Kellegher D	OD
Haskett L	LT DR WEO	Kennard E	EMN L1
Hatton P	CK	Kennedy J	AB
Havis J	PO MEM	Kilbride D	AB
Hawking R	S LT MG	Kilburn G	MEM1
Hayes R	J MEM	Kirk P	CEMN App
Hazle M	PO MEM	Kwok Wah F	Laundry
Healy J	REMN1	Lace W	AB
Henson M	MEM1	Lauder A	PO MEM
Hews D	LT	Laws T	L CEM
Higgins J	MEM	Leach P	OEM1
Hinton N	AB	Lee R	LS
Hirst A	J MEM	Leech G	CEA
Hodgson C	MEM1	Lennard P	RO3 T
Hodson M	L STWD	Littlefair S	SA
Holder J	LT MEO	Lockwood J	C MEA P

Loftus M	MEM1	Oldjham P	L MEM
Low J	OD	Owen D	MEM1
Lynn W	MEM1	Ozbirn D	L REM
Macey D	OEMN1	Partridge C	CEMN1
Mann K	MEM1	Payne S	LRO W
Mapp J	OD	Pendlebury J	AB
Marshall D	PO RP1	Picken J	PO PTI
Mason B	JA CK	Pickering R	OD
Mason J	AB	Piggott G	LT
Matthews A	RO2 W	Pilkington M	STWD
McCarthy J	OD	Pink G	JS
McConnell G	LRO G	Pinn M	AB
McGhee T	CPO	Plummer J	LT ASWO
McGooghan M	MEM1	Plummer T	MEM1
McGuinness J	OD	Pogacic S	CK
McIntosh D	AB	Porter A	PO MEM
McIntosh D	OEA App	Powell C	LS PTI
McIntyre C	JS	Price D	AB
McNally G	MEA H App	Price P	PO
Mellors G	RO2 T	Prior M	J MEM
Miller A	MID	Pritchard G	MECH1
Miln M @ DeVilliers	L WTR	Proctor I	CK
Mitchell A	AB	Pulford M	REMN App
Mitchell R	MID	Purrington C	MEA H App
Moody R	PO	Quarney R	MEM1
Moorley W	AB	Rae G	PO
Murdoch A	LMA	Read P	LS
Muskett D	PO CK	Reed R	LS
Neale T	PO CA	Reid M	AB
Newson R	MEM1	Reynolds P	AB
Noble K	STWD	Rhodes A	JA STWD
O'Donoghue H	AB	Riby T	AB
O'Grady C	AB	Richards J	LS PTI
O'Loughlin P	MEM2	Richardson B	CEMN App

Richardson P	JS
Richardson P	LS RP2
Roberts A	L STWD
Roberts J	MECH3
Robinson J	C MEA P
Robinson K	RO1 G
Rogers G	PO OEL
Rogers R	J MEM
Rooney R	CEA2
Rossi C	RO2 T
Rothery M	
Rudkin R	NAAFI
Russell B	OEA O1
Russon J	L CK
Ryder J	L MEM
Samphire J	PO MEM
Sanderson E	LS RP
Sanderson L	AB
Saunders K	CK
Savage W	LT
Scheel M	OEM1
Scott P	JS
Sell R	RO2 G
Senior R	PO GI
Sewell P	AB
Seymour M	PO MEM
Shaul J	AB
Shaw K	MEM1
Shinkwin M	OD
Short K	J CEM
Silva D	L MEM
Silva J	MEA P2
Skelton J	LT CDR MEO
Slater R	CH OEL
Slaughter J	MEM1
Smith A	L MEM
Smith G	LT S
Smith M	PO MEM
Snell C	CDR 1st CO
Spark S	AB RP3
Spencer–Weare	RL OEM
Spiers M	AB
Sprinks D	OD
Stanfield N	L MEM1
Stanley P	AB
Stephen V	CK
Stephens B	CPO SA
Stephens D	AB
Stevenson R	L CK
Stickley R	OD
Stride A	RO2 G
Sutherland D	AB
Swanston P	L MEM
Taylor M	OD
Taylor O	CK
Taylor R	AB
Temple G	LS
Thompson D	OEA O1
Thomson C	C CEMN L
Thornhill A	MEA P2
Thornton P	OD
Tolman C	AB
Tuck C	
Tung Shing L	Laundry
Turner M	LS
Tustin R	MEM1
Wallace W	J MEM
Ward D	

Ware F	J MEM	**Chinese Laundry crew**
Warner R	AB	Man, Yeung Chun. No1 man
Watkinson M	LT CDR	Wah, Fong Kwok
Webb G	LT NAV	Shing, Lee Tung
Webster L	MEM1	Yee, Choi Chee
Wedge G	MEA H1	
Westlake P	OD	
Weston G	AB	
Whiffin T	L STWD	
White J	CK	
Wilkey R	MID	
Willett P	J MEM	
Williams E	MEM2	
Williams G	LRO T	
Williams R		
Williams S	MECH App	
Williams T	LS	
Williamson A	PO OEL	
Wills F	L OEM	
Wilson N	MEM2	
Winstanley T	MEM2	
Wise D	REA1	
Wood F	COEA L	
Woods F	PO OEl	
Woods L	JS	
Wright P	MEA P2	
Wright P	MEM1	
Wyatt A	CEM1	
Yarham P	MEM1	

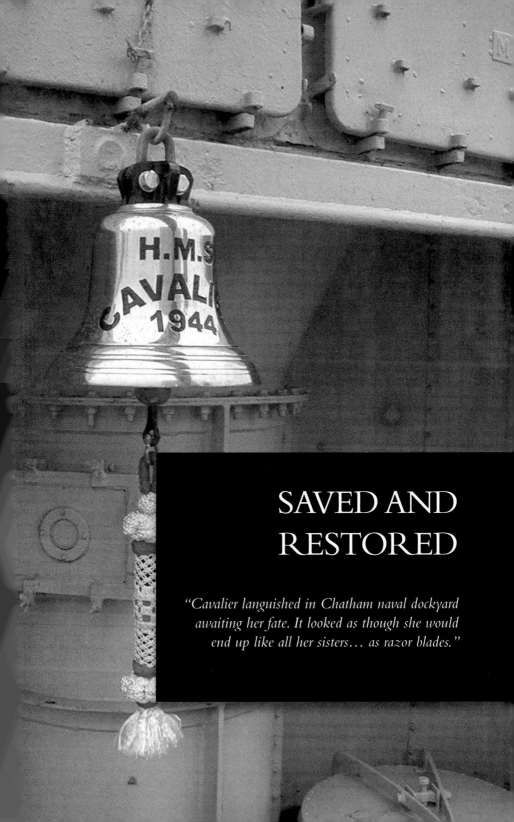

SAVED AND
RESTORED

"Cavalier languished in Chatham naval dockyard awaiting her fate. It looked as though she would end up like all her sisters… as razor blades."

SAVED AND RESTORED

In 1972 'Cavalier' was placed on the disposal list and languished in the then functioning Chatham naval dockyard awaiting her fate. It looked as though 'yet again' she would end up like all her sisters... as razor blades.

Then interest gathered apace by various parties to save her. Wasn't she the last of the Royal Navy's classic WWII destroyers, the Greyhounds of the sea, the ships that had fought the U-Boats, escorted the convoys that had kept open the supply lines to Britain in those dark days? She and her like had contributed so much to the winning of that war and keeping the peace worldwide in the succeeding years.

Principally among those looking to save her was Lord Louis Mountbatten, himself the dashing captain of the WWII destroyer HMS Kelly. It is almost certain that without his influence she would probably not have been saved. His letters from 'Dickie' to 'Harold' the prime minister of the day (to be found in the defence papers in the Public Record Office – Harold Wilson) show that he pushed in the first place to acquire her for a nominal £1, the same conditions under which the cruiser 'Belfast' was sold. This was refused by the Ministry of defence on the grounds that she was worth £100K in scrap and they could ill afford it at that time, the next letter quoted £150K. Eventually, after several other letters from 'Dickie' they agreed to a sum of £75K.

A trust was formed and chaired by Rear Admiral Douglas Parker, former commander of her sister ship 'Cavendish'. They headed an appeal to raise the £75K needed to save her. She was formally purchased and was towed to Portsmouth and then, with Lord Louis on the bridge she was towed into Southampton to go on display to the public. However the catchment area at Southampton was not big enough, the facilities were insufficient to sustain her in this isolated spot and she didn't earn her keep. She was moved to Brighton and failed for the same reasons. Eventually the owners of the land at Brighton Marina, where she was moored wanted to develop the site and she would have to go. Once again she teetered on the brink of destruction. Fortuitously about this time, South Tyneside Council up North was in the process of constructing a ship building heritage centre around the former Hawthorn Leslie & Co's shipyard. It was here that the famous destroyer HMS Kelly, Mountbatten's ship had been built so what better opportunity than to have a destroyer like 'Cavalier', which had the same basic hull structure, as the centre of that attraction. In 1987 they bought her for £91,000, towed her to South Tyneside and placed her in a dry dock. Unfortunately they failed to get funding for their project and 'Cavalier' lay there slowly deteriorating for the next 10 years. Thieves also raided the ship during this period and much of her original equipment and donations were stolen. A later survey showed that her stern which had not been properly supported for such a long period out of her natural element had sagged by four centimetres. Fortunately when she was refloated, being riveted the hull took up its original shape.

Although all the previous efforts in the different venues eventually failed it was the people at these places that kept her going. A series of volunteers, amongst them old sailors and the local sea cadets at South Shields had worked to maintain her. Although their efforts in themselves would never have been enough to preserve her long term it did go towards her eventual salvation, it was disappointing for them but they can take some sort of the credit for her still being here.

Another vital turning point had been reached, for the umpteenth time it looked as though the grim Scrap Reaper with his cutting torch was hovering nearby. With the lack of funding for their great project she had to go. She was placed on the market and, horror of horrors an offer of a token £1 to remove her from the dock was made by Star Cruises, a company based in Malaysia, who intended to make her into a theme park! This enraged so many people, in particular the men who had served in the Royal Navy in destroyers and especially those of her ex crew. MP's were swamped with letters and at least forty of the MPs wrote letters of protest to the then Minister for Culture, Media and Sport, Christopher Smith. Baroness Strange tabled a searching question in the House of Lords. A temporary order was sought and obtained to stop such a national treasure from obtaining an export license. This gave the several groups time to raise funds and raise awareness in the public. Many banded together under the recently formed HMS Cavalier Association and their chairman Sid Anning who worked tirelessly to save her. He had served on her in 1961/3 as an AB Gunner. The Associations president, Rear Admiral John Hervey CB OBE FBIM (Captain of 'Cavalier' 66/67) added weight 'in the right places'. Other groups such as the 'Friends of HMS Cavalier' under Frank Marsh, based at Chatham were formed and also started to raise funds. Many influential people along with the Association created awareness in the public by way of articles in the national newspapers. Other organizations got involved amongst them the Royal British Legion, HMCS Haida Coordinator (Canada), Warship Preservation Trust, The KGV Fund for Sailors, Heritage Afloat and many other groups and individuals. MPs were lobbied and funds started to pour in. These funds were not sufficient in themselves to buy and preserve the ship, but they did help to keep the fighting fund going.

About this time Admiral Sir William Staveley the Chairman of the Chatham Historic Dockyard Trust in Kent had just crossed the bar (He served on 'Cavalier' in '57 as a LT CDR). The author had written to Sir William on the Thursday asking if he could find a berth for 'Cavalier' as the historic dockyard was a bit sterile without a ship, he died on the weekend and I received a letter from his secretary saying that he had answered my letter before he crossed the bar... I was a bit concerned it may have been something I said!

Admiral Sir Nicholas Hunt took over the reins and he was approached about giving 'Cavalier' a berth and without hesitation agreed to make a dry dock available at a peppercorn rent, provided the funding could be found to purchase her in the first place.

Crucial to the ship's survival was a one day hearing before the Culture Media and Sport select committee. The HMS Cavalier Association committee and particularly their president Admiral John Hervey and Sir George Vallins (Also ex crew) had brought the ship's plight to the attention of some seventy two MPs, twelve of whom approached the chairman of the Parliamentary Select Committee, the Rt. Hon. Gerald Kaufman MP. He arranged for a one day hearing and on the 17th February 1998 he chaired the meeting along with the MP's, Derek Wyatt, Sittingbourne, Chris Fraser, Con. Michael Fabricant, Con. Damien Green, Ashford. Ronnie Fearn, Southport. Roger Stott, Wigan. Alan Keen, Feltham. Lin Golding, Newcastle. John Maxted and Claire Ward, Watford.

The room at the Houses of Parliament was packed with mainly ex sailors of all ranks, representatives from Chatham Dockyard Trust and Medway Council, South Tyneside Council and from the Imperial War Museum. There wasn't even standing room left. Expert witnesses were called and examined in a charged atmosphere, among them Sir Julian Oswald NHSC, Ms Anthea Case from the Heritage Lottery Fund and Mark Fisher then the Minister for Culture Media and Sport. At the end of the day Gerald Kaufman summed up by 'suggesting' that a Trust should be formed by the three main groups involved, the Chatham Historic Dockyard Trust, HMS Cavalier Association and the Friends of HMS Cavalier, this was set up as the 'HMS Cavalier (Chatham) Trust' in May 1998 and was chaired by Mrs Jane Sharman CBE, it was registered with the Central Charities Commission as Charity No. 1074598. He also suggested that the lottery fund should find the funds necessary to buy the ship dredge the dry dock at Hepburn and reinstate it and also to secure a tow for the ship to Chatham Dockyard. He said *'Without this ship and her likes we would not be sitting here now!'* The application was fast tracked as she had a month left before becoming scrap. The sum of £1.68m was eventually allotted her by the National Heritage Lottery fund for this purpose. The HMS Cavalier Association handed over £10,000, the residue of money left over from their campaign to save the ship. She was coming home, back to her old base at Chatham! On leaving the room Mr. Kaufman turned to the sailors crowded in the room and said *'I don't think I've ever seen a committee room so crowded. The fact that I've allowed you to barrack must not set a precedent, now I'll leave before I receive a broadside'.* Cheers echoed round the room.

On a momentous day in May 1999 a huge gathering of ex sailors and public crowds stood on the banks of the Medway to watch this proud ship being towed into Chatham dock by Smith's tugs of Sheerness. She had been carefully prepared for the tow down from the Tyne, with various openings welded up to prevent foundering (A high percentage of ships under tow have been lost). She was painted battleship grey, the wrong colour but once again that went towards preserving her so most people didn't care, we could alter that… she was saved. There were flags flying, a preserved WWII MTB escorted her and an Army re-enactment team fired off a twenty five pounder field gun in salute. She was placed in No3 Commercial basin to await a high tide that would allow her to enter her final resting place in No.2 dry dock. This dock was on the same site as the one where HMS Victory, Nelson's flagship,

Dockyard staff watch their new acquisition being eased into her final home by Smith's tugs.
(Author)

had been built in the 18th Century. Two weeks later when the tide
was right she was finally manoeuvred into that dock where she now
lies alongside the Victorian Naval Sloop HMS Gannet and HMS
Ocelot (submarine), the last warship built for the Royal Navy at
Chatham Dockyard.

On her arrival in Chatham in May 1999 the preservation started
almost immediately. A ship keeper was appointed by the Dockyard
Trust, Brian Sanders an old sailor. This time the restoration, with
the right funding and administration was going to be done properly.
A long term programme was put into place for her preservation by
The Chatham Historic Dockyard Trust. A small group of volunteers,
including the author, along with Mike Fleet and Ken Waddington
made a start on clearing accumulated rubbish and painting the inside
of the forward mess deck. In the early days with just a few volunteers
the painting was a daunting task; normally refitting a ship like this
would take gangs of experienced dockyard workers many weeks
or months and millions of pounds. There are over two hundred
compartments on the ship, one down...!

Some of the early volunteers who worked on restoring 'Cavalier' at Chatham, all brought their own expertise to the project. They worked every Wednesday and some several other days as well. New volunteers continue to join in the work.

It would take ten years to restore and repaint most of the ship and then, like the old Fourth Bridge the maintenance would be a continuous process. Each week Ken Waddington checked the double bottoms from frwd to aft for any signs of leakage. He had never been in the navy but had developed an affinity with the ship at Brighton, he along with his wife Sheila and friends went down every other weekend from Kent and slept onboard. They ran the shop and cleaned and maintained as much as they could. The gang of volunteers at Chatham grew until there would be anything up to thirty five men working every Wednesday removing rust, painting, repairing and reconstructing. Initially most of the volunteers were either retired ex-Navy or Dockyard workers but gradually other volunteers joined the working parties.

One day the volunteers were stripping out the lockers in the frwd petty officers mess to carry out a deep clean when they found several 4.5" shells under a seat! It was suspected by the old sailors that although they were real shells they had been deactivated, however not being able to take any chances the dockyard staff very quickly closed the ship and evacuated the public. The shells were removed to the centre of the helicopter pad in the dockyard and the Bomb disposal squad from Chattenden barracks attended to confirm... they were safe.

Shells in the workshop being prepared to go on show to the public, the larger ones are the 4.5's along with (right) a brass cartridge, the smaller ones are the 40mm Bofors shells.

They all brought their expertise to the project and almost any job could be undertaken. There were welders and sheet metal workers with years of experience and an engineer, Les Haddock from Milton, who had worked in the Dockyard before retiring. The dockyard gave them the use of a workshop adjacent to the ship and with help from his grandson Andrew, Les Haddock was able to set up a couple of ancient lathes left over from the dockyard before it closed. Other machinery such as a sandblasting cubicle and plate bending machines were acquired and brought into use.

Les Haddock engineer, working on one of the restored dockyard lathes that he set up.

One of seven door ammunition hatches (R. before and L. after). They were constructed by Les and would have been prohibitively expensive to have had them manufactured elsewhere.

Before and after, an Aldis lamp holder from the bridge manufactured by volunteer Roy Smith a retired dockyard plate worker.

Men like Mike Fleet an ex salesman and 'Go getter' scrounged equipment and materials from various companies that were relocating or getting rid of redundant machinery. Items that would have been beyond our finances to procure were made on site. A retired navy shipwright Mike Kier, with others repaired and repainted the Motorboat and before 'crossing the bar' he had made a start on the whaler, both boats are now back on the ship where they belong. Brian Lucas, an ex RN Auxiliary Reserve signalman, repaired and brought back into use the ship's entertainment system and radio. By using the Radios in the wireless office onboard he obtained a license for and set up a radio with the Call sign 'GB2 CAV'. He was able to connect with other organizations and restored ships throughout the world. He also helped to repair and run the ship's lighting by using the ship's own original cables. Tim Stopford would take parts from the ship home with him and the following week they would reappear completely renovated or reconstructed.

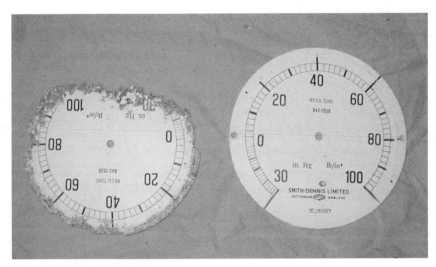

Some of Tim Stopford's work

Once or twice a year the 'Cavalier' association had a working weekend when many of the old crew would turn up to work onboard. In the early days they slept on camp beds in the sheds. They would spend the whole weekend chipping, painting and cleaning ship. In the evenings the lamps were 'swung' over one or two tots of bubbly and they didn't miss an opportunity to have a laugh and play the fool again, for a short while they were back in the days of their youth.

The ship's whaler and motorboat before work began on restoration.

Enter the Fairy Queen ('Katie' Ironton 60/61 commission) at a working weekend.

Many old sailors donated equipment, kit and other items from their past to stock the various compartments.

Tom Warden SBA: Donation of instruments. When the destroyer HMS Cossack (Of the 'Altmark' fame) was torpedoed in the Atlantic on 27th October 1941 she broke in half and the survivors were ordered to abandon ship.

For some reason Tom grabbed his surgical instruments from the sick bay and took them with him into the lifeboat. He kept them in their canvas roll and in 2005 George Toomey on behalf of the 'Cossack' association donated them to the 'Cavalier' in memory of those of their shipmates who were lost. Ex SBA Bob Morgan and friends of the RN SBA's and Surgeons Association adopted 'Cavalier's' sickbay and not only restored it but provided 'Pusser's' blankets and a full set of instruments to re-equip it. New mattresses were made for the sick cots and donated by Nestledown Ltd of Strood. Smith's Tugs donated Paint brushes, kettles and chipping hammers for seventy two Cavalier men on their working weekend.

HMS Cossack broken in half and sinking after being torpedoed in the Atlantic. She was one of the one hundred and forty two Royal Navy Destroyers lost during the five years of WWII. Nearly thirteen thousand men were lost serving on those ships. (Cossack Ass.)

Some of the Royal Navy (Gruesome looking) surgical instruments donated for the sickbay. They are lying on the blue 'pusser's' bed covers.

Donation of china: In 2004 Gillian Wettern, the widow of Desmond Wettern a Daily Telegraph reporter who covered the 'Great race', donated a set of original naval wardroom crockery which her husband had collected over several years. This good china has the Royal Navy 'fouled anchor' motif on it, it was used by the wardroom on special occasions such as when entertaining foreign ambassadors and other VIP's, in foreign ports.

Normally at sea ordinary heavy duty crockery was used in the wardroom to stand up to rough handling.

The newly restored sickbay and the two cots down aft.

Toy Chest: There was a serious shortage of materials during the war and the scrap wood from the recent bombing at Whites yard, where the ship was built was recycled. In 2002 a child's small toy chest of drawers was found in a garden shed in Edinburgh by ex-Royal Marine Frank Toak, it was being used to store screws and nails. When told of the significance of it, he donated it to the ships' collection without hesitation and went to the trouble and expense of having it delivered. It transpires that this chest was made from mahogany from the wrecked office furniture left over from the bombing. Cutouts for a hinge and a lock escutcheon can still be seen underneath a drawer and on an end panel, leftovers from its original incarnation. Toys in wartime Britain were not available in the shops and it was normal for carpenters in particular to make them. This toy appears to have been made by someone at the yard for one of the naval officers who were 'standing by' 'Cavalier' whilst she was being built. The signature on the underside of a drawer is of a 'C, Baker', believed the Gunnery Officer. It may be that it was intended for his daughter, who presented the flowers to Lady Glyn at the launch. The captain did have a daughter but she was not born till after the war so it couldn't have been for her. There is a stamp on the plywood bottom; *Admiralty Principal, (Ship) overseer. 14.1.45. Messrs. J. S. White & Co Lt.* The name Bell is also associated with it which may have been the shipwright who made it.

The ship sailed to join the 6th Flotilla at Scapa Flow in late December 1944 and the chest would have been sent later to catch up with her. The details are written in ink under one of the drawers. It is believed there was also a matching toy wardrobe to the chest but its whereabouts is unknown. Three naval medals were found in one drawer, the Pacific and Atlantic Stars and the 1939/45 war medal, somebody serving on the ship in that period would been entitled to wear these medals. The medals were re-mounted and both chest and the medals are now in the 'Cavalier' collection at Chatham Historic Dockyard.

Left; child's toy chest of drawers, (restored by author) made from scrap mahogany at Whites Yard during the war, it is 21"x18"x11" deep, and Right: The underside of one of the drawers. The address would have been the ship's wartime postal address.

'Mike' Jones Lt Cmdr, the 1st lieutenant of the last Commission: Whilst attending a 'Cavalier' reunion at Chatham and visiting the ship in 2004;

'I have here the silver plated candelabra that used to grace the wardroom table. I have been 'looking after them' all these years and I think it is time they went back onboard where they belong! Oh and here is the 'Cavalier'

badge from the front of the bridge'. The badge has now been re-gilded and is affixed to the front of 'Cavalier's' bridge.

Peter Goddard Cmdr: Captain of the last commission on the same occasion:

'I am bringing in the silver platter which was presented to the ship on the occasion of the winning of the race with HMS Rapid. I've brought it in now because I am fed up with having to polish the damn thing'!

In the meantime the Historic Dockyard Trust, which administers the ship, put into place the large long term projects which were beyond the capabilities of the volunteers. The ship was docked down on several occasions for the hull to be repaired and painted. With financial help from the Heritage Lottery Fund a fire alarm system was fitted throughout and an alarm system was placed in the bilges to warn the security office if sudden flooding should occur at any time. By the spring of 2000 the ship's lighting system had been restored and connected to shore. This enabled the No 2 deck level to be opened to the public for the first time and the volunteers to do more restoration work.

On the 2nd May 2004 'Cavalier's' sixtieth year was celebrated at Chatham Historic Dockyard. A grand weekend was organized mainly by David Thompson (OA 70/71 commission). Countess Mountbatten of Burma, whose father the late Lord Louis had been the captain of the WWII destroyer HMS Kelly, took the salute as nearly three hundred men of the old Ships' companies marched by headed by the Royal Marines band from Portsmouth. Thirty two standards were carried, amongst them the standard of the Royal Regiment of Fusiliers who had been carried by 'Cavalier' in the past. A platoon of Gurkhas represented those from the past who had been carried more than once into war by the ship. They marched past the head of the dock whilst the countess took the salute.

Countess Mountbatten takes the salute. On the left Admiral of the fleet Sir Alan West the First Sea Lord, in the centre Rear Admiral John Hervey CB OBE, a former captain of the ship and president of the HMS Cavalier Association, and in his red robes the Mayor.

The ship was looking as good as new, a tribute to all the men who worked on her. On the stand with the Countess was Admiral Sir Alan West the First Sea Lord, and a previous captain, now Rear Admiral John Hervey CB OBE the president of the HMS Cavalier Association.

Looking as good as new in her
new home. Although not now in
commission she has been given special
dispensation by the Admiralty to fly the
white ensign and the Union Jack.

Roger 'Iggy' Bliss as a cavalier.
(Medway News)

Overlooking the whole
procedure was a 'cavalier' on 'B'
gun mounting. Roger 'Iggy' Bliss
had stood there thirty two years
before when the ship entered
Chatham to pay off on the 7th
July 1972.

Heads held high, over three hundred of her old crew proudly march past
Countess Mountbatten during the 60th anniversary celebrations.

Both of 'Cavalier's' propellers were removed from the ship to reduce
the stress on her hull. One was dedicated to the builders on the
Isle of Wight at a service attended by Cavalier Association members.
That propeller there is the one that had a repair made on it and is
mentioned in the Gibraltar docking during the last commission, the
repair is still evident. The other lies on the dockside alongside the
ship in Chatham.

The Gurkhas, who had several times been carried by 'Cavalier'
to various war zones, were also represented.

One of 'Cavalier's' propellers now
mounted on a plinth on the seafront at
Cowes, Isle of Wight. It was dedicated to
the men of S J Whites who built her.

The ship now lies silent but walk around her and you may hear the ghostly echo of laughter or the rush of the sea thumping the ship's side.

First verse of the Sailors hymn always sung at prayers at church service onboard ships of the RN.

Eternal father strong to save,
Whose arm abounds the restless wave,
Who bidst the mighty ocean deep
Its own appointed limits keep:

Chorus

O hear us when we cry to thee
for those in peril on the sea.

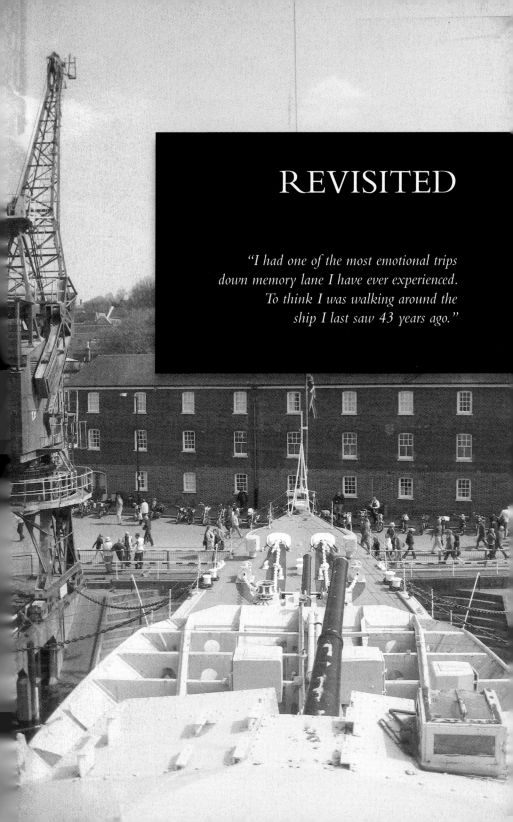

REVISITED

"I had one of the most emotional trips down memory lane I have ever experienced. To think I was walking around the ship I last saw 43 years ago."

REVISITED

During the first commission in 1945 at South Shields we saw Mary Rutter onboard 'Cavalier' celebrating her 21st birthday. Some 62 years later and aged 83 years, Mary was surprised to learn that 'Cavalier' not only still existed but had been restored and was open to the public at the Historic dockyard at Chatham. Bernie Hepplewhite, a ship's volunteer worker and an old family friend arranged for Mary to spend a day onboard reliving her memories. She was able to do this before she sadly passed away shortly afterwards.

Mary Marshall-Taylor nee Rutter revisits 'Cavalier' 62 years later and relives some old memories.

Brian Beniston the Royal Marine transported to Brunei by 'Cavalier' along with his Land Rover in December 1962, re visited the ship in 2012, fifty years later. Now registered blind he is seen here on the iron deck where his Land Rover had been loaded for the Borneo incident.

Brian Beniston on the iron deck where his Land Rover was loaded.

Edith Becker nee Bennett, L WREN, 'Just an office job'. At the outbreak of WWII Edith was just fourteen and a half. She had passed her 11+ exam with 100 per cent in Maths and had gone on to a special school specializing in Maths and commercial studies. Her father had been in the Navy and all the family was doing something towards the war effort… except her. So as soon as she was old enough, seventeen and three quarters, she enlisted into the WRENs. She trained at Westfield College Finchley and then at HMS Pembroke at Chatham. After her training she was hoping to become a member of a boats crew, however when the drafting list went up she found she was being posted to Buckinghamshire, about as far as you can get from the sea. She queried this and was told to 'just obey orders'. She was directed to catch a train from Euston to a small village called Bletchley. On arrival there she reported to the RTO's office and they took her by RN lorry to a place called Bletchley Park, the centre of military code breaking in wartime Britain. The first thing she had to do before entering was to sign the official secrets act. She was given a course in Japanese language and put to work in a room in Hut 7, the section dealing with the breaking of Japanese hand codes and super ciphers. She found this work enjoyable because she was using her maths skills. The messages she was decoding were being sent to the forces and ships of the Far East including one called HMS Cavalier. She was only twenty years old at war's end and was very proud of what she had been doing. Her only regret was that both her parents died before the security was lifted on her work and she was unable to tell them what her 'Just an office job' really entailed. She and her association were keen supporters of the ship in Chatham.

Joe Redhead AB: Served on the 1944 commission. In July 2001 he visited the ship at Chatham for the first time since leaving her in 1946. Having toured the ship and recalled so many memories he was leaving by the gangway when he bumped into **Bob Puttock** also an AB from 1944, he was coming aboard also for the first time to relive his own memories. The coincidence was difficult to believe, not only had he been his oppo from all those years ago but he had also been his best man at his wedding 56 years previously. They had lost touch after leaving the ship in '46.

Peter Bierne P/KX921115 POME 1960/61 commission: 'I always said that I would never revisit old ground… but inevitably I have. I married Mrs Bierne in April 1960 and six weeks later flew out to join 'Cavalier' in the June. During that action packed commission we won several sporting activities whilst we were housed in HMS Terror for refit and I have fond memories of ten buck Yorkshires (whip rounds) down at Sembawang gate on a blank week. Anyone remember Betty's Café? I well remember the sad loss of our NAAFI Canteen Manager, there's a tale to tell. I remember with a small amount of satisfaction and glee when our Captain, Commander Pritchard (or 'Pricky' to his friends!) was swanning around outside his cabin in his dressing gown when through some unaccountable freak of fate the weather shroud was blown off the donkey boiler uptake and was last seen skimming along the surface of the South China Sea like a demented Frisbee... The look of sheer bemusement on his face was worth all the pain of ageing ten years in the eighteen months of the commission (Let's say my wife wasn't sure who I was when I arrived home). The reason I have hit the keyboard is that as a special request I returned to the Medway with Maureen, she being a maid of Kent and we visited what is left of dear old Chatham Dockyard. Yes you've guessed it; I dragged the poor woman onto the 'Cavalier' and had one of the most emotional trips down memory lane I have ever experienced. To think I was walking around the ship I last saw 43 years ago and in company with the domestic goddess was unbelievable. I was only frustrated in not being able to show Maureen around the Boiler rooms and Machinery spaces which contributed so much to my galloping tinnitus and hearing problems (don't grieve, I have a war pension... but would rather have my hearing back!). Maureen was truly amazed at how relatively small the ship seemed. During our visit I explained how we weaved the nettles to help with slinging your hammock and that the stretchers were restricted to eighteen inches... time to get into my King sized bed!! May the force be with you'?

Old man of the sea, 'Des' Gannon PO with his Russian and British Arctic Convoys medals.

'Des' Gannon, Chief Bosun's mate (who we saw supervising some rope work during the 44/46 commission) proudly wears his WWII medals including the Russian 'Arctic Convoys' medal. He and his shipmates were staunch supporters of the ship and her preservation and visited her regularly. In March 2013 he and the other Arctic convoy veterans were finally awarded an Arctic medal by their own Government.

On the 15th June 2003 John and Margaret Nathan and Roger Hunt and his wife Margaret, who's Banns had been called during the 1961/3 commission, were able to celebrate their 40th wedding anniversary onboard 'Cavalier' at Chatham. They re-affirmed their vows in a ceremony on the quarter deck at a service conducted by the Missions to Seamen and Padre to the 'Cavalier' association the Reverend Andrew Huckett. Afterwards they celebrated with a reception in the newly restored wardroom.

Forty years later, Roger and Margaret and John and Margaret re affirm their vows onboard.

John and Margaret Nathan and Roger and Margaret Hunt celebrate their wedding anniversary in the ship's wardroom. The ship's original candelabra grace the table.

Cavalier Association: The HMS Cavalier association was initially formed by the 1961/3 commission and was chaired by Sid Anning AB. It evolved to include all commissions and an annual get together was arranged where sailors could 'swing the lamp' and remember their days onboard. They put a great deal of effort into saving and preserving the ship and in true tradition they played hard.

A ship's standard was bought and was paraded at meetings, funerals and other functions. The standard bearer for many years was Dennis Curd, a leading signalman from the 1960 commission; he was followed by John 'Katie' Ironton AB. The standard is paraded at all official functions and, shrouded with a black ribbon at funerals.

Dennis Curd (Leading signalman), standard bearer

Keeping up tradition, a SODs opera at the HMS Cavalier re-union, the Burlington Hotel, Eastbourne on the 3rd May 2003. Any excuse for a laugh, the Egyptian Sand Dance and the Mustafa brothers, Mustafa sheet, Mustafa tot, Mustafa bigun and Mustafa larf.

A SODS opera song, sung to the tune 'Side by Side'.

I got married last Fridee
My lass was right here beside me,
The guests were all gone
We were alone,
Side by side.

We were happily wed then
She started getting ready for bed when
Her teeth and her hair
She placed on a chair
Side by side.

One glass eye so shiny
One hearing aid so small,

Then she took her leg off and put it on the chair by the wall
Side by side.

Now I'm sat here broken hearted
Most of my lass has departed
So I slept on the chair
'Cos there was more of her there
Side by side.

Cliff 'Windy' East.

It was suggested by some lower deck literary genius that a good ending to this book would be… 'And they all lived happily ever after'! However…

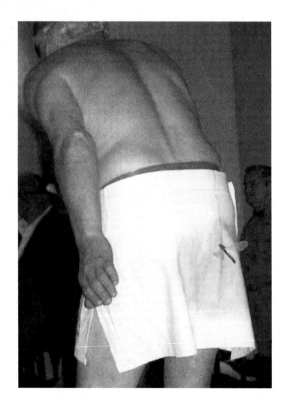

The End!

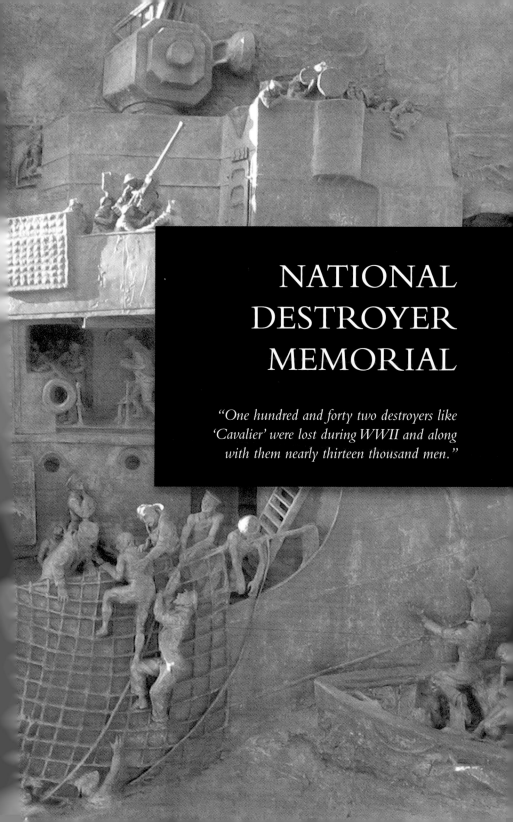

NATIONAL
DESTROYER
MEMORIAL

*"One hundred and forty two destroyers like
'Cavalier' were lost during WWII and along
with them nearly thirteen thousand men."*

NATIONAL DESTROYER MEMORIAL

As part of the Lottery funding agreement the newly formed HMS Cavalier (Chatham) Trust would provide matching funding. Part of that funding had been allocated to providing a monument on the dockside alongside the ship; this was to be dedicated to all the men who died in Royal Navy and Allied Commonwealth destroyers during WWII. Other organizations donated funds, notably among them the Heritage Lottery Fund, The Dulverton Trust (A lost WWII destroyer), HMS Dorsetshire Ass. (WWII cruiser, torpedoed 'Bismarck')

The Memorial:

A Memorial Steering committee was set up chaired by the Rt. Rev. Edward Shotter, Dean of Rochester. The following members represented the various interested groups.

Rear Admiral John Hervey CB OBE	HMS Cavalier Association
Michael Keir BEM	Friends of HMS Cavalier Trust
Barry Knell	Royal Naval Association
Donald MacDonald BEM	8th Destroyer Association
CPT Christopher Page RN RTD	Royal Navy Historical Branch
Jane Sharman CBE	HMS Cavalier (Chatham) Trust
Richard Holdsworth	Secretary – CHDT
Joe Falzon	Royal British Legion

They set about finding a suitable design and sculptor and advertisements for designs were asked for in various naval and other publications. Many designs were received and after much deliberation the committee whittled the designs down to three. The three finalists were invited to submit a Marquette and after three years the final design, by the acclaimed British sculptor Kenneth Potts ARBS from Malvern was chosen. Over a period of a year he produced a mould in wood and clay at his studio in Malvern ready for casting in bronze. It depicts a destroyer rescuing seamen whose ship has been sunk.

The full size clay model in sculptor Kenneth Potts studio in Malvern.

It was finally cast and placed in position on the port side of HMS Cavalier in 2007.

The huge bronze monument alongside the port side of the ship. On the obverse is a list of names of all the 142 destroyers lost. It now provides a focus for those attending the annual Remembrance Day service on the 11th of the 11th (On the day not the nearest weekend).

On the 14th November 2007 His Royal Highness Prince Phillip Duke of Edinburgh KG KT unveiled the monument and dedicated the ship as the National destroyer memorial. It appeared quite an emotional moment for him as it evoked memories of his war time service. Other notable dignitaries present were The Vice Lord Lt of Kent, Viscount De L'isle MBE DL and Admiral Sir Ian Garnett KCB of CHDT. The Royal Marine Band from the Britannia Royal Naval Collage played and a naval guard marched on with the Queen's Colour guard. After the unveiling The Duke toured the 'Cavalier', it must have brought back many memories. He had served on several destroyers during and after WWII and in 1949 he was the Jimmy, (First Lieutenant of HMS Chequers, another 'C' class destroyer.

After the unveiling ceremony HRH boards for a tour of 'Cavalier'. A nice touch, which was noticed by the old sailors, was that he was wearing his old navy great coat which bears the insignia of his father in law King George VI under whom he served.

HRH visits the restored wardroom. On the left, Richard Holdsworth of the Historic Dockyard and right Mike Keir retired CPO shipwright and volunteer worker.

Crossing the bar: A bar is a natural underwater obstruction usually found in the mouth of a river: a sailor is said to have crossed the final bar when he dies and goes to meet his maker.

Sunset and evening star,
And one clear call for me!
And may there be no moaning of the bar,
When I put out to sea.
But such a tide as moving seems asleep,
Too full for sound and foam
When that which drew from out the boundless deep
Turns again for home.
Twilight and evening bell,
And after that the dark!
And may there be no sadness of farewell,
When I embark:
For tho' from out our bourne of time and place
The flood may bear me far,
I hope to see my Pilot face to face
When I have crosd the bar.

Alfred Lord Tennyson

One hundred and forty two destroyers like 'Cavalier' were lost during WWII and along with them nearly thirteen thousand men. You can see from the below list of losses in '40, '41 and 42' why thirty two more 'emergency class' similar to 'Cavalier' were ordered.

1939
Blanche
Duchess
Gipsy

1940
Acasta
Acheron
Afridi
Ardent
Basilisk
Brazen
Cameron
Codrington
Daring
Delight
Escort
Eask
Exmouth
Glowworm
Grafton
Grenade
Grenville
Gurkha
Hardy
Havant
Hostile
Hunter
Hyperion
Imogen
Ivanhoe

Keith
Khartoum
Sturdy
Valentine
Venetia
Wakeful
Wessex
Whirlwind
Whitley
Wren

1941
Broadwater
Cossack
Dainty
Defender
Diamond
Exmoor
Fearless
Gallant
Greyhound
Hereward
Imperial
Jersey
Juno
Kandaha
Kashmir
Kelly
Mashona
Mohawk
Stanley

Thracian
Wryneck

1942
Achates
Airedale
Bedouin
Belmont
Berkeley
Blean
Broke
Cambletown
Electra
Encounter
Eridge
Firedrake
Foresight
Grove
Gurkha
Hasty
Havock
Heythrop
Ithuriel
Jackal
Jaguar
Jupiter
Kingston
Kipling
Lance
Legion
Lively

Maori
Martin
Matabele
Partridge
Penylan
Porcupine
Punjabi
Quentin
Sikh
Somali
Southwold
Stronghold
Tenedos
Thanet
Veteran
Vimiera
Vortigern
Wild Swan
Zulu

1943
Arrow
Beverley
Derwent
Dulverton
Eclipse
Harvester
Holcombe
Hurricane
Hurworth
Intrepid

Lightning
Limbourne
Pakenham
Panther
Puckeridge
Rockwood
Tynedale
Worcester
Loyal
Maharata
Quail
Quorn
Rockingham
Swift
Warwick
Wrestler

1944
Aldenham
Boadicea
Fury
Goathland
Hardy
Inglefield
Isis
Janus
Laforey

1945
Pathfinder
Walpole

HMS CAVALIER
LOG BOOKS

Royal Navy ships log books were designed to cover a month at a time. They were written up by the officer of the watch at sea or by the Quartermaster on the gangway in harbour. Entries were made every hour and contain details of where the ship was and what she was doing, weather and sea state, speed, barometric pressure, wet and dry temperatures, wind strengths, and anything that may affect the security of the ship. The names of VIP's and other persons visiting the ship were also recorded as well as any prisoners sent ashore and any other unusual occurrences. Not too much detail is recorded because firstly there was not a great deal of room on the page and secondly I suspect in an enquiry not too much could then be gained from them! Because of the sensitive nature of some of their work there was a thirty year embargo on them and some were only released in 2001. WWII log books have a one hundred years embargo on them, although they can be accessed under a signed undertaking that certain information will not be disclosed.

On completion of each book the responsibility to ensure they were sent for storage was usually the responsibility of a junior officer. Not all books were saved and it is believed, but not confirmed, that some were either destroyed or secured elsewhere if they contained sensitive information of national importance. Several of "Cavalier's" books are missing, some of which related to the atomic tests at Christmas Island. The following is a list of 'Cavalier's' Log books that do survive and are held in the National Archives in the Public Record Office at Kew. They all come under the Admiralty category (ADM).

1957   From July to December complete.

1958   From January to December complete.

1959   From January to December complete.

1960   From January to December (July missing).

1961   From January to September (Oct. Nov. Dec. missing)

1962   None listed

1963   None listed

1964   A few days of May

1965   None listed

1966   From September to December.

1967   From January to December complete.

1968   November and December only.

1969   February only.

1970   From February to December (January missing).

1971   From January to December complete.

1972   From January to July

GLOSSARY

In the 1970's the titles of various specialist rates changed, particularly the mechanician and artificers.

AB	Able Seaman, next up from O/D
Adrift	Failing to return off leave
App	Apprentice
ASWO	Anti-Submarine Warfare officer
Bish	Padre
Bootneck	Royal Marine
Brown Job	Soldier
Buffer	Chief Bosun's mate
Bulkhead	Walls on a ship
CA	Caterer
CDR	Commander
CEA	Control Electrical Artificer
CEMN L	Control Electrical Mechanician (Electrical)
Charlie Noble	Small galley chimney, sometimes H shaped
Cheongsam	Chinese tight fitting satin dress with long splits in the sides.

CK	Cook
Coxn	Coxswain, expert steersman and small ships policeman
CPO	Chief Petty Officer
CY	Chief Yeoman
Dabtoes	Seamen
Darken ship	Blackout on war footing or to keep quiet
Devil Dodger	Padre
DF	Destroyer flotilla
Dhobey	To wash ones clothes (from Indian for laundry man)
EA	Electrical Artificer
Father Famine	Supply officer
FC	Fire Control
FO2	Flag Officer
G	Gunner
GA	Gun layers armourer
Goffer	A large wave or a cold drink
Guzz	Gosport (Believed from the wartime call sign)
Hairy Fairy	Member of the fleet air arm
Heaving line transfer	A light line used to send small items from ship to ship
Jack Stay Transfer	A heavy line with running pulley wheel for transferring heavy items or personnel
Jimmy	Or Jimmy the one. The 1st LT, next highest to the captain.
JS	Junior Seaman
Lamp Swinging	Sailors retelling stories of their time at sea… very often slightly embellished!

LSA V	Leading Stores Assistant Victling
LS	Leading Seaman
LSBA	Leading sick berth attendant.
LT CDR	Lieutenant Commander
MA	Medical assistant
ME	Marine Engineer (Stoker)
MEA	Marine engineering Artificer, P=Propulsion,
H	Hull
MECH	Mechanician
MEM	Marine Engineering mechanic
MEO	Marine engineering officer
OA	Ordnance Artificer
OD	Ordinary Seaman, next up from JS
OEA	Ordnance Electrical Artificer
OEL	Ordnance electrical
OEM	Ordnance electrical mechanic
Oggin	The sea, from *hogging* and *sagging*.
Out Pipes	Victorian; put clay pipes out resume work.
Phoo phoo dust	Scented talcum powder
Pipe Down	Victorian; put clay pipes out, go to sleep
PO	Petty Officer
Pompey	Portsmouth
Pongo	Soldier, where the soldier goes the pong goes! (Navy vernacular)
PTI	Physical training instructor
Putty	Painter
QA	Quarters Armourer
Q.A.'s & A. I.'s	Queens Regulations and Admiralty

	Instructions.
RAAF	Royal Australian Airforce.
Rabbits (rabbiting)	Presents (searching for attractive items).
RAS	Replenishment at sea
REA	Radio electrical Artificer
REL	Radio electrical
REM	Radio electrical mechanic
RO	Radio operator G = General, T= Tactical, W = Warfare
RP	Radar Plot
RS	Radio supervisor
S	Stores
SA	Supply or stores assistant
Sand scratchers	Seamen
SBA	Sick Birth Attendant
Scran	Food
Scrumpy	Very rough cheap cider favoured by sailors on blank week!
Sea Dad	Older seaman who gives moral guidance to junior seamen.
SEATO	South East Asia Treaty Organization
Shitehawks	Sea gulls
Shit on a raft	Devilled kidneys, see below for recipe
Skipper	from Dutch Schipper, meaning Captain
Sky pilot	Padre
Slop chit	A bill for pusser's equipment
SLT	Sub Lieutenant
Spithead pheasant	Smoked fish, kippers
STD	Steward

TAS	Torpedo and Anti-submarine
Train smash	Tinned tomatoes
TS	Transmitting station, for the weapon systems
WEO	Weapons electrical officer
YS	Yeoman of signals

Recipe:

Shit on a raft

Take 30lb of Ox or lamb kidney.
15lb of onions (peeled).
10lb bread making flour.
1/4lb gravy browning.
2lb of Bisto.
A hand full of pepper and salt.
250 thick slices of bread, fried.
For 'Mit guard rails' add one large bag of potato powder (Smash).
(This for the piped potato round the edge to stop the kidney running off the fried bread in rough weather.)

Using a clean bucket that has been used to scrub out the galley, put all this in a copper and boil, remove any residual soap suds and any floor cloths. Stir regularly with the head of a broom. When served stand back to avoid the rush to consume!

It is suggested you scale down the ingredients for home use!

Civilized recipe:

Dice kidney after removal of any gristle and suet. Peel and finely chop onions and sauté both. Add flour then add the brown stock bring back to the boil then simmer for 25/30 mins.

The Author

Barry Knell, was born in Teynham, Kent in 1939 and now lives in Whitstable, he has a few vivid memories of WWII. The second eldest of eleven children he signed on for nine years in the Royal Navy three days before his eighteenth birthday 'because he didn't want to be called up for National Service and become a 'brown job'. He was trained as a Seaman and specialized in gunnery; he qualified as a marksman with small arms. His first ship was the anti submarine frigate HMS Hardy based in Portland. Three months of this eighteen months commission was spent at sea in one stretch off Iceland on Fishery protection. In 1960 he was drafted to HMS Cavalier based in Singapore. He spent eighteen months on her travelling all over the Far East.

Later, after undergoing a Gun layer's Armourers course in 1962 he trained on and took part as the aimer for the surface trials of the Seacat missile on the destroyer HMS Aisne. The Seacat was the Navy's first close range missile system. He served on several other ships and at the end of his nine years was offered an officers course and a cash incentive if he signed on for a further five years as a weapons mechanician. However having just married his wife Valerie he declined the offer and left the service. On his first day home he took his wife in to hospital for the birth of their first daughter, Andrea. He served as a Police Officer with the Kent County Constabulary for twenty five years at Rochester (and Strood as a beat officer), then as the village PC of Lamberhurst, Matfield and Brenchley with a final move to Whitstable and becoming the intelligence officer for the sub division. He and Val have two daughters and four grandchildren. After retirement he was involved in helping to save 'Cavalier' including attending the Parliamentary enquiry. With others he subsequently spent every Wednesday for the next ten years working to restore the ship at Chatham. For nine of those years he was Chairman of the HMS Cavalier Association of ex crewmen.